Julia M. Eckert (ed.)
The Social Life of Anti-Terrorism Laws

Julia M. Eckert (ed.)
The Social Life of Anti-Terrorism Laws
The War on Terror and the Classifications
of the »Dangerous Other«

[transcript]

This book was printed with the financial support of the Max Planck Institute for Social Anthropology Halle/Saale.

Gedruckt mit Unterstützung des Max-Planck-Instituts für ethnologische Forschung in Halle/Saale.

I would like to thank the Max Planck Institute for Social Anthropology, especially Franz and Keebet von Benda Beckmann, Gesine Koch and Kathrin Niehuus for the support of this publication.

Bibliographic information published by the Deutsche Nationalbibliothek
The Deutsche Nationalbibliothek lists this publication in the Deutsche Nationalbibliografie; detailed bibliographic data are available in the Internet at http://dnb.d-nb.de

© 2008 transcript Verlag, Bielefeld

All rights reserved. No part of this book may be reprinted or reproduced or utilized in any form or by any electronic, mechanical, or other means, now known or hereafter invented, including photocopying and recording, or in any information storage or retrieval system, without permission in writing from the publisher.

Cover layout: Kordula Röckenhaus, Bielefeld
Proofred by: Julia M. Eckert
Typeset by: Gesine Koch
Printed and bound in Great Britain by
Marston Book Services Ltd, Oxfordshire
ISBN 978-3-89942-964-0

Contents

Laws for Enemies 7
JULIA ECKERT

Liberalism versus Terrorism:
Warfare, Crime Control, and the United States
after 11 September 33
THOMAS M. HAWLEY

Suspect Subjects:
Muslim Migrants and the Security Agencies in Germany 55
WERNER SCHIFFAUER

Political Rationalities, Counter-terrorism and Policies on Islam
in the United Kingdom and France 79
FRANK PETER

Documents, Security and Suspicion:
the Social Production of Ignorance 109
TOBIAS KELLY

The Danger of 'Undergoverned' Spaces:
the 'War on Terror' and its Effects on the Sahel Region 131
JAN BACHMANN

Islamic Activism and Anti-terrorism Legislation in Morocco 163
BERTRAM TURNER

Notes on Contributors 193

Laws for Enemies

JULIA ECKERT

Introduction

The 'war on terror' has affected anti-terrorism laws and anti-terrorism policies worldwide. New legislation was passed in many countries; laws existing prior to 11 September 2001 have been used with a new focus on security and prevention; and there were attempts to integrate and harmonize national and international anti-terror measures in order to coordinate strategies against what is perceived as a global and globally coordinated threat.

This book addresses two developments in the conceptualisation of citizenship that arise from the 'war on terror', namely the re-culturalisation of membership in a polity and the re-moralisation of access to rights. Furthermore, the book asks in what ways these developments are globalized, and how they are adopted, adapted, instrumentalized, and circumvented in different political and social contexts. It traces the ways in which the trans-nationalisation of the 'war on terror' has affected national (or regional) notions of security and danger and images of 'the dangerous other', asking what changes in the ideas of the state and of the nation have been promoted by the emerging culture of security, and how these changes affect practices of citizenship and societal group relations.

The new security regime comprises legal frameworks, technologies, regional and global alliances, but at the same time it also employs categories and images of danger and the dangerous other. Furthermore it usually entails the securitisation (Wæver 1995; Buzan et al.1998) of ever more policy fields. In the processes of the globalisation of this security regime, laws are harmonized, technologies exported, the production of specific knowledge about threats and conflicts is coordinated. The question is to what extent the export of policy transports not only specific legal provisions and security technologies, but also schemes of understan-ding crime and risk and security as well as categorisations of the dangerous other. The adoption of the security regime by governments and other interested parties always implies a localisation of these technologies, the categories and cartographies. Many countries around the world adopted new or re-enforced pre-existing legislation (e.g. Bascombe 2003) after 9/11, and were obliged to do so by the U.N. Security Council Resolution 1373. Most of the legislation now enacted entailed measures that had been debated for a long time in connection with other perceived threats such as 'organized crime', drug trafficking etc. (see, e.g. Crenlinsten 1998). Some new legislation revived earlier security laws; some built upon existing legislation (for Germany see Hirsch 2002: 7; for India see Krishnan 2004; for the U.S. see Cole 2003; for Malaysia see Bascombe 2003). Most see new forms of cooperation between the different security agencies, i.e. the police, internal and external intelligence services and the military, the path for which was prepared in many countries with reference to the new challenges posed by globalisation and by transnational criminal networks. In the wave of legislative activities throughout the post-9/11 world we can also see a reclassification of domestic conflicts into the anti-terrorism strategy and a tendency to relate both specific types of conflicts and various policy fields to the phenomenon of terrorism and to security concerns.

Thus, the introduction of new security measures has had repercussions in the legal organisation of fields not immediately related to terrorist activities. In fact, the identification of the fields that are considered to be directly related to the threat of terrorism and which, therefore, have to be addressed by the new security measures, is a matter of contestation.[1] Because of the allegedly diffuse nature of the terrorist threat, policy makers and different state agencies adopt encompassing visions of the new necessities of preventive control: Not

---

1 Terrorism was often defined in the new legislation in a rather vague manner that allows to cover all sorts of actions, including association or even simple contact, as in the now repealed Indian anti-terrorism law, the Prevention of Terrorism Act (POTA); the expression of support for the 'causes' of terrorist organisations (as in Turkey); or material support even if unintentional, as in the U.S. PATRIOT ACT. The term 'terrorism' is used not in a neutrally descriptive way, describing specific forms of political violence, but in a normative way, and some scholars have held that it can only be used in such a pejorative manner and have therefore abandoned the term entirely, claiming, like Cynthia Mahmood, that 'terrorism is a concept that mystifies rather than illuminates; it is a political and not an academic notion' (Mahmood 2001: 528). But it is, of course, precisely the insinuation of a normative judgement, as well as the vagueness with which the term is used, which shapes the politics of security. The problems of defining terrorism are discussed by Charles Tilly (2004), among others.

only financial transactions, organized crime and illegal border crossing are under observation, but whole geographical areas were classified as potential 'bases' of terrorist organisations that demand intervention (such as the Sahel region, and of course Taliban Afghanistan; see Bachmann in this volume). Moreover, policies towards minorities, towards migration and immigrants (whether naturalized or not – see Schiffauer this volume),[2] towards religious (Islamic) or minority rights organisations (see Peter this volume) and, of course, towards data protection have been rethought in connection with current perceptions of the threat of terrorism.

This securitisation of various policy fields not only changed administrative priorities within these fields; it has also affected administrative practice and practical interpretations of norms and policies, as Werner Schiffauer and Frank Peter show in their contributions to this volume.

Thus, despite the precedents, it appears that the 'war on terror' gives these developments a new quality: Firstly, it globalizes them to a new degree and with a new urgency and force; secondly, it merges more tightly independent developments in policing, in development cooperation, in policies concerning migration and in notions of citizenship; and thirdly, it introduces the culturalisation of membership and moralisation of rights to a new degree and with new legitimacy.

However, the war on terror was adopted and adapted differently in different countries: Not all countries jumped onto the bandwagon of the new discourse of security; some, of course, were excluded from the outset, being considered an enemy; and some only joined the agenda after they had been pressured by the U.S. and the EU, for example under threat of withholding aid. There were several governments which hesitated to join the war on terror or to link their domestic problems to its agenda, such as Indonesia and Morocco (see Bertram Turner in this volume). Both joined the war on terror only after they had experienced 'their own' terrorist disasters: Bali and Casablanca.

What differed was, however, not only the individual country's readiness to join the agenda, but also the ways in which the agenda was used and implemented. For different governments it served different ends. Some, such as those of Russia, China, Uganda or the Philippines, used the politics of security mainly to justify their own wars against insurgents. Others instrumentalized the measures to cope with political opposition, a tendency observable for example in Egypt, Malaysia, or Uganda. The governments of India and Pakistan engaged in their own race to be regarded and treated as an ally, motivated by their own regional conflict and the hope for financial, technological and political U.S. American support for their strategies within this conflict. Yet

---

2 In debates of the European parliament, a close connection between terrorism and immigration is frequently claimed; see Bigo (2002); see also Tsoukala (2004: 3).

other governments, such as those of Mali or of Djibouti,[3] sought out the new possibilities in acquiring aid inherent in the anti-terrorism strategies of the U.S. Others were forced to introduce anti-terrorism measures (Bascombe 2004: 4), mainly the small islands of the Caribbean and the Pacific, which were compelled to change their financial or gambling laws to facilitate the surveillance of transnational financial transactions and money laundering operations. They were pressured both by the U.S. and the EU under the threat of withholding financial aid.[4] The introduction of anti-terror measures in line with the new international architecture of security became part of development politics worldwide (Large 2005: 3; see also Bachmann in this volume).[5] Thus, legal innovations, technologies and ideas about security and danger entered different countries in ways related to their local tensions and concerns and their position within the global order, a global order now interpreted in terms of its security implications. As Jan Bachmann shows in his contribution to this volume, the geography of security is one of friends and foes, save havens and areas of withdrawal, of failed states and rogue states.

The processes of adopting the models and ideas underlying the new security regime were shaped by these factors: by the local tensions and conflicts which were now interpreted in the light of the globally unified security paradigm, or for which the latter was now used if only as a legitimation; and by the position of a state in the global geography of security. The measures entered political structures at different levels: They were responded to at national level, had their effects at the local level, and were made use of by different societal agents in conflicts of diverse nature, local, national, transnational. Each appropriation spun off its own social effects, and each connected differently to other implementations of security measures, as Turner shows vividly in his chapter on Morocco in this volume.

Despite the differences in the ways the 'war on terror' entered into national and local politics, and although the ways of adopting a policy is shaped by regional or local concerns, the ideas and procedures characteristic of the 'war on terror' also seem to be exported. In their encompassing and rather unspecific nature, they offer themselves for various purposes to different actors.

---

3   Djibouti for example received $ 30 million for letting the U.S. establish a permanent military base.
4   Another means of pressure is the blacklist of Non-Cooperative Countries and Territories of the Financial Action Task Force (FATF).
5   Little material is available as yet to answer the question of whether the securitisation of development relates to aid objectives such as poverty alleviation beneficially or detrimentally. Since large funds are designated for security enhancement, such as police training, air safety, etc., priorities within aid allocation are definitely changing. See for example: http://www.bond.org.uk/advocacy/globalsecurity.htm

The Omnipresent Threat

Particularly influential in the realisation of security measures all over the world seems to be the specific construction of danger in the contemporary context. The 'new terrorism' is said to be inspired by religious fanaticism (e.g. Laqueur 2000). Since 11 September 2001, this so-called 'new terrorism' is first and foremost Islamist terrorism. There are competing criminologies of Islamist terrorism, referring to either cultural or political causes. However, security policies and measures taken are neither related to the assumed causes of terrorism nor are they designed to remedy those causes. Instead, they are related to a specific perception of risk. This risk is shaped on the one hand by the specific structures of organisation attributed to the 'new terrorism', and on the other hand, by the dynamics attributed to religious fanaticism. This risk is perceived as potentially immense, yet at the same time elusive. Possible damages are considered possibly apocalyptic (cf. Morgan 2004: 30) due to the potential access of terrorists to biological weapons, nuclear and other dangerous materials inherent in advanced technology (e.g. Laqueur 2000). At the same time the perpetrators are seen to be, firstly, highly dispersed and only loosely connected to a transnational network. Secondly, they are well-nigh 'invisible', and most so as 'sleepers'. Thirdly, they are regarded as beyond negotiation or deterrence, since they are said to be inspired by religious fanaticism and an alleged general hatred of the West (or modernity). They are perceived as largely 'aimlessly' or nihilistically destructive. 'Today's terrorists seek destruction and chaos as ends in themselves' (Morgan 2004: 30). 'New terrorists want only to express their wrath and cripple their enemy' (Stevenson 2001-2002: 35). These opinions echoed many analyses of the alleged specificity of religious terrorism (e.g. Laqueur 2000). The novelty of Islamist terrorism, it is said, lies in the fact that it is de-territorialized in two ways: It is neither based in any one territory, from which terrorists operate or whereto they can withdraw, but it is potentially everywhere, hidden in loosely connected undiscoverable sleeper cells of amateur terrorists; nor does it aim at territory, as insurgent or secessionist terrorism used to (e.g. Diner 2004). Rather, it is claimed to be merely destructive, with a complete, indiscriminate contempt for life. Suicidal terrorism above all, allegedly inspired by mere hatred and alien in its motives, renders not only bargaining but also deterrence impossible.

Thus, the 'new terrorism' is perceived and presented as external to society to a new extent. The question of 'Why do they hate us so much', which initially arose in the U.S. and was revived in a British version after the 7 July bombings of the London Underground with the additional shock of home grown Muslim terrorists, in some ways never quite sought an answer. Terrorism's causes or its relation to the society it targets became secondary to an assumed essential alienness and a religious fanaticism that is beyond reason, beyond understanding, and allegedly disconnected from a social and political context. Thus, there is also a new concept of danger. Danger, legally defined as a specific action that will, if not hindered, lead to the damaging of a good that is protected by law, is now no longer connected to the actions of individuals, but to a general situation of threat (Bender 2003: 138, 139; Lepsius 2004: 66, 67, 83). This general situation of threat is emanating from an elusive network[6] and its fundamental 'occidentalism' (Buruma/Margalit 2004), in which individuals are replaceable. 'We do not know where, and precisely who, the enemy is', felt one member of the EU parliament.[7] Because of the characterisation of the 'new terrorism' as an omnipresent but elusive threat, arising from a de-individualized (Lepsius 2004: 66) general and diffuse Islamist terror, security measures are said to be necessary which presume that the enemy could be everywhere and everyone – nearly. Makdisi speaks of a 'spectral terrorism' that offers the 'foundation for a universal campaign of investigation, interrogation, confiscation, detention, surveillance, torture and punishment on, for the first time, a genuinely global scale [...] not only where it [terrorism] does manifest itself but where it might manifest itself, which could, of course, be anywhere' (Makdisi 2002: 267).

No matter how realistic or unrealistic a description of the 'new terrorism' is,[8] the claims to the diffuseness of the threat, the new invisible nature of the

---

6 On the network thesis see also Mayntz (2004).
7 Mogens Camre, Danish member of the UEN (Union for a Europe of the Nations), European parliamentary debate 6 February 2002 quoted in Tsoukala (2004: 6).
8 There is, of course, the question to what degree the 'new terrorism' is actually so new and whether it is really so diffuse, de-territorialized and 'aimless' as is being claimed. See also David Tucker (2001) on the similarities between old and new terrorism; as well as Peter Waldmann's (2004) critique of the theses of alleged novelty of the network structures. It is easy to demonstrate that there have been, and still are, clear and identifiable aims, even rather territorial in nature, of transnational Islamist terrorism (see also Steinberg 2005), such as the removal of the U.S. army from Saudi Arabia and now also from Iraq, or the destruction of Israel. Moreover, many of those Islamic insurgencies which are now considered to be connected to the transnational networks of Al Qaeda, and which constitute this network, have, of course, very 'conventional' aims, such as the independence of Chechnya, the withdrawal of the Indian army from Kashmir, the independence of Aceh or of Mindanao. The security discourse related all sorts of Muslim led insurgencies to 'global terrorism' and thereby justified strategies for regions of unrest accordingly. Of course, new relations might in fact have been established between different local or regional armed groups and others, or with Al Qaeda. Most importantly, the characterisations of the 'new terrorism' mostly fail to see or, because of the apparent enormity of the attack of 9/11, refuse to take into account any political context within which the 'new terrorism' arose. There have been references to the chosen traumata of the Muslim world and the grievances of Arab populations. But the idea that the 'new terro-

perpetrators, the unparalleled potential for destruction and the allegedly novel form of organisation in transnationally loosely connected cells, all have been the main grounds for the justification of the specific measures taken against 'the new terrorism'. 'Terrorism has been used in a calculatedly undefined and indefinite, rather than specific, way. It names not a specific Other, but a general and omnipresent threat' (Makdisi 2002: 266).

Prevention

The idea of the omnipresent, elusive threat has shaped a new type of security measures in that they now raise 'suspicion' to a new importance as grounds for action. Previous legal distinctions between suspicion (entitling the police to investigate) and prognoses or probable cause, that is: The well-founded expectation of an event to occur entitling the police to use preventive measures, have been abandoned in many places. 'Prevention', this seemingly innocent word, relates to the idea of controlling potentials, of surveying future possibilities, of controlling not what people did or do or are planning to do, but what they *might* at some point do. Prevention furthermore changes security from a matter of politics into one of technology, involving specialists' knowledge of risks and their pre-emption (see also Bigo 2002: 74; on experts see also Peter this volume).

Most countries, therefore, detect new forms of cooperation between the different security agencies, i.e. the police, internal and external intelligence services and the military, the stage for which was set in many countries with reference to the new challenges posed by globalisation and by transnational criminal networks. There is, accordingly, a certain diffusion of the distinction between internal and external security (Bigo 2001), practically expressed in the new tasks of collaboration between the above mentioned services or legislated in new competencies for some sections of the army, border security, etc.[9]

Some shifts in the division of power are encoded in law, as for example the extended periods of legal detention in many countries before an arrested person must appear before a magistrate. This has always been one of the most

---

rism' might not constitute a rejection of modernity as such but a rejection of being shut out from it (Mamdani 2004: 19) or losing out within it or not being able to define it oneself has been obliviated by the construction of an essential alienness rooted in 'culture' and fundamentalist religion.

9 Didier Bigo interprets the developments within the security agencies as a move on their part to develop a new field of activity and give themselves a new lease of life after the end of the Cold War made them well-nigh redundant (Bigo 2002: 64). Richard Rorty warns of the advent of the security agencies as 'de facto rulers' (Rorty 2004: 11).

common measures of anti-terrorism legislation (Crenlinsten 1998: 405) and is being employed again, for example, not only in the PATRIOT ACT of the USA, which allows indefinite detention of non-deportable non-U.S. citizens, but also in the British Anti-terrorism law; the now repealed Indian anti-terrorist law POTA; in Singapore; in South Africa's anti-terrorism bill; or in the Philippines, where the immigration law is used for indefinite detention. Encoded in law are also the new surveillance measures, stop and search licenses or similar methods without judicial warrant as in the USA, in Belarus, in Germany and France (see Amnesty International).

Many laws, particularly those concerning changes in arrest laws and detention laws and the expansion of police powers, explicitly sideline the judiciary or reduce its role. Thus, Rorty's warning that 'the courts would be brushed aside, and the judiciary would lose its independence' (Rorty 2004: 10) might already be beginning to take shape, and possibly with the connivance of the judiciary.

Not in all cases, however, is the shift towards further competencies for the executive and for security agencies encoded in law. Often it is produced by the practices of state agencies, such as the greater reliance of the judiciary on intelligence reports (taking them as proof that makes further evidence unnecessary), and generally the enhanced status of intelligence information for political decision-making. Werner Schiffauer in his contribution to this volume explores the processes whereby a consensus is forged within a state apparatus and beyond on the necessity of changes in the structure of the state implied in the new measures. This also relates to the apparently increased legitimacy of secrecy of governmental activities within democratic regimes. Secrecy is couched not only in terms of security needs but also in terms of expert knowledge. It relates to an increased authority of specialized agencies to 'know best'. This curtails the powers of legislatures. Added to this is often a new level of 'loyalty' of the fourth estate, the media, in relation to governmental policies towards Muslims and Islam. Thus, this innocent word 'prevention', so much less brutal than 'repression', so much less vindictive than 'punishment' entails possibilities for the expansion of state powers that potentially undermine not only civil liberties but also procedures of political deliberation.

Not everywhere unanimity reigns about the necessity of a shifting balance of power, as Thomas Hawley indicates for the USA in his contribution to this volume. The conditions for and precise processes of generating a consensus and overcoming competing interests or oppositional positions within the state apparatus are thus in themselves a matter for analysis. And, as Frank Peter shows in his contribution to this volume, anti-terrorism measures can take an altogether different form, attempting to administer an Islam suitable, that is: incorporable into the nation state.

Identity

Consequently, the conceptualisation of citizenship has undergone implicit but fundamental changes. Firstly, there is a shift of rights and duties in favour of the state related to the new role of suspicion: Suspicion as grounds for governmental action undermines the presumption of innocence. 'Because "the risk" exists always and everywhere, it becomes normality; to be harmless is then the exception that has to be proven by the citizen for his or her own person' (Denninger 2001: 472, my translation).

Although this was posed as a general description of anti-terrorism measures by those who fear for the future of civil rights, not all people are equally likely to be suspect and come under observation. The first task of prevention is, of course, to separate the potential threat from the protected.

The 'war on terror' operates with categories that are for the most part ascriptive categories; the classification of people as potentially dangerous relates only secondarily to their actual activities. Rather, because of the alleged elusiveness of 'the enemy', suspect subjects are classified according to their religious or national background, their ethnicity, their associations or other so called 'characteristics'. These form the basis of the current data gathering and surveillance activities. Surveillance, registration, the gathering of personal data, tracking emails and internet usage, monitoring financial transactions and, above all, stop-and-search and 'sneak-and-peak' searches are, in the end, not undertaken indiscriminately but according to criteria like race, religion and national background. All involve categories and classifications that are not related to the actual activities of those targeted but to their legal status, their history (migration), their nationality or their religious affiliation. Above all it is the construction of 'supporting milieus', those social groups that terrorists might hail from, hide in or that are believed to 'breed' terrorist mindsets, that extends the preventive measures and their categories to include innumerable people who have no other connection to the perceived threat than their religious identity or regional background (see Schiffauer and Turner in this volume). 'Seeing like a state' (Scott 1998) in the war on terror involves categories that are at the same time selective and distinctive, but also broad and vague.

Attempts to fix identities, to create secure knowledge about individuals, such as are discussed by Tobias Kelly in his contribution to this volume, always produce their specific possibilities of fraud and conceal-ment — and thus further perceptions of insecurities for the state. Kelly shows why attempts to make people more legible through biometric identity documents actually force security personnel to resort back to the actual bodies of people, and thus promotes a racialized approach to security measures. 'Precisely because identity cards do not tell the state everything they want to know, state officials are forced to resort to reading bodies for marks of suspicion, feeding into racialized notions of danger.' Connected to the categories and classifications of security measures, a new focus on national homogeneity is emerging; heterogeneity is perceived as a 'problem' to be tackled and, potentially, a security risk. Of course, heterogeneity has often been considered and treated as a problem, not only since the rise of the idea of the nation-state, and particularly in Western immigration countries.[10] However, the current idea of homogeneity, implicit as it is in the categories of 'potential danger', does not only supersede heterogeneity (or specific kinds of ethnic or religious forms of heterogeneity), but instead introduces a dichotomy related to the spectre of the clash of civilisations. The idea of a clash of civilisations, and particularly its implicit or explicit applications in security measures, employs a concept of culture as being of a deterministic nature.

Some forms of heterogeneity are thus not a matter of difference or plurality, but of alienness. This firstly targets Muslim minorities. While distinctions are made on all levels of the new security discourses (mostly by non-Muslims) between 'good Muslims' and 'bad Muslims', between Islam and Islamism, and – despite the references to the similarities – between the Abrahamitic religions, the implicit labelling of people (and of types of conflicts) under the quasi-explanatory heading of Islam constructs Muslims as the 'other'. This construction, rooted as it is in the history of Western imperialism (Mamdani 2004; Agnes 2005), also relegates Islam to the realm of the innately pre-modern. Unlike others designated as pre-modern, Muslims are assumed to be also largely anti-modern, thus replacing philanthropic or paternalist relations designed for the purely pre-modern with those of 'fear and pre-emptive police or military action' (Mamdani 2004: 18). This spawns two seemingly divergent types of administrative and legal strategy. On the one hand we have those counter-terrorism strategies which are 'played out in the incorporation, administration and regulation of Islamic institutions and practices', as Frank Peter shows in his contribution to this volume. For him, civil Islam, as he calls it, is a governmental strategy, 'a state policy aiming to refashion a certain number of institutions and practices among immigrants from Islamic background in order to reduce the risk of socio-political conflicts and terrorism'. It risks, however, 'entrenching the perception of Islam as a potential threat'. On the other hand we have policies that aim at exclusion, banishment or containment, such as those discussed by Schiffauer, Kelly and Hawley.

---

10 As Nina Glick Schiller has pointed out, in the U.S. there often existed a relationship between anti-immigration laws and assimilation campaigns and measures against religious and political diversity, which even included de-naturalisation. See also Cole (2003).

Social discourses of 'othering' differ and connect to local plausibilities. Islamophobia (cf. EUMC 2006) and the fear of ethnic heterogeneity reign large in countries of immigrant Muslim communities, but also in India, a country with an indigenous Muslim population of about 140 million. Muslim majority countries differed widely in their reactions, depending not so much on their democratic or authoritarian set-up, but on the status of religion in their state ideology (Middle East Working Group 2002). As Bertram Turner shows in his chapter on Morocco, social patterns of othering there took on different forms of distinguishing between 'others' who could be re-integrated – 'lost sons', so to say – and those who were constructed to be foreign, dangerous and essentially alien. Thus, the dichotimisations of the war on terror take root wherever and to the degree that societal fissures and tensions correlate to the categorisations of security.

The impact of such dichotomies on group relations, both the relation between majority and minority populations and social relations within targeted groups, has yet to be explored, and even more so, since the concept of 'the sleeper' as the undiscovered and undiscoverable 'dangerous other' has complicated the relation between assimilation and 'otherness'. 'The sleeper's' is an idea of invisible otherness; it questions commonly held ideas of similarity and belonging. While those who are clearly identifiable as (practizing) Muslims in Europe have gained the nimbus of the quintessential 'other' and are therefore often considered and even treated as potentially suspect, the real danger is now seen in those who cannot be distinguished as being different, but are assumed to be essentially so. The allegedly malevolent concealment of their essential otherness justifies the return to criteria of 'heritage' in blood or ethnicity for distinguishing between 'us' and 'them'.

Related to this, conceptualisations of different 'degrees of membership' in polities have gained a new saliency. The idea of a national core culture, be it the so-called 'Judeo-Christian tradition' of Europe – which, of course, officially became 'Judeo' only after the annihilation of six million Jews in Europe – or, for example, Hinduism in India, which different groups can be more or less close to, and which bestows on them more or less legitimate claims to membership, re-emerges as a notion of political organisation. Claims to membership and membership itself can own different degrees of legitimacy, and this legitimacy is being grounded more generally in a *ius sanguinis* or a religio-cultural complex, that is something of a *ius culturae*. Culture here again is perceived as a quasi-natural disposition. It is clearly demarcated according to one's religious background.

This culturalisation of membership rights enters legal categories in naturalisation procedures, legal grounds for expulsion or denial of entry, observation, screening and inspection of whole categories of the population (rather than of individuals). It is thus not mere rhetoric; it undermines our very principles of universality by re-introducing systems of dual law.

Dual Law

The attachment of civil rights to membership ideas that rely not on formal criteria but on criteria of 'culture' or 'blood' is visible in the developments leading to unequal structures of access to law. The tendencies towards a shift of the burden of proof onto members of certain social categories, and very concretely the policing laws that ground legitimate police action on mere suspicion or even merely the 'potential' of a person committing a crime is possibly the foremost instrument of this development: If whole categories of people are considered potential threats, individuals belonging to these categories have to prove their non-dangerousness. This abandons the presumption of innocence and introduces a measure of *Sippenhaftung*, i.e. the collective liability of family members, co-religionists, or others categorized as having the 'same' characteristics. If ascriptive membership or a legal or merely 'biographical' status such as that of being an 'immigrant' – and particularly a Muslim one, whether naturalized or not – is enough to provide grounds for suspicion, and suspicion now provides grounds for police action, this shift of the burden of proof is extended to people who have not engaged in any criminal activity but are suspected of having the potential to at some point do so simply because of their religious or national background, their legal status, their acquaintances or possibly their extended family relations (see also Cole 2003: 2). The presumption of innocence is restricted to 'us', for 'them' there is the suspicion of guilt.

Werner Schiffauer in his contribution to this book explores the ways in which unequal access to law is established in Germany. He shows how dual law tendencies are often not explicit in legislations. The ways in which such unequal access to law or dual law is de facto created lie in the practices of judges and administrators and their interpretations of norms.

Not only citizenship rights but even basic civil rights and human rights, that should pertain to all persons on the territory of a state, whether citizen or not, whether legally or illegally present, attain a new character as they become attached to conditions either of membership or of 'worth'. Adding to a culturalisation of membership is a *moralisation of rights*.

As becomes apparent in Thomas Hawley's discussion of the 'citizen terrorist', the two processes are related. 9/11 brought onto the stage terrorists as foreigners. Hitherto, most terrorists had been nationals of the state they attacked. The foreignness of Islamist terrorists was in line with the construction of their cultural alienness and their status as outsiders. However, there were the perplexing cases of nationals who joined the Islamist cause. This was a matter of betrayal. The perception that terrorists were aliens in a legal sense gave way to the perception that terrorists were aliens in a social sense, whereby nationals also became outsiders to the moral realm of the community.

The new moralisation that re-attaches rights to the moral worth of a person – as judged by those who can provide access to or deny rights – is visible in extremis in the treatment of 'unlawful enemy combatants' in Guantanamo and other places of detention, and in its justification by Dick Chaney when he said: 'The people that are at Guantanamo are bad people.'[11] These detentions not only contravene any code of international law, but also introduce the logic of the rights of (assumed) terrorists to be less important, less valuable than the rights of others, since they are 'bad people'. There are two versions of this argument. Firstly, it has been held that the protection of the rights of (alleged or convicted) terrorists is not compatible with justice since the protection of their rights would violate the rights of their victims and even their potential victims (see for example the debates of the European parliament as described in Tsoukala 2004: ft 27 and 28). The denial of rights with the argument that a person is 'bad' goes in some ways even further, since it categorically denies those deemed to be 'bad' the right to have rights. Jakobs defined the duty of the state for a 'law for enemies' (*Feindstrafrecht*) in the following manner: 'Whoever does not provide sufficient cognitive securities of behaviour as a person cannot expect to be treated as a person. Even more, the state must not treat him as a person since he would otherwise violate the right to security of other persons' (Jakobs 2004: 93, my translation).

The re-moralisation of rights in this manner, of connecting access to law, or the right to have rights to the moral value of a person – a moral value, that is defined, of course, by those who have the power to determine access – and the new role of the state in defining morally worthy citizens or people adds new forms of legitimizing (and legalizing) inequality before the law to old forms of exclusion.

The construction of a normative community which is evident in all the Manichaean and belligerent oppositions of civilisation vs. barbarism, freedom vs. hatred, 'with us or against us' etc. condemns certain categories of people who are not considered morally to be members of the normative community to the status of outlaws. This exclusion, again, is not achieved with respect to the activities or actual deeds of the persons concerned but with respect to their religious or national background. 'If to live by the rule of law is to belong to a common political community, then does not the selective application of the rule of law confirm a determination to relegate entire sections of humanity as

---

11 Dick Chaney on Fox News Channel, Monday 13 June 2005.

conscripts of a civilisation fit for collective punishment?' (Mamdani 2004: 257). This dual system of law finds its climactic formulation in the debate on a special criminal law for 'enemies' as practically invented by the USA in its detention centres (of which Guantanamo is only one), or the '*Feindstrafrecht*' as it has been called in German (Jakobs 2004). A special criminal law for 'public enemies' is emerging. It differs from other criminal law in that it creates different legal standards for 'enemies', whatever or whoever that may be, and even for 'potential enemies'. Since the point of the law for enemies is prevention of future deeds (Jakobs 2004: 92), an enemy cannot be distinguished from a potential enemy. The identification of a potential of a person to become an enemy will differ: It can either rely on previous deeds, or on intentions and processes of planning, or on membership in specific organisations or on categories of people who are deemed potentially hostile. Guantanamo and other centres of detention, and the whole concept of 'unlawful enemy combatants', are the beginnings of such special criminal law for 'enemies'. However, it is also visible in the circumvention of 'normal' criminal law and its safeguards by the use of administrative law in security measures.

Philosophically, these ideas of dealing with 'the enemy' were frequently related to the fundamental distinction between friend and foe that was for Carl Schmitt, the German jurist whose ideas gave Nazism a justification in legal philosophy and political theory, the essence of the political. Schmitt, unlike the propagators of the 'war on terror', did not write about morals;[12] he insists that the opposition between friend and foe underlying the political is in no way related to the opposition between good and evil (Schmitt [1932] 1963: 27) or any other such opposition. Schmitt does, of course, hold that the existence of the state (state security) supersedes all other legal norms: 'In a state of emergency the state suspends law by virtue of its right to self-preservation' (Schmitt [1934] 1979: 19, my own translation). This is reminiscent of the U.S. justifications for the suspension of rights during the 'war on terror', although U.S. officials usually employed a more mundane language than Schmitt's theoretical elaborations.

The law for enemies also differs from ordinary criminal law in that it does not intend to rehabilitate, reform or even punish, but, above all, to banish (see Jakobs 2004: 89). Banishment, of course, can be a punishment more severe than other kinds of penalties. All measures, the seemingly banal ones of gathering data on the religious belonging of a person, or the dramatic ones applied at the detention centres, are justified largely with reference to 'banishing dan-

---

12 Denninger (2005) therefore sees Fichte as the original thinker of the law for enemies, the *Feindstrafrecht* (Denninger 2005: 9), and Fichte's ideas on the outlaw are also cited by Jakobs (2004) in his advocacy of this kind of law.

ger' or preventing it from materializing: Indefinite detention at Guantanamo has been justified by pointing out that some of the detainees who had been released had taken up the fight against U.S. forces again and that this needed to be prevented.[13] In Germany the use of the Law for Foreigners (*Ausländerrecht*) and its provisions for deportation and denial of entry, rather than of criminal law in order to deal with people considered to potentially pose a security risk, is justified by the idea that this way, potential danger can be banished from German territory.[14] The securitisation specific to the 'war on terror' made possible such uses of administrative and procedural law for security concerns. Procedural and administrative law is used in many places to circumvent the safeguards built into criminal law (see Cole 2003: 14). Administrative procedures are used where criminal law would not hold as those targeted cannot be convincingly accused of committing a crime recognized by penal law (Schiffauer in this volume). Legal status thus attains a new significance in matters of fundamental rights and the access to law, since the universality of protections under criminal law does not pertain to administrative procedures or immigration law etc., for which legal status is of course central (see also Bender 2003).

Banishing danger is the core idea of the preventive state. It relates to what Garland has described as the 'culture of control' that de-socializes crime, and gives up on rehabilitation or reform, but restricts itself to 'retribution, incapacitation and the management of risk' (Garland 2001: 8). The enemy (and the criminal) are perceived to be beyond redemption or the possibility of (re)integration because their deviance is seen to be rooted in their 'nature' or personality (Garland 2001: 181), rather than in the social context.

'Intrinsic evil defies all attempts at rational comprehension or criminological explanation. There can be no mutual intelligibility, no bridge of understanding, no real communication between "us" and "them". To treat them as understandable [...] is to bring criminals into our domain, to humanize them, to see ourselves in them and them in ourselves' (Garland 2001: 184).

The externalisation of 'the enemy' is, of course, all the more plausible when the explanation for their 'difference' is strengthened by reference to 'a different culture' and its fundamental 'otherness' or the perception of a 'new terror-

---

13 Dick Cheney, quoted in *Süddeutsche Zeitung*, 15 June 2005, "Schlechte Menschen", p. 10.
14 The contradiction inherent in the call for a global 'war on terror' and the practice of banishing people considered to be potentially a security risk beyond national boundaries is not addressed. In this way, the U.S. detention centres and all forms of indefinite detention are consequent to the proclaimed globality of the 'war on terror'.

ism' that is fuelled by an innate hatred of modernity. Because the 'enemy', the deviant or the criminal is in this way treated as essentially different and thus beyond (re-)integration, they primarily need to be banished, excluded, incapacitated. For Garland, it is the prison that is 'located precisely at the junction point of two of the most important social and penal dynamics of our time: risk and retribution' (Garland 2001: 199). Of course, expulsion, deportation or the denial of entry have the same potentials for the management of risk, and they have similar, if sometimes more fundamental aspects of retribution or punishment (see Bender 2003: 132).

Banishing danger de-socializes conflicts; it de-politicizes terrorism and merges ideas of innate alienness with (in many cases largely) administrative procedures of exclusion. Technologies of prevention and neo-liberal thinking about crime as discussed by Garland (2001) prepared the ground for thoughts about terror. The crime regime Garland describes presents itself as 'un-ideological' 'technical', preventive and incapacitating, etc. It is, of course, ideological in its interpretation of social relations and the individual, depicting crime as resulting from a natural disposition rather than from circumstances. With the war on terror this whole way of thinking is pushed further into a field of morals ('evil'). And culture enters into the equation replacing the nature of character or psyche with a quasi-natural cultural disposition, as implicit in any notion of a clash of civilisations. In this way, the neo-liberal philosophy of crime prepared the grounds for the neo-conservative philosophy of cultural enmity and its translation into policy. The belligerent opposition of 'good and evil', 'freedom and hatred', 'civilisation and barbarism' is thus no mere rhetoric or the creation of enemy images, but has already entered the procedures of law and administration.

The inadvertent proximity of general trends in policing, of the preventive posture of the war on terror, and the ideas of Schmitt have triggered a debate on the advent of the permanent state of emergency (Agamben 2003). But just as debates on the general threat to civil liberties posed by security measures – which is, of course, also a valid criticism – overlook the development of a dual class system of rights, the idea of the age of exceptionalism also seems to miss the asymmetry of the state of emergency. Of course, all states of emergency do not target all citizens equally; usually they target certain forms of behaviour and certain activities equally, regardless of the person in question – denying rights to these actions. The current situation, however, treats certain activities differently according to who 'commits' them. 'While there has been much talk about the need to sacrifice liberty for a greater sense of security, in practice we have selectively sacrificed *non-citizens'* liberties while retaining basic protections for citizens' (Cole 2002: 955, emphasis in the original).

Since citizenship now comes in different degrees,[15] the protection of someone's liberties and rights also depends on his or her degree of legitimate membership. Generally, criticism and opposition to the politics of security were not forcibly stifled. Indeed, there are many dissenting voices from human rights organisations, lawyers and academics. Beyond a potential general threat to civil liberties entailed in the new measures, it is the idea of equality before the law that seems to be undermined in a new manner – and with a new degree of legitimacy.

Consensus

In many countries, especially those in the West, previous resistance to far-reaching security measures seems to have dissolved.[16] This is due, it seems, firstly to the emergence of dual law: Since most people actually do not feel – rightly or wrongly – they might become a target of the new laws, since they do not belong to the categories of people addressed by them, they also do not

---

15 A case in point beside the various cases of the revocation of citizenship when the persons concerned hold a double citizenship and one of them is revoked, is one case in which German citizenship was revoked despite the person in question having no other citizenship, and having committed no deed other than not declaring his membership in an organisation that is under observation by the German Federal Security Agency. The organisation in question is not outlawed and has not even been accused or is suspected of promoting violence or similar such unconstitutional activities. In 2007, the Administrative High Court overturned the ruling and granted the plea for the retention of German citizenship.

16 There are many voices of dissent, such as human rights organisations, immigrant rights and asylum groups, concerned lawyers, etc. As suggested above, they were not forcibly silenced. Their media presence is, however, marginal. Moreover, their dissenting opinions remain marginal also in the face of the social dichotomisation already prevalent. In a few countries, resistance to the expansion of anti-terrorist measures seems to have borne fruit – for different reasons. In Kenya, their introduction was prevented by public protests (Bachmann 2004: 5), apparently largely because of the memory of authoritarian rule is still fresh in the public's mind. In Mauritius, both the president and vice president refused to give assent to the Prevention of Terrorism Special Measures Regulations, which were enacted in 2003, and resigned. In India, the new anti-terrorist law POTA passed by the BJP was resisted by opposition parties (and of course many civil rights activists), and it was repealed by the Congress-led government which came into power in 2004. This might not have been for the love of civil liberties but rather for other political reasons, and it also does not necessarily mean that the new Indian government employs entirely different practices against what it classifies as terrorism. Nonetheless, these examples raise the question of what the conditions are for 'logics' other than that of the preventive state to be effective, other perceptions of the situation to be accepted and other voices to be heard – and why elsewhere this is not so.

oppose measures they would otherwise find unacceptable (see also Hirsch 2002: 6).[17] The production of clarity by locating societal troubles in a foe – who is without history or cause – potentially overcomes the deep ambivalence towards some surveillance measures and other expansions of state control. The dichotomisation of good and (potentially) dangerous, of worthy members and suspicious subjects, and the apparent bifurcation of the threat (of falling victim to terrorist attacks and of falling victim to the war on terror) reproduce the dichotomy of 'us' and 'them' underlying the dual law system.

Secondly, there seems to be a new consensus on a conceptualisation of security and risk that relates individual, national and international security in a new manner. The security discourse elevates state security as the precondition for other forms of (individual or societal) security above all other forms of security, especially above social security, but also above civic security (i.e. the security from the state, habeas corpus, privacy, etc.). The distinction between private and public enemies is dissolved (Bigo 2002: 81). The politics of 'unease', as Bigo called it (Bigo 2002), the new role of fear that can be witnessed in the dramatic scenarios of the media, the moral panics, as several authors have described the new Islamophobia (Schiffauer 2005); bring about a return to Hobbes – who had probably never been very far anyway. New ideas of security become common sense in the acceptance of governmental authority to know best how to protect, and from what. 9/11 provided an opportunity for many governments to overcome some – or most – of the resistance posed by parliaments, the media, civil rights groups or the judiciary.

Consensus seems to be dependent either on the successful portrayal of an 'us vs. them' distinction so as to make security measures appear to target only 'them' and identify the state with 'us', rendering public enemies and private enemies quasi-identical. Wherever such a dichotomy could not be convincingly established – either, it seems, because the targeting of all citizens by state security measures was still too vividly remembered, like in Kenya, or, as in many Muslim majority countries, because no essential alienness could be argued – the plausibility of the necessity of the security measures, or their beneficial nature for the 'good citizen' seems to have been less evident. Decisive for the social life of anti-terrorism laws seems to be whether there is or emerges a congruence between governmental categories of 'the dangerous other' and societal forms of othering. Unanimity on securitisation apparently progresses best alongside the dichotomisation of society.

On another level, and in some ways even more subversive, the new laws served as powerful instruments in conflicts entirely unrelated to security is-

---

17 An indication of this is also the outcry in Britain about the suggestion to extend the powers of detention without trial inherent in the British anti-terrorism law to all Britons in order to make the law less discriminative (Large 2005: 3).

sues and thus were embedded in the structures of political competition. They became indispensable, and even in places were they were revoked, like in India, where the anti-terrorism law of 2002 was repealed in 2004, they found new forms in criminal law reforms or in other extraordinary laws.[18] In India like in Morocco, the new possibilities for damaging an opponent inherent in the laws also entered into local quarrels, being used as a weapon in struggles and disputes at the neighbourhood level, or in local rivalries amongst different economic groups (Turner in this volume), and became a powerful weapon for the police and anybody in league with them.[19] They had the potential to change local power relations by providing new measures of legitimate participation. Individuals or groups, the legitimacy of whose membership could be questioned along the lines of the new culturalisation of membership and the moralisation of rights, now find it harder to articulate their claims. Not only governments made use of the new possibilities for 'pre-emptive punishment' and control inherent in the security measures; civil society actors, too, adopted the measures for their own purposes. As Turner writes in his contribution to this volume: 'The fact that local people make use of Moroccan anti-terror legislation for their own purposes implicitly keeps it operative.'

Thus, the structures created and the laws passed in the course of the 'war on terror' can affect political practices and social relations far beyond their immediate goal. They become embedded in the political structures through their usefulness for diverse strategies. Through the adoption of the measures, their justificatory imagery of friend vs. foe, of the unworthy other, of the moralisation of rights also enters into the practices of those using the measures. This imagery can be as useful as the measures in themselves, since subsuming diverse conflicts under one banner potentially creates new alliances[20] that strengthen different agendas, thereby uniting against a common enemy.

The export of ideas through the export of policy, however, succeeds best when there is an additional local use for the exports. So far it is mainly in countries and societies where social tensions can be interpreted along the lines

---

18 India amended its unlawful activities (prevention) bill to include some of the provisions of the repealed POTA. However, it abolished the provisions for indefinite detention and for confessions to the police being admitted in court, thus abandoning the measures most prone to misuse.

19 The measures were more easily instrumentalized in this manner when the targets were Muslim, since then they could more plausibly be connected to the global discourse of the 'dangerous other'; but some prominent cases also involved non-Muslim politicians opposed to the regional leading parties.

20 One striking new alliance is the one in Germany between left-wing feminists, such as Alice Schwarzer, and right-wing politicians, who both oppose Islam in the name of protecting women against 'tradition'. In India, on the other hand, the hijacking of women's issues by the Hindu Right was resisted by the feminist movement, albeit not always successfully.

of the 'war on terror', that is, where the foe can be externalized from society and such externalisations have a history that dual law emerges, and the culturalisation of membership and the moralisation of rights takes root.

Reactions

There are as yet no investigations into the reactions of those groups specifically targeted by anti-terrorist measures and their categorisations of labeling and of unequal access to law. One question is whether these developments actually serve to diminish the threat of further terrorist activities and recruitment (see Crenshaw 1991). Since they fail to isolate terrorism from widely felt grievances, but rather seem to further the plausibility of this link, one could claim that they are likely to produce more anger and hatred among the targeted and thus possibly produce more terrorists or at least sympathies with their ideas.

The actual 'production of terrorists' is possibly hard to prove, since causative explanations must be more complex. The reactions of those belonging to targeted categories can be assessed, however, in terms of their withdrawal from social relations beyond their group and in terms of their identification with and use of norms and institutions of a polity. Both are possibly strongly affected by the experience of labelling and of unequal access to law. From what we learned from research into individual and collective identity formation, the measures implemented under the 'war on terror' are likely to produce a social dichotomisation that leads to experiences of alienation and processes of self-segregation. These may trigger militancy and anti-systemic violence.

The social and political costs of escalation seem obvious, but also the retreat and further segregation of groups considered and treated with distrust, and faced with a constant suspicion must cause social costs. Organisations which are being criminalized or forcibly dissolved might go underground, where they will most likely develop new internal dynamics, new structures of leadership and new ideologies of integration or alienation. Moreover, social segregation also often means new social relations within one group, and a strengthened exclusivity of identification with that group which entails new dependencies, new hierarchies and new structures of communication and trust.

Conclusion

The globalisation of the 'war on terror' operates on at least two levels: One is the explicit export of security technologies, legal arrangements, knowledge, and the coordination of alliances and forms of cooperation in various policy fields. These efforts take different courses, some relying on pressure, others on financial incentives, or both, and yet others on a moral economy of alliances.

On another level, the 'war on terror' is globalized by the various forms of appropriation of its specific ideas of security and danger, its categories and maps as forms of knowledge, its interpretations of conflicts. It is established on different levels, entering into political relations as a new tool and steering ideas about security and danger in a specific direction: Ideas of security are, again, first and foremost ideas about state security, subsuming other forms of security under the former. This also entails renewed sources of nationalism, relying, of course, on enemy images that have always accompanied such sentiments. Thinking about difference, belonging and alienness, however, is increasingly shaped in broader, more global and therefore in more inescapable and fundamental terms of 'civilisational' core cultures.

The 'war on terror' seems to have globalized the de-socialized conception of conflict that stems from neo-liberal thinking about crime prevention. It has added the cultural dimension, albeit treating culture as a non-social, quasi-natural disposition. Moreover, the notion of 'evil' and the concomitant moralisation of rights affect the ways conflicts are dealt with. The emergence of dual law, explicitly legislated or implicit in the practices of administrators, is due both to the technicist approaches of the preventive state and the culturalisation of belonging and the moralisation of rights. Ideas of 'civilisational' unity and homogeneity shape the ways various forms of social difference are dealt with and are the base of offers of different degrees of membership or exclusion.

Each adoption of the tools provided, for whatever purpose, embeds them in political structures. Power relations between societal groups change or are re-enforced due to differences in the legitimacy of claims to membership and participation established by the model of rights entailed in the security regime of the 'war on terror'. Reactions of the individuals and groups who are targeted by these measures might differ; they might take the form of resignation and withdrawal, radicalisation and the escalation of conflict, or the protest might be voiced by other means. The social and political conditions of each need to be explored.

Thus, we are left with the question of which changes in the ideas of the state and of government have been promoted by the emerging culture of security, and how they affect notions and practices of citizenship. What does the securitisation of politics mean? Is it the advent of a general state of exception? (Agamben 2003) The claim was made that these changes serve long-term goals of altering state structure. Makdisi (2002) as well as Düx (2003), for example, maintain that we are observing the final push for a general shift from a providing state (either of welfarist or developmental nature) to a controlling or preventive state for which 'terrorism' is merely an occasion for expansion. This thesis is supported by the fact that most legislation allegedly necessary because of the novelty of the 'new terrorism', or the general merger of internal and external security, was not new but had long been debated in many countries. 9/11 provided an opportunity for many governments to overcome some – or most – of the resistance posed by parliaments, the media, civil rights groups or the judiciary. Likewise, the re-emergence of retribution and incapacitation as a way of dealing with conflicts or with crime has been developing ever since the late 1990s, as Garland (2001) has shown. Despite these precedents, it appears that the 'war on terror' gives these developments a new quality: Firstly, it has established the dispositive of security as the globally predominant one, at least for the time being. It has made plausible the employment of specific expertises about social conflict (rather than others), and it has furthered a specific merger of social and governmental practices of othering, resulting also in the culturalisation of membership and the moralisation of rights.

Acknowledgements

I thank Nina Glick Schiller and Tatjana Thelen for their insightful and inspiring comments on an earlier version of this chapter. I am grateful to the participants of the workshop 'The Social Life of Anti-Terrorism Laws' held from 26 to 27 May 2005 at the Max Planck Institute for Social Anthropology in Halle/Saale for the fruitful discussions on the issue. I am indebted to the initiative *'Justizgewährung, Staatsraison und Geheimdienste'* of the Berlin Brandenburg Academy of Sciences from which I have gained valuable insights into the legal debates on the topic. I thank Werner Schiffauer for many engaged discussions on the politics of security which have inspired this chapter.

References

Agamben, G. (2003): *Stato di Eccezione*, Torino: Bollati Boringhieri.

Agnes, F. (2005): 'Citizenship and Identity in Post 9/11 Nations'. In: A. Fitz/M. Kröger/A. Schneider/D. Wenner (eds), *Import Export. Cultural Transfer. India, Germany, Austria*, Berlin and New Delhi: Parthas Verlag and Katha, pp. 182-88.

Amnesty International (no year): Charting the 'War on Terrorism', at: http://www.amnestyusa.org/amnestynow/war_terrorism.html (accessed 25 June 2005).

Bachmann, J. (2004): '"Leave no Continent Behind'. Die Integration Afrikas in den Krieg gegen den Terror und ihre Folgen', *Afrika im Blickpunkt*, 3: 1-7.

Bascombe, D. (2003): Anti Terrorism Legislation in the Commonwealth, at: http://www.humanrightsinitiative.org/new/anti_terror_legislationcw2003.pdf (accessed 25 June 2005).

—— (2004): *An Update of Anti Terror Legislation in the Commowealth*, at: http://www.humanrightsinitiative.org/new/anti_terror_legislationcw 2004.pdf (accessed 25 June 2005).

Bender, D. (2003): ''Verpolizeilichung' des Ausländerrechts? Die ausländerrechtlichen Maßnahmen des Gesetzgebers nach dem 11. September 2001', *Kritische Justiz*, 36: 130-45.

Bigo, D. (2001): 'The Möbius Ribbon of Internal and External Security(ies)'. In: M. Albert/D. Jacobson/Y. Lapid (eds), *Identities, Borders and Orders*, Minneapolis: University of Minnesota Press, pp. 91-116.

—— (2002): 'Security and Immigration: toward a Critique of the Governmentality of Unease', *Alternatives*, 27, Special Issue: 63-92.

Buruma, I./Margalit, A. (2004): *Occidentalism; the West in the Eyes of its Enemies*, New York: Penguin.

Buzan, B./ de Wilde, J./Wæver, O. (1998): *Security. A New Framework for Analysis*, Boulder, CO: Lynne Rienner.

Cole, D. (2002): 'Enemy Aliens', *Stanford Law Review*, 54: 953-1004.

—— (2003): 'The New McCarthyism: Repeating History in the War on Terrorism', *Harvard Civil Rights-Civil Liberties Law Review*, 38(1): 1-30.

Crenlinsten, R. (1998): 'The Discourse and Practice of Counter-terrorism in Liberal Democracies', *Australian Journal of Politics and History*, 44: 389-413.

Crenshaw, M. (1991): 'How Terrorism Declines', *Terrorism and Political Violence*, 3: 69-87.

Denninger, E. (2001): 'Freiheit durch Sicherheit?', *Kritische Justiz*, 4: 467-78.

—— (2005): 'Recht, Gewalt und Moral', Frankfurter Rundschau, 20 June 2005, at: http://www.fraktuell.de/ressorts/nachrichten_und_politik/dokumenta tion/?cnt=690272 (accessed 27 June 2005).
Diner, D. (2004): 'Steht das *jus in bello* in Frage? Über Regulierung und Deregulierung der Anwendung von Gewalt'. In: E. Reiter/W. Matyas (eds), *Jahrbuch für Internationale Sicherheitspolitik*, Hamburg: Mittler & Sohn, pp. 59-71.
Düx, H. (2003): 'Globale Sicherheitsgesetze und weltweite Erosion von Grundrechten', *Zeitschrift für Rechtspolitik (ZRP)*, 6: 189-95.
European Monitoring Centre on Racism and Xenophobia (EUMC) (2006): 'Muslims in the European Union: Discrimination and Xenophobia', Wien.
Garland, D. (2001): *The Culture of Control*, Oxford, New York: Oxford University Press.
Hirsch, B. (2002): 'Der attackierte Rechtsstaat: Bürgerrechte und "Innere Sicherheit" nach dem 11. September', *Vorgänge*, 3: 5-9.
Jakobs, G. (2004): 'Bürgerstrafrecht und Feindstrafrecht', *HRR-Strafrecht*, 3(5): 88-95.
Krishnan, J. (2004): 'India's Patriot Act: POTA and the Impact on Civil Liberties in the World's Largest Democracy', *Law and Inequality*, 22: 265-300.
Laqueur, W. (2000): *The New Terrorism; Fanaticism and the Arms of Mass Destruction*, Oxford: Oxford University Press.
Large, J. (2005): 'Democracy and Terrorism'. Paper presented at the International Summit on Democracy, Terrorism and Security, 8-11 March 2005, Madrid, at: http://english.safe-democracy.org (accessed 27 June 2005).
Lepsius, O. (2004): 'Freiheit, Sicherheit und Terror: die Rechtslage in Deutschland', *Leviathan*, 32(1): 64-88.
Mahmood, C. (2001): 'Terrorism, Myth, and the Power of Ethnographic Praxis', *Journal of Contemporary Ethnography*, 30(5): 520-45.
Makdisi, S. (2002): 'Spectres of 'Terrorism'', *Interventions*, 4(2): 265-78.
Mamdani, M. (2004): *Good Muslim, Bad Muslim*, New York: Pantheon Books.
Mayntz, R. (2004): 'Hierarchie oder Netzwerk? Zu den Organisationsformen des Terrorismus', *Berliner Journal für Soziologie*, 14(2): 251-62.
Middle East Working Group (2002): 'Summaries of the Papers presented at the Annual Meeting of the American Political Science Association', *Middle East Policy*, 9(4): 75-101.
Morgan, M. (2004): 'The Origins of the New Terrorism', *Parameters*, XXXIV(1): 29-43.
Rorty, R. (2004): 'Post Democracy', *London Review of Books*, 1 April 2004: 10-11.

Schiffauer, W. (2006): 'Enemies within the Gates: the Debate about Citizenship of Muslims in Germany'. In: T. Modood/A. Triandafyllidou/R. Zapata-Barrero (eds), *Multiculturalism, Muslims and Citizenship: a European Approach*, London: Routledge, pp. 94-116.

Schmitt, C. ([1932] 1963): *Der Begriff des Politischen*, Berlin: Duncker & Humblot.

—— ([1934] 1979): *Politische Theologie*, Berlin: Duncker & Humblot.

Scott, J. (1998): *Seeing like a State: how Certain Schemes to Improve the Human Condition Have Failed*, New Haven: Yale University Press.

Steinberg, G. (2005): 'Entwicklungstendenzen im militanten Islamismus'. In: Senatsverwaltung für Inneres, Abteilung Verfassungsschutz (ed.), *Islamismus: Diskussion um ein vielschichtiges Phänomen*, Berlin: Senatsverwaltung, pp. 44-59.

Stevenson, J. (2001-2): 'Pragmatic Counter-terrorism', *Survival*, 43: 35-48.

Tilly, C. (2004): 'Terror, Terrorism, Terrorists', *Sociological Theory*, 22(1): 5-13.

Tsoukala, A. (2004): *Democracy and Security: the Debates about Counter Terrorism in the European Parliament, September 2001 - June 2003*, at: http://www.libertyandsecurity.org/article137.html (accessed 29 November 2004).

Tucker, D. (2001): 'What is New about the New Terrorism and how Dangerous is it?' *Terrorism and Political Violence*, 13(3): 1-14.

Waldmann, P. (2004): 'Islamistischer Terrorismus; Ideologie, Organisation und Unterstützungspotenzial', *Kriminalistik*, 12: 740-45.

Wæver, O. (1995): 'Securitization and Desecuritization'. In: R.D. Lipschutz (ed.), *On Security*, New York: Columbia University Press, pp. 46-86.

Liberalism versus Terrorism: Warfare, Crime Control, and the United States after 11 September

THOMAS M. HAWLEY

The United States' 'war on terror' has drawn widespread criticism in the years since the attacks of 11 September 2001. For some, it not only entails major violations of human rights but signals an active effort to dismantle legal protections refined over the course of centuries and is therefore a mortal threat to the liberties enshrined in the Constitution. For others, it demonstrates the continued ascendancy of the executive branch in a manner at odds with the principle of checks and balances. Still others resent the United States waging war against a country with no demonstrable relationship to the horrors of that day. By contrast, those fighting the war on terror argue that the president enjoys sweeping powers during wartime that constitutional protections are reserved for Americans who choose to obey the law, and that international legal frameworks improperly limit the sovereignty of nation-states under attack. While these issues are undoubtedly important, they also tend to assume the relevance of the classically defined liberal state for purposes of understanding the United States' war on terror. That state, so the story goes, exercises sovereignty over a given territory and hence has certain rights and responsibilities which are simultaneously limited by a social contract that requires the protection of the natural rights and freedoms of its citizens. This framework, of course, sets the stage for the heated debates since 11 September about the use and abuse of state power in the war on terror. It also inhibits a more comprehensive analysis of the changing nature of political power and the citizen-state relationship in the early twenty-first century.

In this chapter, I argue that the American response to 11 September cannot be adequately understood if we assume the continued relevance of the classically defined liberal state and the accompanying division of state violence into an external warfare mode and an internal domestic crime control mode. Instead, we must recognize the ambiguities that trouble the liberal state's use of violence and take seriously the ways in which these uncertainties reshape the relationship of citizens to their state. Terrorists figure prominently here because they pose a unique challenge to the credibility of the state's exercise of sovereignty over a given territory as well as its claim to secure the lives of its citizens against external aggression. As we know from Locke and Weber, among others, the legitimate use of violence in accomplishing these tasks is one criterion by which the liberal state is distinguished from other sources of authority whose violent possibilities have been gradually expropriated over time (Kaufman-Osborn 2002). When this is a question of either arresting criminal activity within or of combating aggression from without, the use of liberal violence is a relatively straightforward matter. In the former, the state exercises its statutory right to detain offenders and deprive them of either life or liberty (the state in crime control mode as ensurer of domestic tranquility), while in the latter the state combats acts of war against it by matching force with force in a manner that can be provided by no other entity within the polity (the state in warfare mode as provider of common defense).

Things become more complicated, however, when the categorical distinctions upon which liberal violence is predicated become blurred as they do when the danger to which the state must respond comes from 'unlawful combatants', meaning those whose violence fails to come from within the confines of state sovereignty. Matters are complicated still further when the combatants in question are also citizens who have allegedly sided with non-state terrorists, as was the case with Yaser Hamdi, John Walker Lindh, and Jose Padilla. The problem lies not so much in identifying the perpetrators as in how to think about them. Not quite domestic criminals (calling the cops seems a bit feeble), not quite soldiers fighting in war (sending the military seems oddly inapplicable), citizen terrorists, theoretically speaking, are something of a paradox. Simultaneously members of the commonwealth and allegedly committed to its destruction, they are those whom the liberal state promises both to protect and destroy. That the United States chose the second of these two options has understandably been criticized as a departure from liberal principles that accord citizens certain legal protections. Yet it is important to situate this departure within the increasing tendency to regard liberalism's warfare mode as the default response to disorder. In other words, the tactics employed against Lindh, Hamdi, and Padilla indicate not simply a frustration with the constraints imposed by the contractual dimension of liberalism – the dimension that requires governmental protection of individual rights as a condition of legitimacy – but also the conviction that responding to terrorists as if they were mere criminals is insufficient. The terrorist is simply too evil, too radically 'other,' to qualify for law's privileges and the sorts of correctionalist interventions that have for many decades been the standard response to domestic malefactors. The preferred result involves a shift away from the liberal state's crime control mode and towards the tactics peculiar to warfare that have come to characterize American society more generally (witness the 'war on cancer,' the 'war on drugs,' the 'war on terror,' etc.).

It is in light of the increasing application of warfare to disorder that we should understand the United States' response to the events of 11 September. Among other things, this approach trivializes liberalism's legal rights and presumptions of innocence as cumbersome at best or even aids to the enemy when applied to accused terrorists like Hamdi, Lindh, and Padilla. So too does it render 'quaint' the protections of the Geneva Conventions concerning prisoners of war in the eyes of U.S. Attorney General Alberto Gonzales (Cohn 2004). It also entails a qualitative shift in the nature of the citizen's relationship to the state, one whose defining elements were perhaps best captured by White House Press Secretary Ari Fleischer when he issued his immediate post-11 September warning 'to all Americans that they need to watch what they say, watch what they do' (White House 2001b). Presented thusly, individual reaction to 11 September boiled down to a choice between the freedom of expression or cautious silence. Americans, Fleischer implied, should assess the options and then reason their way to appropriate modifications of their behaviour or else risk some unspecified reprisal. Orwellian overtones notwithstanding, Fleischer was on familiar liberal ground when he insisted on reason as the unique faculty that impels man to forsake the state of nature in favour of life in the commonwealth. Presented with the inconveniences and risks that accompany life without government, humans voluntarily accept certain restrictions on their liberty in exchange for the superior freedom that occurs in a society governed by laws. Newly liberated, citizens are now free to pursue their self-interest without worrying about attacks from their neighbours or excessive meddling by their government. What makes this work, in turn, is the neutrality of the government that then enforces those laws. It must not become a participant in the affairs it claims to regulate, nor can it have a predetermined interest in the outcome of those disputes it must from time to time resolve. The state, therefore, relate to citizens as an umpire to players: there when needed, silent and unobtrusive when not.

It is precisely this relationship that gets perverted when the state's warfare mode is employed as a response to disorder. Most noticeably, the forms of rationality specific to warfare become goods in themselves. Not only must citizens reason correctly between competing alternatives, so too must the state become a rational actor, its erstwhile regulatory function transformed by the norms appropriate to combat. So too does the state increasingly participate in the affairs it claims to supervise, as when it establishes incentive structures that reward citizens who reason 'correctly' while punishing those who do not. Still more, disorder-as-warfare reorients the liberal compass away from punishment and rehabilitation and towards repulsion and destruction. An ethic of absolute enmity gradually transforms difference into alterity, with consequences for those who depart (willfully or otherwise) from accepted forms of personhood. Citizens now relate to the state not as players to an umpire but as choosers whose efforts to reason through what they say and what they do is represented as a matter of life or death. Accordingly, I think it helpful to conceptualize the war on terror not so much as a complete dismantling of liberalism but as a strategy for the administration of disorder in late-modern society, one that not only mocks liberalism's traditional limitations on power but fundamentally reframes critical components of the social contract.

By way of contextualizing these developments, I begin by presenting a version of liberalism attuned to the ways in which the social contract amplifies precisely the forms of enmity it claims to minimize when it puts forth the state as a mediator of disputes. The social contract, in other words, *worsens* the seriousness of domestic conflict and external aggression when it embodies the citizenry in an imagined community that now thinks in terms of inside and outside. Because citizens are members of a group defined by territorial borders and specific identity configurations, threats are no longer simply threats to an individual as was the case in the state of nature but to the political order as a whole. Abetting this tendency to inflate the threat posed by disorder are recent criminological theories which emphasize the absolute otherness of the criminal temperament. In particular, the 'criminology of the other' (Garland 2001) explicitly favours retributive punishment in the belief that illicit behaviour arises out of dispositional factors that are beyond the reach of the interventionist strategies of penal welfarism. As will be shown, it is the interaction between the criminology of the other and liberalism's warfare mode that enables the unsavoury practices of the war on terror and contributes to the changing nature of the citizen's relationship to the liberal state.

By way of example, I briefly discuss the indefinite detention of unlawful combatants at the United States naval facility at Guantanamo Bay, Cuba. Despite being a clear departure from liberal principles in the eyes of the United States Supreme Court, this tactic has nevertheless been accepted as a necessary element in the war on terror by substantial majorities of the American public. This apparent necessity is fueled by endless fear-inducing warnings from government officials that characterize terrorism as not only a pure form of evil but a permanent feature of life in the twenty-first century that requires both a militarized response and measures designed to curb forward behaviour before it occurs. Accordingly, I conclude with some reflections on the implications of the war on terror for the future of the citizen-state relationship. As indicated, that relationship is decreasingly amenable to comprehension solely on the basis of the liberal social contract and increasingly governed by norms proper to the marketplace that fetishize reasoning choosers while simultaneously constricting (for those who make the wrong choices) the liberty which social contract theory promises will follow.

John Locke's Disciplinary Liberalism

In *The Second Treatise of Government*, John Locke argues that what differentiates men living in the state of nature from those living in society is the absence among the former of a neutral means of settling disputes. The term 'disputes' is undoubtedly meant to have wide-ranging applicability but it is instructive that Locke draws his examples from activities that are distinctly criminal, as opposed to, say, economic or athletic. In other words, the sorts of conflicts for which Locke seeks a remedy are serious to the point of death and have a conspicuously Hobbesian feel. Not surprising, therefore, is Locke's (1988: 278) use of an overtly martial vocabulary in describing them. Occurring in either nature or society, the 'state of war' arises when someone exhibits 'a sedate settled design upon another man's life,' a problem for which Locke sees very few alternatives. He argues (1988: 279) that 'when all cannot be preserved, the safety of the innocent is to be preferred: and one may destroy a man who makes war upon him, or has discovered an enmity to his being, for the same reason that he may kill a wolf or a lion; because such men are not under the ties of the common law of reason, have no other rule, but that of force and violence, and so may be treated as beasts of prey, those dangerous and noxious creatures, that will be sure to destroy him whenever he falls into their power.' While Locke is clearly no Hobbesian, one can nonetheless see that the fear of violent death so familiar in *Leviathan* plays an equally pivotal, if smaller, role in Locke's account of the virtues of the social contract.

Said contract is the mechanism by which humans are able to exit the state of nature and enter into society, that unique form of fellowship which permits a modulation of the state of war by providing for third-party resolution of conflict. I say modulation because of Locke's insistence, *pace* Hobbes, that the state of war can still exist in society. Locke, in other words, acknowledges that some will have 'sedate settled design[s]' on the lives and property of others regardless of whether they live within the confines of civil society.[1] The

---

1   Locke's imagery again illuminates just how seriously he regards these conflicts. As he says (1988: 280) by way of example, 'But force, or a declared design of force, upon the person of another, where there is no common superior on earth to appeal to for relief, is the state of war: and it is the want of such an appeal gives a man the right of war even against an aggressor, tho' he be in society and a fellow subject. Thus a thief, whom I cannot harm, but by appeal to the law, for having stolen all that I am worth, I may kill, when he sets on me to rob me but of my horse or coat; because the law, which was made for my preservation, where it cannot interpose to secure my life from present force, which, if lost, is capable of no reparation, permits me my own defence, and the right of war, a liberty to kill the aggressor, because the aggressor allows not time to appeal to our

all-important difference lies in how those designs are to be met, which is by society as a whole serving as the maker and enforcer of laws which are 'indifferent, and the same to all parties' (Locke 1988: 324). Now, when confronted by an aggressor, citizens must defer to the authority of the government and the laws created thereby rather than draw their swords. The result, ideally, are conflicts mediated by the community for whom the common good (understood as the protection of property), is the highest priority and under which is subsumed the private interest of any single member. Put differently, Locke does not see the social contract as a means by which force and violence are to be eliminated. Rather, they are to be redressed through superior versions thereof, both in terms of overall strength and in terms of the legitimacy bestowed when government settles disputes according to neutrally administered laws.

By virtue of his contractarian approach to conflict resolution, Locke can now make a distinction unavailable in the state of nature, namely between inside and outside.[2] Those who have given their express consent to the contract are properly understood as members of the commonwealth and therefore on the inside, while those on the outside are either members of a different commonwealth or remain in the state of nature. The importance of this distinction lies in the way it conditions the understanding of disputes, which, in a manner that I doubt Locke quite realizes, become more acute and fundamental than the disunited confusion that characterizes violence in the state of nature. In other words, conflict is now a far more totalizing 'us against them' sort of scenario. Attacks from without become a calculated form of aggression by one commonwealth against another, while domestic criminal activity morphs into an attack on the social body as a whole rather than the individual victim per se. The authors of disorder become wholly alien and fundamentally other, as indicated by Locke's claim that such people do not live under the common law of reason and hence may be treated as beasts of prey. Such circumstances are not mitigated by the legal mechanisms of dispute resolution put forth as one of the prime virtues of civil society. Instead, those mechanisms become weapons that must necessarily be deployed when Locke commits to managing inter-human conflict by folding it within the institutional complex we call the liberal state.

---

    common judge, nor the decision of the law, for remedy in a case where the mischief may be irreparable. Want of a common judge with authority, puts all men in a state of nature: force without right, upon a man's person, makes a state of war, both where there is, and is not, a common judge.'

2   Locke (1988: 325) argues in this context that the principal role of government is 'to judge by standing laws, how far offences are to be punished, when committed within the commonwealth; and also to determine, by occasional judgments founded on the present circumstances of the fact, how far injuries from without are to be vindicated; and in both these to employ all the force of all the members, when there shall be need.'

Derived from the opposition between inside and outside is a second distinction that has long been one of liberalism's hallmarks, namely that between the violence brought to bear on external aggressors and that employed against domestic criminals. Because those on the inside are members of the commonwealth, they enjoy certain rights and privileges the protection of which is the state's responsibility. Consequently, the liberal state cannot simply destroy the body of the criminal as was routine under the *ancien régime* without jeopardizing, among other things, its sovereign pretenses and the clear line of demarcation between public and private violence.[3] Instead, the state's power to punish must be grounded in laws that recognize the offender's status as a member of the commonwealth and consequently a bearer of natural rights which the state exists to protect, and all this no matter how heinous the criminal act in question. The liberal state's warfare mode, however, knows no such limitations.[4] There, it is understandable, and Locke gives ample support for thinking, that the state should regard external aggressors as radically other. After all, what else could such aggression portend but an end to the social contract and a return to the state of nature? Liberal states thus tend to wage total warfare because their theoretical foundations incline them to view such conflicts as a matter of life or death. Issues of justifiability aside, the point is that liberalism intends a qualitative distinction between the forms of violence employed in the crime control and war making contexts. It is ultimately this difference that enables the escape from the state of nature to take on the character of a reasoned act.

From Welfare to Warfare

With this brief sketch of Lockean liberalism in mind, we can now take stock of changes in the American approach to crime that help explain many of the tactics now being brought to bear in the war on terror. Throughout most of the twentieth century, that approach embraced the doctrines of penal welfarism, which argued that the punishment of criminal activity ought to take the form of rehabilitative interventions rather than retributive sanctions. Accordingly,

---

3   As Foucault (1995: 58-69) has pointed out, the public executions of the ancien régime often devolved into festivals of illegal and other insubordinate behaviour that actively contested the sovereign's right to punish. Rather than reconstitute the sovereignty injured by the criminal act, such events showed just how fragile the king's authority actually was. As for public versus private violence, Kaufman-Osborn (2002: 70) argues that the line separating these is blurred when, as sometimes occurred during public executions, members of the condemned's family intervened to ensure a quick death for their loved one by pulling down on his feet as he swung from the gallows.
4   Theoretically speaking, at least. Clearly, international accords governing state conduct in times of war have led to practical modifications of this point.

imprisonment was generally de-emphasized in favour of social and psychiatric inquiry, criminological research and social work, and sentencing laws that could be tailored to the individual in question. When used, prison in the penal welfare model was designed to be corrective and to include the possibility of early release and parole supervision (Garland 2001: 34-35). Such strategies were supported by two maxims that were as unquestioned as they were influential. The first held that social reform and economic prosperity would eventually reduce the incidence of crime. Criminal activity was caused not so much by corrupt character but by economic and social deprivation, particularly among the lower classes. Fix these underlying problems, the thinking went, and you solve the problem of crime. The second axiom held that the state was responsible for the care of criminals as well as their punishment and rehabilitation. In an overtly Lockean sense, the state was figured as something like a parent, responsible for both reform and repression, care and control, welfare as well as punishment. In lieu of retribution, 'one needed expert knowledge, scientific research, and flexible instruments of intervention, as well as a willingness to regulate aspects of life which classical liberalism had deemed beyond the proper reach of government' (Garland 2001: 40). The Lockean idea of third-party dispute resolution was broadened to include a range of social services aimed at reducing the problem of crime by eliminating its causes.

In the years after 1970, however, what David Garland (2001) has called the 'criminology of the other' gradually began to supplant penal welfarism. This new way of thinking about crime resulted in part from the gradual demise of penal welfarism, itself prompted by major losses of faith in the power of the state to address social problems (Garland 2001: 55-57). If anything, the civil rights and anti-war movements had starkly revealed the state's complicity in *causing* widespread social problems through its often unconscious tendency to promote class and racial biases. Crime rates in the United States also rose dramatically in this period, peaking by the early nineteen-eighties at three times what they had been twenty years previously (Garland 2001: 90). The significance of these changes lies in the responses that were deemed necessary as a result. Virtually everyone from policy makers on down to prison wardens blamed the failure to control crime on the theory of penal welfarism itself rather than with faulty implementation (Garland 2001: 115). Wholesale changes in both philosophy and strategy were needed, changes which drew far more heavily from the control side of the authority coin than did penal welfarism with its more explicitly liberal ethos.

Grounding this change in attitude was the 'assumption that certain criminals are "simply wicked" and in this respect intrinsically different from the rest of us' (Garland 2001: 184). Rehabilitation and therapeutic intervention were essentially wastes of resources because there could be no rapprochement between good and evil. Penal welfarism could therefore be represented as a 'failure of moral nerve,' an unwillingness to judge and condemn, and a strategy that had 'unleashed the floodgate of crime, disorder and social problems that have characterized the late modern period' (Garland 2001: 184). In place of investigations into causation and prevention, the criminology of the other substituted the desire to punish. High crime rates generated an emphasis on control and discipline rather than the penal welfarist concern with etiology and reform because criminal activity resulted from the voluntary choices of essentially evil people.[5] Resentment was transformed into a political project as the victims of crime came to be regarded as 'righteous figure[s] whose suffering must be expressed and whose security must henceforth be guaranteed' (Garland 2001: 11).

Here again it is worth recalling the ways in which the Lockean social contract generates this sort of totalizing response. As seen, that contract tends to inflate the seriousness of disorder by lending it an 'us versus them' quality. The criminology of the other, while distinctly illiberal in many respects, is nonetheless highly dependent on the liberal notion of an essentially embodied collectivity, united by contractual consent, which can then be understood as threatened either from within or from without. Yet even this, I would argue, is not the most distinctive feature of the current approach to crime. What should also catch our attention is the susceptibility of this framework to an 'us versus us' mindset. Because domestic criminals are already on the inside, they are arguably even more dangerous than those who would wage war from without. The citizen terrorist, of course, ratchets up the threat still further by having allied, in the case of al Qaeda, for example, with those on the outside who have declared a sedate settled design on the American body politic.

Yet it is equally important to note that the Lockean social contract is not ideally suited to this 'us versus us' mentality. In other words, Locke's overriding concern is with the solidarity generated by express consent to the laws of the commonwealth rather than with drawing up elaborate lists of potential threats to it. Accordingly, lawbreakers are still members of the compact despite their untoward behaviour.[6] It is because the criminology of the other substantially alters this arrangement that it becomes key to an understanding of the war on terror and the many objectionable practices that have become its hallmark. By virtue of the interaction between the ethic of absolute enmity that belongs to liberalism's warfare mode and the belief in the radical alterity of the authors of disorder characteristic of the criminology of the other, the terrorist (citizen or otherwise) becomes the most mortal of threats to the body politic. It is the 'us versus them' outlook supplied by liberalism's inside/outside distinction and embraced by liberalism's warfare mode adapted

---

5   The enthusiasm for the death penalty in the United States can be understood along these lines.
6   The contrast with Hobbes (1996: 106) is noteworthy in this regard. According to his Fifth Law of Nature (Compleasance), citizens are to strive to get along with each other. However, he who 'for the stubborness of his Passions, cannot be corrected, is to be left out, or cast out of Society, as cumbersome thereunto'.

for use both within and without the body politic as a general response to disorder. In this context, penal interventions aimed at rehabilitation are reserved for the naïve, those who do not understand the true nature of the threat posed by terrorism. In what follows, I document the application of this strategy in the years since 11 September. I begin with the aforementioned citizen terrorists, Hamdi, Walker, and Padilla, to show how the rationality specific to warfare results in the jettisoning of basic legal protections such as habeas corpus and the right to counsel even though the danger allegedly posed by these three individuals has never been adjudicated before a neutral arbiter. I then briefly discuss the indefinite detention of unlawful combatants at Guantanamo Bay to show how warfare's violence can be inflicted without a shot being fired. In these instances, the thoroughgoing antagonism characteristic of liberal warfare translates into the creation of spaces entirely outside the law where terror suspects can be kept indefinitely and where the freakish violence of the state of nature masquerades as policy. It is here where we see with alarming clarity just what President Bush means when he talks of the 'sacrifices' necessary to secure freedom (Fox News.com: 2005).

Citizen Terrorists: Hamdi, Lindh, and Padilla

In light of the pronounced shift towards the modalities of warfare inspired by the criminology of the other, an account can now be offered of the American response to 11 September that reflects the tensions within liberal violence noted earlier and shows how frustration with the legal protections extended to those on liberalism's inside leads to reactions formerly reserved for those on its outside. Those tensions are revealed when, as the monopolist of legitimate force, the United States government seeks to eradicate terrorist violence through recourse to its violent prerogatives. But when those terrorists also happen to be citizens, the state opens itself up to the contractarian side of the legitimacy coin which includes the right of citizens to appeal state actions taken against them. This conundrum became apparent almost immediately after 11 September and the Congressional passage one week later of the Authorization for Use of Military Force (AUMF), which permitted President Bush 'to use all necessary and appropriate force against those nations, organisations, or persons' responsible for the attacks (Authorization for Use of Military Force 2001). During the resulting invasion of Afghanistan in October, Yaser Esam Hamdi was detained by the Northern Alliance, turned over to the U.S. military and held first in Afghanistan, then at the U.S. detention facility at Guantanamo Bay, Cuba.

In the spring of 2002, Hamdi was designated an 'unlawful combatant', which meant he could be held without being charged, deprived of the ability to challenge his detention in a court of law, and denied access to counsel.[7] The sole basis for the designation was a statement by Michael Mobbs, Special Advisor to the Under Secretary of Defense for Policy (now known as the 'Mobbs Declaration'). According to Mobbs, Hamdi travelled to Afghanistan in July or August 2001, affiliated himself with the Taliban for purposes of military training, and then engaged in operations against the United States. In addition, Mobbs stated that because the Taliban and al Qaeda '"were and are hostile forces engaged in armed combat with the armed forces of the United States," "individuals associated with" those groups "were and continue to be enemy combatants"' (*Hamdi v. Rumsfeld* 2004: 5). This remains the only evidence ever provided by the United States in support of Hamdi's detention and enemy combatant status.

In June 2002 Hamdi's father filed a petition for a writ of habeas corpus alleging that, as an American citizen, Hamdi enjoyed the protections of the United States Constitution, particularly those of the 5th and 14th amendments (*Hamdi v. Rumsfeld* 2004: 2-3). The Eastern District Court of Virginia initially found in Hamdi's favour, appointing him counsel and ordering access to Hamdi. On appeal, the Fourth Circuit Court of Appeals reversed this order, arguing that the District Court 'had failed to extend appropriate deference to the Government's security and intelligence interests' (*Hamdi v. Rumsfeld* 2004: 4). It also ordered the district court to conduct an inquiry into Hamdi's status, an inquiry which found that the Mobbs Declaration fell 'far short' of supporting Hamdi's detention and was 'little more than the government's "say-so"' (*Hamdi v. Rumsfeld* 2004: 5). The district court itself then ordered a far more comprehensive review of Hamdi's status and the legality of his detention, which the Bush administration appealed. Again the Fourth Circuit found in the government's favour, arguing that the AUMF and the Mobbs Declaration were sufficient to render Hamdi's detention constitutional. It consequently directed Hamdi's habeas petition to be dismissed (*Hamdi v. Rumsfeld* 2004: 6). In June 2004 the United States Supreme Court vacated the findings of the Fourth Circuit, arguing that the due process requirements of the Constitution did, in fact, apply to Hamdi and that 'the threats to military operations posed by a basic system of independent review are not so weighty as to trump a citizen's core rights to challenge meaningfully the Government's case and to be heard by an impartial adjudicator' (*Hamdi v. Rumsfeld* 2004: 28-29). Further, while not invalidating the government's right to indefinitely detain unlawful combatants, the Court asserted its right to review such detentions in spite of the Bush administration's strident opposition on the basis of

---

7   According to the Department of Defense, an enemy combatant is 'an individual who was part of or supporting Taliban or al Qaeda forces, or associated forces that are engaged in hostilities against the United States or its coalition partners. This includes any person who has committed a belligerent act or has directly supported hostilities in aid of enemy armed forces' (U.S. Department of Defense 2005).

the separation of powers doctrine. Lacking the ability to keep Hamdi legally, the United States agreed to release him to Saudi Arabia (where he was also a citizen and had lived since childhood) on condition that he gives up his U.S. citizenship and agrees to certain travel restrictions for the rest of his life.

The situation can hardly be said to have improved for John Walker Lindh, the other American captured in Afghanistan during the United States' 2001 invasion and who subsequently came to be known as the 'American Taliban'. Indeed, it was Lindh rather than Hamdi who became the public face of Islamic radicalism in the American imagination, thanks in no small measure to his conversion to Islam during high school. This conversion eventually led him to Afghanistan in the spring of 2001 where, at the age of twenty, Lindh joined the Taliban in its struggle against the Northern Alliance. According to the United States, he also attended a military training camp affiliated with al Qaeda, twice met with Osama bin Laden, and remained on the front lines even after the events of 11 September and the American invasion of Afghanistan (*United States v. Lindh* 2002). Though he was not designated an enemy combatant, the details of Lindh's capture, interrogation, and prosecution suggest that the United States also regarded him as someone so threatening as to be ineligible for the legal protections of citizenship. Captured with his Taliban unit, Lindh was held incommunicado for the next fifty-four days as he was interrogated by agents of the U.S. government. During this time, Lindh's parents hired a lawyer and sought to inform him of this through the State Department, the Department of Defense, and their Congressional representatives. All these efforts were blocked by American officials. In the meantime, Lindh gave a confession to an agent of the Federal Bureau of Investigation which Lindh was not allowed to read or sign, was not taped, and which, in violation of FBI protocol, did not include the presence of a second agent (Mayer 2003: 57).

Lindh was subsequently indicted on ten federal charges related to his Taliban activities, including aiding the Taliban, conspiracy to kill nationals of the United States, and providing material support to al Qaeda, offenses for which he faced three life sentences plus an additional ninety years in prison if convicted (Mayer 2003: 50). In July 2002, two days before Lindh's defense planned to challenge the legitimacy of his confession in court, the government abruptly offered Lindh a plea bargain which entailed his serving a twenty-year prison term on one of the charges (aiding the Taliban) in exchange for the other nine being dropped. Since early 2003, Lindh has been at a medium-security federal prison in California, where he will remain until 2022 (Mayer 2003: 50).

While Lindh's circumstances certainly differ from Hamdi's, the space he occupies in the American response to 11 September does not. Not simply denied the privileges of citizenship, Lindh became one of 'them,' an American Taliban whose 'allegiance to those fanatics and terrorists never faltered, not even with the knowledge that they had murdered thousands of his countrymen', to quote Attorney General Ashcroft (in Mayer 2003: 50). Never mind that none of these allegations was ever proven in a court of law, that Lindh's Islamic fundamentalism bears a strong resemblance to its Christian counterpart so fashionable in the United States, or the possibility that Lindh may simply have been tremendously naïve and consequently in the wrong place at the wrong time. Each of these interpretive possibilities was outweighed by the threat he allegedly posed to the body politic and obscured by the inflationary pressure of the social contract that transformed his deviance into a mortal danger. It is the ethic of destruction that belongs to warfare. As one of Lindh's attorneys remarked, 'It's part of the change in approach to the law in this country, to prevention. You can detain people without evidence, make allegations, then develop the evidence later. If you have no evidence, you drop the charges. The only problem is, you've destroyed someone's life in the process' (in Mayer 2003: 59).

A third American caught up in the American offensive against terror is Jose Padilla, apprehended on 8 May 2002 by federal officials in Chicago as he stepped off a plane recently arrived from Pakistan. Padilla was initially held in federal criminal custody as a material witness in a grand jury investigation into the 11 September attacks. Accordingly, an attorney was provided for him by the Southern District of New York. On 9 June, however, President Bush designated Padilla an enemy combatant and ordered him into military custody for detention at the naval brig in Charleston, South Carolina. The basis for the designation was Padilla's alleged conspiracy to detonate a 'dirty bomb' in the United States, as well as his suspected links to al Qaeda. Like Hamdi, Padilla was a United States citizen and therefore sought to challenge the legitimacy of his detention via a habeas petition filed in district court for the Southern District of New York alleging violations of his Fourth, Fifth, and Sixth Amendment rights. The petition ultimately reached the Supreme Court, which in June 2004 rejected Padilla's claim on a jurisdictional technicality (*Rumsfeld v. Padilla* 2004).[8] During the appeals process, however, the Second Circuit Court of Appeals declared that the president lacked constitutional authority to detain citizens indefinitely without charge. When Padilla refiled his habeas petition, the South Carolina district court agreed with the Second Circuit Court concerning the president's lack of constitutional authority. On appeal in September 2005 the Fourth Circuit Court of Appeals reversed, setting the stage for another review by the Supreme Court.

It is here where things get interesting. Facing another challenge to its practice of indefinitely detaining citizens without charging them with a crime, the government accused Padilla of conspiracy to 'murder, kidnap and maim' people overseas and requested that he be transferred from military to civilian custody to stand trial. No mention was made of the dirty bomb allegation or

---

8 Padilla filed his habeas petition in the Southern District of New York, which is where he was held immediately after his arrest. The Supreme Court found, however, that because he was transferred to South Carolina, he should have filed his petition in that state.

any of the other circumstances that had led to his enemy combatant designation. Unimpressed, the Fourth Circuit rejected the government's transfer petition while pointedly criticizing the government's bizarre legal maneuvering. Judge J. Michael Luttig observed that the ever-shifting rationale behind Padilla's detention created the impression that 'Padilla may have been held for these years, even if justifiably, by mistake', and that the government seemed to believe it could engage in such behaviour 'with little or no cost to its conduct of the war against terror'. Luttig concluded with the warning that such conduct might in fact entail 'substantial cost to the government's credibility before the courts' (in Frieman 2006). Undeterred, in January 2006 the United States government asked for and received Supreme Court permission to transfer Padilla back to civilian custody, where he now awaits trial scheduled for January 2007 (JURIST Legal News and Research 2006).

Noteworthy in each of these cases is just how little the privileges of citizenship actually helped the individuals in question, a circumstance indebted to the criminology of the other and its tendency to view the authors of disorder as fundamentally evil. No longer offenders from liberalism's inside, Hamdi, Lindh, and Padilla became part of the outside when they affiliated with those who, by attempting to harm the body politic, intended its death by definition. Yet the paucity of actual evidence in support of the government's contentions suggests that the real offence here is betrayal of the norms and ideals that define what it means to be an American and of which citizenship has increasingly become the legal expression. Lindh, as an upper-middle-class white male, is especially instructive in this regard. As the government's strangely evaporating case against him suggests, Lindh was quite likely never a material threat to the United States and was most certainly not threatening to the degree suggested by the ten crimes with which he was initially charged. However, with his conversion to Islam, he departed from the view that sees in Christianity divine inspiration for the existence of the United States. His act of religious difference (admittedly more thoroughgoing than most), was transformed in the aftermath of 11 September into a total repudiation of the republic and effortlessly linked to the horrors of that day. As a result, claimed the Bush administration, Lindh forfeited the rights that belong to citizens (despite this being a legal impossibility absent a judicial procedure). Likewise might Hamdi's and Padilla's transgressions be seen as less significant for the threat they posed (quite little in the former, as it turned out; still to be seen, in the latter), than for what they indicated about the status of Islamic Americans, who rightly fear the very real possibility of being cast into a zone beyond the law at least partly on the basis of who they are. Such responses are animated by the belief that liberalism's warfare mode is the appropriate solution to disorder and that such disorder permits the exclusion of citizens from the legal and political order of which they are nevertheless members. Citizenship itself becomes an artifact of executive branch determinations made in response to the imperatives of the 'war on terror'.

Guantanamo Bay

Guantanamo Bay, Cuba, has been under United States jurisdiction since the conclusion of the Spanish American War in 1898 and, since 2001, has served as a prison for suspected Taliban and al Qaeda members detained during the war on terror. From the beginning, Guantanamo detainees have been denied basic legal protections, including access to counsel, knowledge of the charges against them, and the right to file habeas corpus claims in the court system of the United States. Likewise have Guantanamo detainees been denied Geneva Conventions protections as prisoners of war. Despite international outrage over these circumstances, the United States have consistently claimed that foreign fighters captured in the war on terror do not deserve Constitutional protections because they are not citizens and are ineligible for Geneva Conventions protections because they are non-state enemies. They are, in a very concrete sense, no longer persons. Instead, Guantanamo detainees are unlawful combatants, a legal non-status beyond the reach of law that has made it nearly impossible for them to contest the circumstances of their detention, much less to defend themselves or secure their release.

Legally speaking, the practice of indefinite detentions is rooted in both the Authorization for Use of Military Force and in an executive order signed by President Bush on 13 November 2001 authorizing him to detain persons who are members of al Qaeda, who engaged in or conspired to commit acts of terrorism against the United States, or who have harboured anyone in these two categories. While such authorisation might be seen as more or less legitimate considering the circumstances, it is language near the end of the order which signals the administration's conviction that belligerents on the wrong side of the war on terror deserve nothing less than the full force of liberalism's war making capacity. In particular, the order stipulates that 'military tribunals shall have exclusive jurisdiction with respect to offenses by the individual,' and that 'the individual shall not be privileged to seek any remedy [...] in any court of the United States, or any state thereof, any court of any foreign nation, or any international tribunal' (White House 2001a). In short, no judicial review of unlawful combatant status or the indefinite detentions that result.

During legal proceedings pursued on behalf of the Guantanamo detainees by American legal rights organisations, both the district court and the Washington DC circuit court of appeals agreed that the courts of the United States lack jurisdiction to consider habeas petitions filed by aliens held outside the sovereign territory of the United States. In June 2004 the United States Supreme Court vacated these findings, arguing that American courts have the power to determine the legality of alien detentions regardless of where they're held, and that at any rate, the United States government exercises exclusive jurisdiction over Guantanamo Bay, thus bringing it within the purview of the American court system. The Supreme Court further pointed out that nothing in any of its previous decisions categorically excluded aliens from invoking habeas privileges, again irrespective of whether they are held by the military or by the civilian criminal justice system (*Rasul v. Bush* 2004, Center for Constitutional Rights 2006).

Thanks to *Hamdi* and *Rasul*, it momentarily appeared as though the war on terror and the Bush administration's efforts to keep accused terrorists in a zone beyond the law would be reined in by liberalism's traditional limitations on the power of government. Faced with this prospect, Congress in 2005 elected to strip the federal courts of jurisdiction over Guantanamo detainees via passage of the Detainee Treatment Act of 2005. According to Section 1005(e)(1), 'no court [...] shall have jurisdiction to hear or consider [...] an application for [...] habeas corpus filed by [...] an alien detained [...] at Guantanamo Bay' (Detainee Treatment Act of 2005). Of even greater concern, from the detainees' perspective, at least, was the Bush administration's intent to interpret the act as applying to all pending Guantanamo habeas petitions, thereby jettisoning the legal protections recently conferred by *Rasul*.

However, a second Guantanamo-related case was gradually making its way towards the Supreme Court, one that would not only bear directly on the jurisdiction-stripping provisions of the Detainee Treatment Act but other elements of the war on terror as well. Broadly speaking, *Hamdan v. Rumsfeld* (2006) pertained to that part of the president's 13 November executive order creating military tribunals for the trial of Guantanamo detainees. The petitioner in the case was Salim Hamdan, a Yemeni national captured in Afghanistan in 2001 and who, it turned out, had formerly been Osama bin Laden's driver. The circumstances of Hamdan's detention were familiar: he was held without charge for a year at Guantanamo, at which point 'the President deemed Hamdan eligible for trial by military commission for then-unspecified crimes' (*Hamdan v. Rumsfeld* 2006: 1). Another year passed, at which point Hamdan was charged with conspiracy 'to commit [...] offenses triable by military commission' (*Hamdan v. Rumsfeld* 2006: 1). Via pro bono counselors acting on his behalf in the United States, Hamdan argued that Bush's military commissions lacked authority to try him because such commissions were not created by a specific act of Congress and that the procedures adopted for purposes of his trial violated both military and international law.

The Bush administration's initial response was to seek dismissal on the basis of the Detainee Treatment Act's jurisdiction-stripping provision. The Supreme Court demurred, arguing that the act failed to specifically include pending cases. The Court also had much to say concerning the substantive points raised by Hamdan. First, it found that Congress' Authorization for Use of Military Force did not contain specific language authorizing the creation of military tribunals and that therefore the president's 13 November executive order could not be justified through reference to that act. Accordingly, the legally binding provisions for military tribunals were those provided by the UCMJ, which are in turn bound by the Geneva Conventions. However, the Court found numerous violations of the provisions of these two laws. In particular, the commissions not only enabled the admission of hearsay evidence but provided that the accused and his attorney could be denied access to evidence presented during any part of the proceedings declared 'closed' by the presiding officer, the grounds for which included vague 'national security interests' (*Hamdan v. Rumsfeld* 2006: 4). Still more to the point, the Court concluded that 'there *is* a basis to presume that the procedures employed during Hamdan's trial will violate the law: He will be, and *indeed already has been* excluded from his own trial' (*Hamdan v. Rumsfeld* 2006: 5). As for the Geneva Conventions, the Court cited Common Article III's 'prohibition on "the passing of sentences [...] without previous judgment [...] by a regularly constituted court affording all the judicial guarantees [...] recognized as indispensable by civilized peoples"' (*Hamdan v. Rumsfeld* 2006: 6). Further, the Court pointed out that while Common Article III's requirements 'are general, crafted to accommodate a wide variety of legal systems [...] they are *requirements* nonetheless' (*Hamdan v. Rumsfeld* 2006: 7).

In late September 2006, however, Congress once again joined the fray with passage of the Military Commissions Act of 2006 (Military Commissions Act of 2006). Acting as though the Supreme Court had uttered nary a word on the subject, the Act gives Congressional support to precisely the sort of military commissions so roundly criticized in *Hamdan*. In particular, the Act specifically authorizes the president to establish such commissions, prohibits an individual subject to trial by commission from invoking the Geneva Conventions as a source of rights, and permits the admission of hearsay evidence at the discretion of the presiding officer. As for habeas corpus, the Act specifically prohibits any court, judge, or justice from considering a habeas petition related to any aspect of the detention by the United States of unlawful combatants anywhere in the world. Further, the new law applies this provision to all pending habeas claims. On 20 October 2006, (the day after President Bush signed the measure into law), the government informed the U.S. District Court for the District of Columbia that it no longer had jurisdiction over 196 habeas petitions brought by Guantanamo Bay detainees. At a minimum, the new law indicates that the legislative branch is now also committed to marginalizing the judiciary's role in the 'war on terror'. Despite repeated judicial opinions concerning the right of detainees to access the federal court system, Congress has decided to bypass those rights by providing legislative validation of executive fiat. It also indicates that the particulars of the United States' conduct of that war will remain shrouded in secrecy, which is to say that the war on terror will be waged outside the parameters of the law. Only the overwhelming force of the state's war making capacity, so it seems, is adequate to the task of eliminating the radical evil of terrorism.

Conclusion

Certainly it is tempting to explain the United States' response to 11 September in terms of an enthusiasm for wild west-style justice on the part of President Bush or through reference to the extreme version of Christianity and its simplistic division of the world into good and evil which guides his conduct. Alluring though this may be, it fails to describe how an established system of national and international laws has been so easily subverted for purposes of waging war against those deemed responsible for the attacks of that day or how an entire nation can accede to acts of torture and abuse committed in its name. It is for these reasons that I have highlighted the importance of recent developments in the national attitude towards domestic criminals. Only when the authors of disorder are represented as fundamentally other and therefore implacably opposed to the social order does it become possible to imagine the suspension of basic human rights which domestic and international law formerly regarded as sacrosanct. As threats multiply and become increasingly atavistic, so too does the horizon of possible responses expand, even to the point of discarding the very rules for managing interhuman conflict laid down in the social contract. Yet the United States has faced grave threats in the past without having to torture, indefinitely detain, abuse, or otherwise compromise the principles in defense of which it was allegedly founded. Accordingly, in the space that remains I wish to highlight some of the implications of these developments, particularly as they concern the future of the citizen's relationship to the decreasingly liberal state.

I say 'decreasingly liberal' because of the ways in which the state's dispute resolution function has been displaced by the norms of the neoliberal marketplace in which rationally informed 'choice' serves as the orienting principle of both individual and state behaviour. Locke's use of the term 'umpire' in describing the state's function is instructive here because it implies a state that *regulates* the realm of rational decision-making without itself participating in that realm or endorsing one version of rationality over others. It is by virtue of this neutrality that the state can make good on its promise to protect the members of the commonwealth even when they make poor decisions. Simply put, from the state's point of view, protection is the higher value. In the agent-centric orientation of the criminology of the other, however, crime is explained as the outcome of a flawed calculus that can and should be punished. It's less the deed itself that matters than the calculations that led up to it. After all, choosing between competing alternatives is what liberal, reasoning man does, and the social contract is clearly preferable to the state of nature in the eyes of any rationally thinking being. Accordingly, said beings choose to abide by its mandates and the modification of their behaviour these entail. No coincidence, then, that the criminology of the other represents criminal behaviour as a similar type of choice made in the opposite direction by fundamentally wicked people.

As Wendy Brown (2005: 39-40) has argued, this neo-liberal version of citizenship involves 'extending and disseminating market values to all institutions and social action' as well as the development of 'institutional practices and rewards for enacting this vision'. Even decisions made in what Locke would undoubtedly regard as the private sphere come to be viewed in terms of market criteria, with all the associated rewards and penalties. So, for example, individuals' 'moral autonomy is measured by their capacity for "self-care" – the ability to provide for their own needs and service their own ambitions. In making the individual fully responsible for her/himself, neo-liberalism equates moral responsibility with rational action [...] no matter how severe the constraints on this action – for example, lack of skills, education, and childcare in a period of high unemployment and limited welfare benefits' (2005: 42). Along the way, the citizen-state relationship is radically transformed. The state is no longer that unique associational form for the resolution of disputes but an actor like any other which 'must not simply concern itself with the market but think and behave like a market actor across all of its functions, including law' (2005: 42). Not surprisingly, the model citizen in this context 'is one who strategizes for her/himself among various social, political and economic options, not one who strives with others to alter or organize these options' (2005: 43).

The effect of extending the mores of the marketplace to liberalism's formally non-political spheres is twofold: the production of subjects for whom a highly depoliticized version of rationality becomes the highest priority, and the implementation of controls for those deemed incapable of adhering to the dictates of reason. After all, the criminology of the other presumes that the capacity to reason correctly is not equally present in everyone and therefore takes for granted the existence of a class of people who are 'strongly attracted to self-serving, anti-social, and criminal conduct unless inhibited from doing so by robust and effective controls' (Garland 2001: 15). Accordingly, behavioural interventions 'should centre not upon individuals but upon the routines of interaction, environmental design and the structure of controls and incentives that are brought to bear upon them. The new policy advice is to concentrate on substituting prevention for cure, reducing the supply of opportunities, increasing situational and social controls, and modifying everyday routines' (Garland 2001: 16). That the state has become an active participant in the implementation of these controls ought not come as a surprise given the increasing fluidity of liberalism's inside/outside distinction. Now itself a rationally calculating 'being', and consequent to its enthusiasm for looking upon war and crime as flip sides of the same coin, the state now has little choice but to regard everyone as a potential combatant/criminal.

Of course it is precisely within the context of the 'war on terror' that the embrace of an overtly martial and therefore highly restrictive rationality comes to seem most necessary and most logical. Especially for those citizens raised on the virtues of the social contract as a mechanism for resolving disputes, terrorism – and especially that perpetrated by citizens – is the most comprehensive repudiation of the body politic and therefore the ultimate irrational act. Consequently, it becomes rational to reduce the opportunities for terrorist activity through constraints on personal freedom, the hardening of public spaces, and the spending of untold billions on the military. So too does warring against terror further abet the tendency of the criminology of the other to regard acts of disorder as rooted in dispositional factors rather than concretely situated political circumstances. In what has become an interpretive double standard, 'we' are waging war in the sedate, settled sense implied by liberalism, whereas 'they' are akin to Locke's 'dangerous and noxious creatures' beyond the pale of civilisation and who must therefore be eliminated because they cannot be rehabilitated to the norms of liberal reason. The recent fondness for civilisational comparisons can thus be read as shorthand for the rationality/irrationality divide that allegedly differentiates those committed to freedom and those not. Criminology's 'evil other' becomes applicable on a global scale, embodied in the person of the 'terrorist'.

The modifications to the citizen-state relationship entailed by these developments are therefore far from haphazard. The citizen needs the state now more than ever, not simply as a protector from external dangers and as a regulator of internal affairs but also as a bulwark against the irrationality now regarded as omnipresent and implacably opposed to the interests of those reasoning choosers who remain committed to the social contract. Yet there is ultimately an additional paradox here, insofar as the fear inspired by the war on terror is so utterly *irrational*. After all, the chances of dying in one's bathtub are many thousands of times greater than that of dying in a terrorist attack. But fear, of course, has a way of inducing its own forms of rationality, such that the citizen can be forgiven for occasionally relating to the state as someone in need of protection might, and whose contractual obligation now includes acquiescence to whatever forms of behaviour are deemed necessary. In such an environment, passivity, too, becomes a rational, reasoned act designed to ensure one's survival.

Predictably, fear also stimulates a pronounced turn towards the executive branch and its version of events, versions that are as damaging as they are fantastical. I refer here to the July 2006 Harris poll which found that half of all Americans still believe Iraq possessed weapons of mass destruction at the time of the United States' 2003 invasion. Analysts and pundits put forth all sorts of explanations, including repeated assertions to the effect of same by the White House, right-wing talk radio, and a general need to justify the war in Iraq (*New York Times* 2006). Undoubtedly each of these explanations is plausible in its own way. Yet they each fail to account for the ways in which belief in such ephemera is the concomitant of the state's monopolisation of what it means to be rational and of the highly restricted options for thinking about threats and dangers that result as a consequence. Increasingly deprived of the ability to fashion the reality to which they now relate as consumers, citizens frequently have little choice but to acquiesce to the version of truth formulated by those at the helms of control. Accordingly, along with the legal protections ideally afforded by liberalism, we might also list a meaningful sense of citizenship as an additional casualty in the war on terror.

References

Authorization for Use of Military Force. (2001): *Public Law* 107-40, 115 Stat. 224, 107th Congress: 18 September.
Brown, W. (2005): *Edgework: Critical Essays on Knowledge and Politics*, Princeton: Princeton University Press.
Center for Constitutional Rights. (2006): *Synopsis of Rasul v. Bush: The Guantanamo Detainee Cases Decided by the Supreme Court*, http://www.ccr-ny.org/v2/rasul_v_bush/home.asp (accessed 29 August).
Cohn, M. (2004): *The Quaint Mr. Gonzales*, http://www.truthou.or/doc _04111304A.shtml: 13 November (accessed 15 August 2006).
Detainee Treatment Act of 2005(2005): http://jurist.law.pitt.edu/gazette/ 2005/12/detainee treatment-act-of-2005-white.php (accessed 29 August 2006).
Foucault, M. (1995): *Discipline and Punish: The Birth of the Prison*, 2nd edn, New York: Vintage.
Fox News.com (2005): *Bush: Freedom Requires Sacrifice*, http://www. foxnew.com/story/0,2933,166363,00.html: 23 August (accessed 4 September 2006).
Frieman, J.M. (2006): 'Padilla's Real Message: the Grace Period is over', *JURIST Legal News and Research*: 4 April. http://jurist.law. pitt. edu/ forumy/2006/04/padillas-real-message-grace-period-is.php (accessed 10 August 2006).
Garland, D. (2001): *The Culture of Control: Crime and Social Order in Contemporary Society*, Chicago: University of Chicago Press.
Hamdan v. Rumsfeld (2006): 548 U.S. ____.
Hamdi v. Rumsfeld (2004): 542 U. S. 507; 124 S. Ct. 2633.
Hobbes, T. ([1651]1996): *Leviathan*, ed. R. Tuck, Cambridge: Cambrid-ge University Press.
JURIST Legal News and Research (2006): *Federal Judge Delays Padilla Trial until January*, http://jurist.law.pitt.edu/paperchase/2006/08/fe-deral-judge-delays-padilla-trial.php (accessed 17 August 2006).
Kaufman-Osborn, T.V. (2002): *From Noose to Needle: Capital Punishment and the Late Liberal State*, Ann Arbor, MI: University of Michigan Press.
Locke, J. ([1690]1988): *Two Treatises of Government*, ed. P. Laslett, Cambridge: Cambridge University Press.
Mayer, J. (2003): 'Lost in the Jihad: Why Did the Government's Case against John Walker Lindh Collapse?' *New Yorker*, 10 March 2003, 50-59.

Military Commissions Act of 2006 (2006): Pub. L. No. 109-366, 120 Stat. 2600: 17 October.

New York Times (2006): *Half of U.S. Still Believes Iraq Had WMD*, http://www.nytimes.com/aponline/us/AP-Iraq-Believing WMD.html: 6 August (accessed 6 August 2006).

Rasul v. Bush (2004): 548 U.S. ___.

Rumsfeld v. Padilla (2004): 542 U.S. 426; 124 S. Ct. 2711.

United States v. Lindh (2002): 212 F.Supp.2d 541.

U.S. Department of Defense (2005): *Guantanamo Detainee Processes*, http://www.defenselink.mil/news/Sep2005/d20050908process.pdf: 8 September (accessed 15 August 2006).

White House (2001a): *President Issues Military Order*, http://www.whitehouse.gov/news/releases/2001/11/20011113-27.html: 13 November (accessed 15 August 2006).

—— (2001b): *Press Briefing by Ari Fleischer*, http://www.whitehouse.gov/news/release/2001/09/20010926-5.html: 26 September (accessed 19 August 2006

Suspect Subjects: Muslim Migrants and the Security Agencies in Germany

WERNER SCHIFFAUER

Ever since 9/11, security political questions have increasingly been dominating the discussion about the integration of Muslim immigrants into German society. This is a result of the new security policy, which is characterized by an expansion of 'repressive' measures and their supplementation and extension through 'preventive' measures. In the jargon of the security agencies, 'repressive' measures are those which – as did the laws enacted in the first security package issued shortly after 9/11 to increase air travel security – target direct prevention of crimes and/or improvement of criminal prosecution. To the extent that measures are adopted in advance of an incident, they are to deflect immediate danger. 'Preventive' measures, on the other hand, are concerned with abstract danger situations. In this context, matters preliminary to, and associated with, possible crimes are interpreted in a significantly broader manner. The emphasis placed on such measures recently is the expression of a 'comprehensive approach to domestic security which is not limited to repressive intervention' or of an 'all-encompassing' concept of security.[1] Preventive measures are not concerned with criminals or crimes, but with 'extremists' assumed to be capable of becoming potential criminals, with 'milieus' producing or providing escape for criminals, and with 'discourses' which could incite crimes. The need for a new concept of security, as Julia Eckert has shown, is based on two figures of thought: the supposed unpredictability and

---

1 Volker Homuth, Director of the Lower Saxony Agency for Internal SecurityAgency, during a conference of the Evangelische Akademie Loccum, 15-17 April 2005.

irrationality of the new terrorism, which can apparently hit anywhere and anytime; and the extent of the danger,[2] which made new measures necessary (Eckert 2005).

In this paper, I will turn to the consequences preventive measures have on integration policy. At the same time, it is of particular importance to me to show that the results do not merely consist in a new legal situation. Of far greater consequence is the fact that a new atmosphere has been promoted, which has an extensive influence on the application of laws in practice. This atmosphere leads to a new and close cooperation among various agencies – especially the *Verfassungsschutz* [the internal security agency for the protection of constitutional order], the immigration authorities, and the courts. As Didier Bigo puts it, a security field with a high degree of internal coordination develops (Bigo 2000). This coordination is only in part consciously created; rather, it seems to develop almost on its own as various partners agree on a common threat scenario, which can be summarized as follows: The central danger facing our state comes from Islamistic terrorism which is penetrating Germany through immigrants from Muslim countries. The acceptance of this scenario has two consequences. The first is that, as far as Muslim immigrants are concerned, the usual checks and balances of various state authorities – vital for the functioning of the rule of law – are reduced. This increases the danger of false decisions, and thus of injustice. The second consequence consists of Muslim residents being increasingly stigmatized, accelerating the dynamics of the isolation by others and self-isolation. Both together lead to unintended consequences which give rise to new dangers.

In the first section, I will deal with the significance of the *Verfassungsschutz* (Internal Security Agency) in the context of prevention and discuss the specific ways it constructs knowledge with regard to the supporting milieus of terrorism. In the sections to follow I will show how this information directs and structures practices of state agencies, with regard to naturalisation, to expulsions, and to the surveillance and disciplining of Islamic organisations. At the same time I will devote particular attention to the cooperation among various state agencies. In a concluding section I will go into the unintended results of new security policies on the integration of Muslims.

---

2   The mathematical definition of risk refers to probability times extent of danger. If the danger is considered extremely high, such a risk estimate is required, even to take measures for a situation whose probability of occurrence is considered relatively unlikely. The problem with this calculation lies in the fact that quite far-reaching measures can be legitimized by it.

The Knowledge of the *Verfassungsschutz*

The German Internal Security Agency plays a key role in the implementation of the security policy inasmuch as it provides the information on whose basis other state instances act.

In accordance with its assigned duties, the agency is obliged to observe not only groups and efforts which – such as the prohibited organisations 'Hizb ut Tahrir' and 'Caliphate State' – are in open opposition to the German constitution, but also those who profess allegiance to the constitution in their public statements, obey the laws, and distance themselves from acts of violence, if there is a justified suspicion of anticonstitutional efforts. Among Islamic communities, this applies to the Islamic Community of Germany (IGD), and especially to the Islamic Community Milli Görüs (IGMG). For them, the 'suspicion' of anticonstitutional efforts is based primarily on their Islamistic past and on the transnational relations both organisations maintain, the IGD with the Muslim Brotherhood in Egypt and Syria, and the IGMG with the Saadet Party of Necmettin Erbakan in Turkey. Both of these organisations are pursuing the goal of Islamisation of their respective homelands and societies. IGD and IGMG admit to these connections, raise the point, however, that meanwhile they are pursuing a different agenda *in Europe*. The change of generations, they say, has led to a shift in perspectives in the European divisions of the organisations. They are committed to Europe with the long-term goal of establishing Islam as a minority religion in the framework of the legal systems of European states. Both organisations claim to have changed and/or to be in the midst of a process of change.

Now, there is a significant interest of society on the whole in an unbiased examination of this claim. For if that should indeed be true, this would mean that in these two organisations' positions have been developed, which attempt to overcome Islamism from within. Such a process would promise a certain sustainability and provide intellectual answers to radical and terrorist Islam. This would signify the chance of preventing young people from drifting off into the sectarian and violent scene.

An independent examination, however, is hindered by the *Verfassungsschutz*'s claim to be 'the Federal Republic's institutionalized distrust of itself' (Claudia Schmid, Director of the Berlin Bureau of the *Verfassungsschutz*). Reading the federal and state Internal Security Agencies' reports, one gets the impression that the agencies' assignment of duties does not result in an unbiased examination of the positions of the organisations observed, but rather in a systematical attempt to counter the public claims made by these organisations – which amounts to showing that 'actually', a secret agenda is indeed being pursued despite constitutional rhetoric. A precise reading of the reports highlights the fact that the Internal Security Agency is very selective with the information it provides. Whatever fits the picture is quoted (anti-Semitic statements in sermons, for instance); what doesn't fit the image (for example, active contacts with the Jewish Community or engagement in inter-religious dialogue), however, is sorted out. The fact that the youth work in these communities attempts to promote Islamic self-confidence is criticized as anti-integrationist; the fact that the communities at the same time encourage sending children, both sons and daughters, to German upper schools, all are not mentioned in any report. When interpreting quotes, the reading most unfavorable for the IGMG is chosen. If contradictory statements from the organisation appear, the agencies only in exceptional cases examine whether this is a result of factional struggles;[3] rather, they are quite simply explained by the image of speaking with a forked tongue (to the outside world, they speak in accordance with the accepted German public opinion, while maintaining other positions internally). Occasionally, statements are turned into their exact opposite.[4] Under the distrusting gaze of the *Verfassungsschutz*, communities are stylized and are portrayed as significantly more extremist and closed off than an unbiased examination of them would indicate.

A specific problem area is to be found in those sections of Internal Security Agency reports dealing with the IGD and the IGMG, in that they quite simply equate the accusation of behaving in an anti-integrational manner, of carrying out 'identity policies', and/or of creating 'parallel society structures' with anticonstitutionalism. Here, the points of view dominating the examination have nothing to do with the constitution. One may indeed have political objections to parallel societies, but no constitutional qualms can be deduced from them. Thus, the line between constitutional and anticonstitutional is completely blurred and the door to arbitrariness is opened wide. For example, Internal Security Agency reports portray activities which are in complete conformity with the constitution, such as the creation of a legal department,[5] as problematic.[6]

Indeed (and this has so far been taken into consideration far too little), the far-reaching assessments of the Internal Security Agency rely on a limited data basis. Analysis is based primarily on the evaluation of written material, but not on systematic interviews, field research, or questioning. 'For legal reasons, Internal Security Agencies are not authorized to conduct broad studies

---

3   The single exception is the Berlin Internal Security Agency report from 2004.
4   Cf. Schiffauer (2004). I have indeed had the personal experience of witnessing the complete perversion of my text. An appraisal I wrote, which was very critical of the Internal Security Agency, was evaluated by that same agency in public as a confirmation of its own position.
5   This assessment of a legal department is particularly touchy considering the serious legal consequences membership in the IGMG entails.
6   I have published a summary listing of these in Die Zeit. To date they have not been contradicted.

on the "Islamic milieu"; these are and remain primarily the tasks of academic research', claims the Cologne staff member of the Internal Security Agency, Tania Puschnerat (2006).

Another limitation must be stressed. The *Verfassungsschutz* creates the impression of being an independent authority charged with investigation on 'enemies of the constitution'. This impression is deceiving. The reports are prepared, according to the official explanation, 'on the basis of the results of the Internal Security Agencies after subjection to a political evaluation by the Ministry of the Interior'. Political considerations thus influence which organisations are mentioned in the report and which are not, and what the extent of the coverage is.[7] Political intervention also appears to penetrate through to the content of what is said. Agency staff members have reported to me that a supervisor's expectations may indeed have an influence of the reports drafted.

There is no mention of these limitations in the reports of the Internal Security Agencies, nor in agency decisions. Instead of providing a differentiated picture listing arguments for and against anticonstitutionalism and pointing out the limitations related to the narrow data basis, authoritative judgments on the constitutionality of an organisation are passed.

In recent years, apparently in connection with security political considerations, Internal Security Agency evaluations have been placed in a new context. Connected with radicalisation scenarios and a broader notion of security, communities such as the IGMG and the IGD are increasingly being portrayed as supporting milieus of radical and terrorist Islamism. What was depicted as anticonstitutional, but not dangerous in any real sense, before 9/11 is now considered a first step towards a security risk. Since then, it was stressed again and again that, in terms of a broader concept of security, investigations of Islamism must not be limited to radical and/or violent organisations.[8]

The link between (inferred) 'anticonstitutionalism' and (vaguely defined) 'security risks', produced in radicalisation scenarios, has a very strong impact because a demand for concrete measures is connected to it. It may lead to a situation in which other agencies are ever less willing to critically examine the statements contained in *Verfassungsschutz* reports, because the fear of making a political mistake is growing. In case of imminent danger, it is better to act overcautiously.

---

7   According to Heribert Landolin Müller, Director of the section responsible for Islam at the State Agency for Political Education in Berlin: 'Islamism – a journalistic challenge' (2/3 February 2006)
8   According to the director of the Lower Saxony agency, Volker Homuth, at the conference of the Evangelische Akademie Loccum from 15-17 April 2005.

Naturalisation

This new dominance of security policy has led to a U-turn in the area of naturalisation policy. This shift in the practice of the naturalisation authorities required no change of legislation. Its legal basis instead rests on a new interpretation of the new law on national citizenship passed in 1999. One component of the law was the introduction of new requirements for obtaining citizenship in addition to the ones already in existence (i.e. long residency, no criminal record, etc.). These consisted of the ability to provide economic support for oneself and one's family. Additionally, linguistic competence and loyalty to the constitution were included as prerequisites. Concerning the latter, the law states: 'No claim for naturalisation exists if [...] actual indications justify the assumption that the naturalisation candidate is pursuing or supporting efforts [...] which are directed against the free and democratic basic order of the state or against the continued existence or security of the federal state or any of its component states [...]' (Bundesgesetzblatt, Jg. 1999 Teil I Nr. 38; 23 July 1999, p.1620).

Interestingly enough, the debate at the time focused on insufficient linguistic competence as grounds for an exclusion from naturalisation. There was an intense discussion of the question as to whether older immigrants can be compelled to learn German. However, what hardly anyone paid any attention to is the stipulation that 'actual indications' for the assumption that someone pursues efforts directed against the free and democratic basic order of the state are sufficient; this clause introduced a very elastic formulation in the text of the law. In order 'to affirm "actual indications for the assumption", no specific factual situation must be proved; rather, the mere possibility that a given situation might exist and that certain evidence provides indications for this indeed suffices' (Bender 2003: 135).

By means of a microanalysis of administrative practice I shall demonstrate in the following how this formulation was turned into a sharp sword with which the original intent of the law was transformed into its very opposite.

On 28 June 2002, the city of G. decided to reject Ayhan Celik's (name changed) application for naturalisation. In its presentation of grounds, the city of R. quotes the above cited paragraph 85 of the law and makes this decisive point:

'Though you indeed professed allegiance to the free and democratic basic order of the Constitution of the Federal Republic of Germany in writing on 12 January, 2002, you actually pursue and/or support activities which are directed against that free and democratic basic order. [...] According to information from the Interior Ministry of the State of North Rhine Westphalia of 13 May, 2002, you have been on the board of the local IGMG organisation since the year 1998. [...] According to the current Internal Security Agency report of the State of North Rhine Westphalia for the year 2001, the efforts of the IGMG are directed against the free and democratic basic order of the Federal Republic of Germany, by which you fulfil the exclusion grounds of § 86 No. 2 AusG (Foreigner Law) and thus have no claim to nationalisation into the German Federation of States under § 85 AusG (Doc.1).'[9]

Mr. Celik appealed this decision. He argued that he would never support efforts directed against the free and basic order and that the agency had no proof whatsoever to the contrary. The agency rejected the appeal on 22 October 2002. It was argued that his engagement in the Milli Görüs was an 'actual indication' for the assumption of anticonstitutional efforts. This, it went on, was determined by the Internal Security Agencies of the federal and state governments. 'It is not the task of the Naturalisation Agency to make judgments about the information collected or evaluations made by federal and state Internal Security Agencies' (Doc. 2).

There are two remarkable aspects of this correspondence.
- The naturalisation authority expressly cedes to the Internal Security Agency the right to define whether an organisation, which has not been prohibited, is anticonstitutional or not. Thus, everyday bureaucratic routine undermines the intended legal procedures which entail a prohibition pronounced by the Interior Ministries of the states or the federal government, against which legal proceedings can be initiated.
- An examination of individual cases is neglected. If you are a functionary in an organisation which an Internal Security Agency deems not to be in conformity with the constitution, then the actual indication for your support of anticonstitutional efforts is considered manifest.

In the case mentioned, a person was concerned who was actively, even if only on the local level, involved. In some federal states (for example Rhineland Palatine), however, also ordinary members are affected. Here, organisation membership and support for the local mosque are presented as grounds for denying naturalisation. Even mere contact is enough to arouse decisive suspicion. Mr. Yildirim (name changed) was denied naturalisation by injunction, again with reference to 'actual indications': His 'vehicle was observed during an event conducted by the IGMG Community of Völklingen-Luisenthal in the local culture center on 27 January 1998' (Doc. 4).

---

9 This document, and those which follow, can be found online under http//viadrina.euv-frankfurt-o.de/~anthro/Dokument_text_verwaltete_Sicherheit.htm.

In cases of this sort, a hearing occurs. The following document, a written rejection after conclusion of a hearing, casts a light on the character of such conversations.

'On the occasion of your personal appearance on 22 May, 2003, you made a statement to the effect that you are not a member of the IGMG. Where the Internal Security Agency obtained the information that you were a member of the above mentioned organisation in the years 1998 and 1999 is unknown to you. It was, however, known to you that the mosque you attended for prayer sympathizes with the IGMG [...]'

'Through your membership in the above mentioned organisation, you declared your agreement with its goals and adopted them as your own. The profession of allegiance you made to the free and democratic order can, in view of your membership in the IGMG, only be regarded as empty talk (Doc. 3).'

Two things are important about this document. Firstly, the hearing is obviously only concerned with the question of IGMG membership. Attending the mosque infers membership, and membership infers agreement with the (supposed) goals of the organisation. This chain of inferences is problematic. There can be very different motivations for membership in a Milli Görüs mosque community. In addition to members who feel politically at home in the Milli Görüs movement, i.e. support actively or passively Necmettin Erbakan's Saadet Party or Tayyip Erdogan's AK Party (about half of all members, by my personal estimates), there is a large segment of completely apolitical members. Also, mosques are centers of social life as well, and it is indeed possible for someone to join the Milli Görüs because he wants to meet friends and acquaintances there. Many second-generation members were quite simply born into the community. And finally, not everyone who attends a Milli Görüs mosque is a member of the community. Unless you have strong reservations, you go to the mosque that is easiest to reach.[10] Even if donations are made to the local mosque community, this is not necessarily a proof of membership in the IGMG. It is a matter of decency to provide financial support for the mosque community whose services you make use of, for these communities, unlike churches, must support themselves.

Secondly, this document shows how the logic of fact-based indications shifts the burden of proof. There is no information in the text about the applicant's arguments, but apparently, the claim that he only went to the mosque to pray was considered mere denial self-defence. A similar helplessness can be deduced from the minutes of a hearing which is in my possession. The appli-

---

10 All observers emphasize this heterogeneous nature of motives. On the second generation, cf. Tietze (2001) or Meng (2004).

cant's statements, distancing himself from violence, anti-Semitism, and religious intolerance as well as his profession of allegiance to democracy prove to be of no use to him.

The impression that an applicant hardly stands any chance in a hearing to disprove the suspicion of being anticonstitutional can be drawn from the other minutes. Those questioned must give detailed information about cross-connections between mosques, about previous memberships, etc. They must describe their reading habits. It is not unusual for the persons questioned to be confronted with statements from *Verfassungsschutz* reports about the IGMG and to have to take a stand on them. The hearings rather resemble cross-examinations; it is very obvious that the aim is to get the persons questioned tangled up in contradictions. During questioning in Nuremberg, an applicant was asked to take a stand on the following extremely confrontational statements: 'What do you have to say about the discussion on veils? The prohibition of symbols has nothing to do with the free practice of religion.' Or: 'If state laws run counter to your understanding of free religious practice, you don't like it. You place the Koran above state laws according to your interpretation of the Koran.'

The developments described up to now concern the executive branch. Within this domain, it is hardly surprising that the interplay among the agencies becomes ever more coordinated. It is, however, remarkable, and can ultimately only be explained by the dominance of security policy, that the judicial branch also increasingly bows to this logic. For example, on 2 June 2003, the Bavarian Administrative Court in Munich (AZ M 25 K 00.5269) dismissed the suit of a Munich IGMG member who had argued that the material presented by the Internal Security Agency provided no support for the charge that he himself had participated in violent activities or called for them to be supported, nor for the claim that the IGMG views the use or approval of violence as a legitimate means for the advancement of its goals. The member claimed that he is highly integrated into his local German community. The court contested none of this, but declared it irrelevant. The plaintiff's argumentation, according to the court, was based on the 'old legal situation'. The new legal situation excludes nationalisation when 'actual indications' are at hand. Proof of anticonstitutional activity is no longer necessary, 'instead, fact-based suspicion of crime suffices' (p. 11). And as far as that was concerned, the court was of the opinion 'that the information presented in the *Verfassungsschutz* reports can in and of themselves be deemed actual indications in the terms of § 86 No. 2 AusG n.F. The *Verfassungsschutz* assessment and evaluation in the annual reports are admissible evidence and are to be accepted by an organisation as long as they are not obviously based on improper considerations' (p. 16). The court did indeed concede that the 'interests of the younger generation today dominating the IGMG are predominantly directed at improving the social, political, and legal conditions of residents of Turkish origin and, in that regard, are oriented along the guidelines of Islamic law concerning Muslims in the diaspora, calling for obedience to the local legal system of the host society and affirmation of the values delineated in its constitution' (p. 20). However, the fact that the activities are only predominantly and not totally constitutional provided sufficient 'actual indications' for the denial of naturalisation.

With this argumentation, the court confirmed the naturalisation authorities' practice of neglecting to examine individual cases. Instead, the concept of fact-based indications is used to treat two in fact loose connections based on suspicion as firm fact-based linkages.

- If the Internal Security Agency suspects an organisation of being anticonstitutional, it is, in the opinion of the court, permissible to treat it as an anticonstitutional organisation.
- If someone is a member of a suspected organisation, he, too, is to be treated as someone who 'pursues or supports efforts [...] directed against the free and democratic basic order or against the continued existence or security of the federal state or any of its component states [...]' § 86 No. 2 AusG.

Admittedly, court judgments are, for the time being, not unanimous. In its decision of 28 February 2003, the Administrative Court of Karlsruhe followed a different assessment. The court argued that the Islamic community of Milli Görüs could not unequivocally be classified as extremist or anticonstitutional on the basis of the information sources provided. Therefore, an evaluation of the individual case was mandatory. The Administrative Court of Hamburg argued along similar lines in its decision of 1 October 2003. This decision was also remarkable because it was not dealing with a simple IGMG member, but with a functionary, the deputy chairman of a mosque community. In its written opinion, the Hamburg court set down more stringent conditions for a 'suspicion based on actual indications'. 'General incriminating factors not supported by demonstrable concrete facts' were insufficient in the eyes of this court.

These verdicts show that other interpretations of the law are possible, differing from the Munich judgment. Though the legal situation still remains unsettled on the whole, there does seem to be a tendency to follow the Munich neglect of strict examination of individual cases. For example, the Superior Administrative Court of Rhineland Palatine may not have explicitly cited the Munich opinion, but it did adopt its contents. In essential passages of their opinion, the judges adopted the arguments of the *Verfassungsschutz* reports.

Judicial opinion took another step when the Administrative Court of Wiesbaden, on 19 May 2005, upheld a decision of the Governing Committee of Gießen to revoke the citizenship of three men, a novelty in the history of the German Federal Republic. In the written opinion (6 E 2225/04(2)), the state of Hessia was declared correct in arguing that the men had deceitfully acquired citizenship because in their application for naturalisation they had declared never to have supported efforts 'which are directed against the free and democratic basic order of the state or against the continued existence or security of the federal state or any of its component states'. They should have mentioned their membership in the IGMG. In the proceedings, the IGMG members argued that in their opinion the IGMG did not pursue any anticonstitutional goals and that no one had informed them that the IGMG was considered an anticonstitutional organisation by any state authorities. The plaintiffs also pointed out that they had actively participated in integration efforts, namely in 'informational events for school students, German courses for women, the coordination of training programmes among students', and 'under the aegis of Caritas (the Catholic charity organisation in Germany), in information sessions on youth crime and so on' (17). The court did not contest their personal engagement, but declared it irrelevant as the *Verfassungsschutz* report had evaluated the IGMG's youth work in toto as disintegrative (17).

Here, too, we can again witness the development of a special logic. In this case, the double linkage upheld by the Munich Administrative Court (i.e. that any organisation the Internal Security agency suspects of being anticonstitutional indeed is anticonstitutional; and that any member of such an organisation is to be treated as someone acting or expressing himself anticonstitutionally) is consistently applied in reverse. Anyone who does not apply this logic to himself has thus 'fraudulently' obtained citizenship.

The dominance of security policy may well explain why courts increasingly tend to accede to the *Verfassungsschutz*, rather than to the Federal Supreme Court for Constitutional Matters, the authority actually responsible for declaring organisations in conformity with the constitution or anticonstitutional. The observation of an attorney who was involved in asylum proceedings for many years is significant: 'In quiet times, judges tend to ask the *Verfassungsschutz* to simply present the facts it has. In tense times, there is, on the contrary, a tendency to simply take over the assessments of the security agencies. The worry about making political mistakes becomes dominant.'[11] An IGMG trial observer formulated another point of view: 'You get the impression that the people on the judge's bench are trembling with fear of being tricked by particularly clever Islamists and later appearing naïve. Those involved in the trial can talk about their inner social commitment as much as they want, it will be viewed with distrust simply on principle.' Aggravating the situation is the fact that the law text is not unequivocal and permits a vari-

---

11 Gottfried Plagemann in a personal communication with me.

ety of interpretations. In making decisions in this wide area, ideas about values and preconceived opinions play a major role. The atmosphere in the society on the whole, as it currently exists with regard to Islam, indeed has a decisive influence on the judgments, according to former Supreme Court Justice, Bertold Sommer.[12]

This agreement on a definition of security shows quite clearly how a far-reaching coordination of the independent executive and judicial branches takes place through a security definition and the constitution of a concept of the enemy, namely the Islamist. Each on their own, the different agencies start to go down the same path without any directive needed. 'We see that the security realm is not so much defined by a power of coercion, as Weber and Hobbes suggest, as by the ability to produce images of the Other who can then be controlled [...]' (Bigo 2000: 93).

The Law on Foreigners as a Weapon: Expulsion

One consequence of the more restrictive naturalisation policy was indeed intentional, keeping Muslim immigrants under the control of the law on foreigners. For example, Representative Grindel, in a Federal Parliament hearing, referred to the initiatives for naturalisation started by the IGMG as early as 1999, 'which limit our possibilities to get rid of some of the ringleaders and thus to stop activities directed against integration' (Representative Grindel, CDU. Deutscher Bundestag, Bandabschrift. Public Hearing on 20 September 2004, p. 66). The Bavarian Interior Minister, Günther Beckstein, according to the *Süddeutsche Zeitung* of 3 February 2006, declared, 'he is "firmly convinced" that the security interests of the citizens of Germany can better be served by a strict application of the foreigner law than by the enforcement of criminal law' (p. 6).

The severity of this weapon becomes particularly clear in connection with expulsions and denials of stay permits. Both methods hit the affected hard and permanently in their personal sphere and are often 'worse than criminal sanctions' (Bender 2003: 132). Here, the foreigner law operates as a pseudo-criminal law punishing with banishment. This is especially precarious, given that foreigner law, as an administrative law, does not recognize the liberal protection of the accused, which is so highly developed in criminal law (e.g. with regard to presumption of guilt or rules on evidence). Also, the principle of official investigation valid in administrative law is limited and/or suspended inasmuch as the foreigner himself is obliged to provide verifiable evi-

---

12 On the occasion of a professional talk on 8 March 2006, at the German Institute for Human Rights, 'Recognition and revocation of legal titles'.

dence for what is most favorable for him (oral information from Heiko Habbe). In short, the burden of proof is reversed.

It is interesting that the debates conducted in 2001 on the second package of security laws took the far-reaching consequences of expulsions and denials of stay permits into account (Bender 2003). The government's proposal for expulsion merely on the grounds of 'actual indications' of anticonstitutionalism was therefore voted down and a proof of actual anticonstitutional activity required. It is then interesting that administrative practice has, in this respect, not followed the intentions of the lawmakers. As I will show in the following, authorities have also deemed fact-supported indications for a lack of loyalty to the constitution as sufficient for decisions to expel. As applies to naturalisation, you don't even have to be a member of an organisation which is considered dangerous, it's enough to be a member of an organisation which is under suspicion of being anticonstitutional to prompt an expulsion, and this is so, even though the two legal matters are not at all on the same scale.

For example, the expulsion order of the city of Frankfurt against Mr. Özturgut (name changed) on 16 June 2005, was served on the grounds that there was knowledge of activities of his indicating he was an active member and functionary of the IGMG. (There was said to be verifiable evidence that he had provided his mobile phone for a Saturday meeting of the youth organisation of the IGMG district Frankfurt am Main-West, that he was cashier for the umbrella organisation of Hessian IGMG associations, that he had moderated a competition for oral Koran readings, etc.) Since there were indications that efforts against the free and democratic basic order of the Federal Republic of Germany originated from the IGMG, an expulsion had to be ordered (Doc. 7). The fact that at that time a proof of anticonstitutional activity was required for expulsions, unlike the requirements for naturalisation, was simply ignored by the authorities.

As with the naturalisation proceedings, here, too, the impression arises that the system is becoming ever more consistent. The County of Schaumburg, for example, argued on 16 September 2005, that the denial of a stay permit to a woman who, at the time of the decision, had been living in the Federal Republic for 12 years, was 'urgently' necessary because of her activity in the Board of Directors of the IGMG. The foreigners' office claimed that it had to act in accordance with the security authorities and had no 'manoeuvring room'. With this decision, they not only neglected to examine the individual case; the alleged lack of manoeuvring room also categorically dismisses any possibility of weighing legal alternatives and rights. According to the County of Schaumburg, obviously an activity as a functionary in an organisation that has not been forbidden necessarily requires the destruction of the framework of a person's life whose focal point of life has been in Germany for the past 12 years.

In this context, again increasing use is being made of the weapon of *retroactive* cancellation of a stay permit. Mr. Akkaya (name changed), for example, was notified by the County Administration of Germersheim on 8 February 2006, that his stay permit granted on 16 August 2005, was being rescinded because it had been an 'illegal administrative act'. His activity as chairman of the local IGMG community gave rise to 'security concerns' (Doc. 9). Inasmuch as the foreigners' office here clearly goes beyond the terms of the *Verfassungsschutz* report, this means an intensification, since constitutional concerns with regard to the IGMG are mentioned in the report, but no security concerns. Aggravating Mr. Akkaya's situation is the fact that he is affected by the rescission of his stay permit despite belonging to the second generation, born and raised in Germany.

With this argumentation, the radicalisation scenario developed by the Internal Security Agencies is put into practice. A further turning of the screw occurred on 20 July 2005, with an expulsion decree of the Mayor of the City of Wiesbaden. During a so-called security interview, the affected party had failed to mention membership in the IGMG when asked about connections with organisations suspected of supporting international terrorism.

'Thus, in the course of questioning serving to clarify concerns about entry or further residency, you made false or incomplete statements to my agency on major points. Thus, you have fulfilled the grounds for expulsion under § 54 Nr. 6 AufenthG, and it is my intention to expel you from the territory of the Federal Republic.'

Here, the criminalisation inherent in the logic of the radicalisation scenario is carried out once and for all. The chain of associations leads from suspicion of anticonstitutionality through accusation of anticonstitutionality, through the supposition of security concerns, all the way to the suspicion of a support of international terrorism. At the same time, anyone who doesn't bow to this logic is accused of making false statements.

There is something undeniably offensive about these decisions. The bureaucrats go beyond the letter of the existing laws, or are expected to do so by superior agencies. They apparently consider themselves in part justified by the concept of a 'democracy that can defend itself'. In addition, there is a certain passion for action in response to public pressure on politicians 'to do something'. This is, of course, directed against groups and individuals who officials, on the basis of *Verfassungsschutz* reports, personally suspect of being anticonstitutional. This selective procedure, contradicting the ideal of state neutrality, does not interfere with their sense of justice, since their decisions can ultimately be reviewed by the courts (just as those who drafted the Baden-Wurttemberg questionnaire were very aware of the fact that it might not be kept up by the courts).[13] Precisely this extremely widespread practice, however, makes a judicial practice which cedes the power of definition to the reports of the Internal Security Agencies especially problematic. For this way, any counterbalance to measures which acquiesce in injustice for the individual on the grounds of what is good for the state, or for political reasons, disappears.

In Islamic circles there are fears that the IGMG and the IGD could be only the first victims of the bureaucratic strategies described. Newspaper reports such as the one about the expulsion of three members of the Quietist (and explicitly pacifist) organisation Tabligh-i-Jamaat by the Bavarian state in September 2004, nourish these fears.

All these cases clearly show the dangers which arise when the foreigners' law is employed as a juridical weapon in political debates. It is increasingly turning into a weapon against individuals active in disliked, but not prohibited, organisations. At least in some federal states, they must expect the destruction of their social and professional context of life through expulsion, practical banishment. Increasingly, not deeds, but convictions are being punished.

Surveillance and Control

Muslim organisations had to a remarkable extent already been the object of surveillance by the Internal Security Agencies and police even before 9/11. After 9/11, the intensity of surveillance practice increased. A new method consisted of the *Verdachts- und Ereignisunabhängige Kontrollen* ('checks unrelated to suspicion or event') and raids. There had indeed been raids before (against Caliphate State mosques, for example), but the goals had always been specific. Today, the raids seem to be mainly directed against the mosques of the Milli Görüs and the IGD, but they also include other mosques, without the selection criteria being obvious to outside observers. The majority of raids occurred in Baden-Wurttemberg. I personally know of eight larger operations. The following summary listing, produced on the basis of police reports, reveals a remarkable discrepancy between the mission conducted and the results achieved.

- On 13 December 2002, 750 police officers were involved in a mission in Baden-Wurttemberg which examined over 600 people. It was called a 'raid against criminal Islamists in Stuttgart, Mannheim, and Freiburg'.

---

13 'Of course nobody now knows what the courts will say. But let's just stay calm, wait, and not give up in advance.' This can be found in the 'minutes' of talks with naturalisation agencies, p. 15/16 (AZ 5-1012.4/12 Doc. 11).

They discovered 'eight crimes and/or misdemeanors against stipulations of the foreigners' law (illegal residency, violation of location restrictions), two forgeries of documents, and one offence against property' (Press release from 16 December, 2002).

- On 28 November 2003, 380 police officers on a mission in Baden-Wurttemberg checked 360 individuals. They detected 'one violation due to illegal residency, one violation of the law on asylum procedures, two insults of police officers, and two traffic violations' (Press release from 2 December 2003).
- On 6 February 2004, controls took place in Rhineland Palatine to combat international terrorism. 270 officers examined 168 individuals. They were able to find one violation of the law on narcotics, four violations due to illegal residency, and two misdemeanors (violations of the restrictions on localities for asylum seekers).
- On 23 July 2004, a mission was conducted in Rhineland Palatine for a 'combat against international terrorism', in which 230 police officers were involved. 235 individuals and 102 vehicles were examined. Five crimes (suspicion of illegal residency) were registered.
- On 23 July 2004, about 400 officers in Baden-Wurttemberg inspected 18 organisation sites and mosques. Four crimes were registered, namely one violation of immigration law, one violation of asylum law, one violation of weapons law, and one misuse of identity documents (Press release from 27 July).

The state government of Lower Saxony, in reply to a parliamentary inquiry by representative Dr. Lennartz (GRÜNE), was unable to document a single search success. To the question as to the state government's estimation of the relation between the costs of the measures and their results, the laconic reply was that the cost of the measures conducted could not be calculated (Lower Saxon State Parliament – 15th legislative period. Printed document 15/60).

Politicians like the CDU Commissioner for Integration, Bosbach,[14] occasionally try to play down the raids by comparing them to traffic checks. This is deceptive. These police actions take place in an incomparably more severe manner, as the description of one such mission by the Bochum police shows:

Bochum, 16 April 2004

'Well, no one could leave the mosque or the mosque's courtyard. The driveway is maybe 20 meters wide and three or four VW police vans were standing there

---

14 During a discussion with graduates of the Axel Springer Journalist School in Berlin on 16 November 2005.

bumper to bumper so nobody could climb over, and everywhere somebody might have been able to get out there were at least two police officers in full gear, with helmets, not on their heads, but attached, billy clubs, but not drawn yet, handcuffs, and of course these completely puffed-up jackets. Those weren't regular police officers; they belonged to these special troops like for riots on 1 May in Kreuzberg [...] You had to line up. Then two of those troops took you to a mobile office where they checked your identity, checked whether each one was really registered at some address and if his identity papers were in order. Then they sent it out over radio and walkie-talkie, whatever, and they probably compared the data with those of the city of Bochum. Because a couple of computers were down, this took from quarter past three till nine-thirty in the evening. Then they finished up the last ones [...]' (Interview with Mohammed Nabil Abdulazim, Berlin, 25 October 2004).

Waiblingen and Fellbach, 23 July 2004

'[...] Our mosque and the DITIB mosque are in an industrial area. After Friday prayers, the gates to the industrial area were blocked by about forty or fifty police officers and their police vans. They stopped everyone leaving the mosque [...] The names and addresses of every Muslim leaving the mosque were taken down. Two young men who didn't have their IDs with them were taken to the police station and kept there for five hours. They were photographed. These two young men reported that another 25 Muslims were held at the police station [...]'

'During the same raid, the mosque in Fellbach [...] was checked. According to our information, barricades were set up at a distance of 150 to 200 meters from the mosque [...] Our people panicked. Because of these procedures, they couldn't get back to their jobs on time [...] The controls lasted until four o'clock in the afternoon. If you asked, different reasons were given. 1) They were looking for Islamists; 2) they were searching for criminals; 3) it was only a normal traffic check; 4) they weren't allowed to give any information; 5) it was a search for drugs' (Minutes of a conversation with Ugur Ataman, 23 July 2004).

The general problem with these 'checks unrelated to suspicion or event' is, of course, that by definition they affect innocent citizens belonging to a certain category of individuals. These measures were therefore, not surprisingly, perceived as extremely discriminatory by the faithful. 'They would never dare do that in a church', said one Muslim student. Many viewed the procedures as being specifically directed against Islam. 'They won't be satisfied until we completely give up Islam.' 'They want to scare people off so they won't go to a mosque at all.' (Interview with Mohammed Nabil Abdulazim)

Particularly in smaller cities, where they had struggled for years for recognition of their mosque community, people find it embarrassing and humiliating to be subjected to controls openly on the street for everybody to see after attending mosque services. The Waiblinger and Fellbacher Muslims viewed themselves as being portrayed as Islamists in the public eye. The report about the action in the local newspaper, the *Rems-Murr-Rundschau* (24 July 2004) bore the headline: 'Search for Criminal Islamists'. 'Once the police are there, whether you're innocent or not, people say the police were at your place.' (Mohammed Nabil Abdulazim op.cit.) The investigations were especially traumatic for individuals who had been subject to political persecution in their homelands. 'They now feared the worst; that just has to well up inside them. And you had to get them to calm down first. There was an old man crying and he didn't want to go outside. He saw the police and turned around and went back in. One man, he is 50 or 60 years old, was just bawling because he was afraid and said, "I haven't done anything, I'm innocent, they shouldn't take me", and such things.' (Mohammed Nabil Abdulazim)

After the raid in Bochum, those attending the mosque were divided into two factions. Some said, 'They don't have anything on us.' And the others said, 'Yeah, they've got lists now of who's comes to the mosque. They organized the whole shebang to get that kind of list together.' This fear exists. The ones with a German citizenship are therefore less worried [...] but everybody here who's a foreigner could be expelled tomorrow. Statements from the community after the raid in Braunschweig on 30 July 2004, are typical: 'Soon they'll give us all a crescent moon sticker like they did with the Jews and the Star of David in the old days.' (Report of an eye-witness) For the people attending mosques of the Islamic Community Milli Görüs, the situation is aggravated by the fact that they must fear substantial disadvantages, for the reasons mentioned earlier, if they are registered during such controls.

Checks without regard to individuals or grounds for suspicion are, meanwhile, not the only type of data collection. In Bavaria, for example, communities of the IGMG and the IGD are increasingly being treated as foreign political organisations and required to hand over names and addresses of members as well as information about their citizenship.

How vague the term 'political' is can be seen in the answer to an appeal from the County Administration Office of the state capital of Munich on 20 October 2004. The community was first informed that, as a member of the IGMG, it belonged to an organisation directed against the free and democratic basic order and one which is considered a political organisation. More interesting is the second argument:

'According to its bylaws, the goal of the organisation is the representation of the common interests of Muslim organisations in Bavaria, the protection of the rights of Muslims living in Bavaria, as well as the advocacy of the social, religious, legal, and cultural interests of Islam. In addition, one declared goal of the organisation is to attain state recognition as a religious community and thus to be entitled to state support [...] The representation of these interests in the society as a whole, in its all-encompassing manner, in fact represents a political activity which, in view of the close link between Islam's religious message and its concept of the state and the lawmaker and public life, can in principle not be separated from the rest' (Doc. 14).

For all practical purposes, this argument contains the claim that Islamic organisations are per se political, and that their activities are thus not protected under the right to freedom of religion.[15] In connection with the denials of naturalisation and expulsion decrees described above, the demands for membership lists appear to be a massive form of interference in the freedom to organize and assemble peaceably. They appear to be primarily motivated by the desire to pressurize unpopular groups, about which the authorities lack sufficient materials for proceedings for prohibition, for as long as it takes to destroy them.

In connection with the genesis of the security realm, then, it is interesting that not only the agencies subordinate to the Interior Ministries, but also the tax offices meanwhile tend to put pressure on Islamic organisations. I am in possession of a letter from the tax office of Rheingau-Taunus which shows that the tax-free charitable status of the local IGMG community was revoked because of the *Verfassungsschutz* reports.

The impression arises that the population does not perceive, and does not want to perceive, either, the intense feeling of insecurity such measures produce among Muslims. Muslim immigrants are confronted with the precarious status that many of them have. They are unashamedly placed under the general suspicion of being enemies of an open society and therefore subjected to special procedures for naturalisation. The foreigners' law is increasingly used as a weapon against them. They suffer restrictions on freedom of religion, of opinion, and of assembly. And finally, they are placed under an irritating extent of surveillance as well as controlled, and registered.

With all this, they are treated as enemies of an open society and lumped together with violent criminals. This leads to Muslims feeling unprotected and homeless. 'Since 9/11, many Muslims are incredibly frightened of ending up on some list or other', says Burhan Kesici to describe the atmosphere. Ever more often in discussions with Muslims, they refer to the fate of the Jews. 'Before 11 September, I had the feeling I was simply supposed to break with Turkey. What do I have to do with Turkey anymore? That country has become foreign to me. In the meantime, I no longer believe it would be a good

---

15 This is no single case. A letter from the Administrative Office of Miltenberg, for example, states, 'In its bylaws, in § 10, the general principles of the organisation's work is formulated. At least those principles formulated in no. 7 and no. 8 prove that the organisation is politically active by taking positions on current socially relevant questions from an Islamic point of view as well as by publishing violations of law against its members in suitable form.' (Doc. 16)

idea for us to burn our bridges to Turkey. Maybe we'll need that country one of these days.' (Minutes from memory of a conversation with Mustafa Yeneroglu)

Unintended Results of Security Policy

Because of security authorities' broadened concept of security and radicalisation scenarios, security policy is increasingly concerned with the 'preliminary stages' of revolutionary and/or violent Islam, i.e. with communities defined as 'legalistic Islam'. For it can of course be argued that, in view of the immensity of the terrorist danger, a balancing of legal interests must be undertaken. Restrictions on the freedoms of one group of the population would be acceptable, if a larger legal interest, namely prevention of bodily injury, could this way be secured. The question is whether the measures described can at least achieve what they promise in terms of security policy. Since not even the security authorities believe that communities of legalistic Islam pose any danger, the radicalisation scenarios presented must be examined especially in this context. They may be summarized as follows: In communities of legalistic Islam, socialisation takes place within an 'isolated Islamic view of the world' which, if appropriate chances and structures are present, makes a transition to more radical forms of Islam possible or even likely. Communities of legalistic Islam are, so to say, regarded as the milieu in which revolutionary, or even violent, Islam finds a protected space and can recruit. Here, common ideas are produced which permit access to more radical circles.

First of all we should note that despite having some points in common in terms of their view of the world, there are radical differences between legalistic Islamists and revolutionary Islamists, related to the overall context. On the one hand, an ethical conviction of ideological purity is to be found which regards any compromise with the West as treason (cf. Schiffauer 2000); on the other hand, a practical politics logic of compromise which insists that a Muslim can engage in the Western system as a Muslim without relinquishing his character, that basically the 'West' [democracy and the legal system] and Islam can be combined. Representatives of the first position will reject all cooperation and dialogue; representatives of the second position tend to seek them. While an 'isolated' Islamic image of the world can indeed be assumed in communities of revolutionary Islamism, the legalistic communities are characterized by a clear plurality of opinions.[16] Just as important is the fact that communities of legalistic Islamism place key terms (such as *jihad* or *Sharia*) in a new overall context and thus 'redefine' them. This way, the fas-

---

16 This is also confirmed by the observations of Tietze (2001) and Meng (2004).

cination with revolutionary Islamism finds a counter position, inasmuch as it is demonstrated that Islam can also be understood differently.

Even more important are the sociological differences between communities of 'legalistic Islamism' and those of 'radical-revolutionary Islamism'. While the former are characterized by an open network structure and maintain relations with other Islamic communities (for example, in umbrella organisations, by mutual assistance, or through cooperation in foreigner advisory councils), revolutionary communities close themselves off. During my study of the Caliphate State (2000), I detected a circle constitutive of a sect. Demarcation from other communities, elitism, the pronounced development of a view of the world contrary to that of other communities, inner authoritarianism, and a cult of revolutionary purity increasingly went hand in hand. Here, largely isolated '*in groups*' develop which 'get themselves worked up about something' and formulate an ever more deviant view of the world. This sectarian circle increasingly caused members of the Caliphate State to regard the communities of the Milli Görüs, which were closest to them in their ideas, as their biggest enemies, namely the ones who had deviated from the pure teachings and against whom they should therefore fight the most decidedly (Schiffauer 2000: 197). In fact, there were only violent altercations between members of these two communities (in the form of fist fights). The Caliphate State's distancing itself from the 'compromisers' was met with a response from the IGMG. They viewed the followers of the Caliphate State as deluded and dangerous nuts, who in essential points (especially in terms of their revolutionary intolerance) had deviated from Islamic teachings. This mutual resentment led to the two communities largely avoiding contact with each other. On this basis, quite distinct organisational cultures developed. While the communities of legalistic Islam confronted the world, acted with political pragmatism, and were therefore in principle ready to compromise, the communities of radical-revolutionary Islam are inimical to the world, have ethical convictions, and maintain a rhetoric of radical opposition.

All indications are that there is no continuity between the communities of 'legalistic' and 'radical-revolutionary' Islam, but rather a clear divide. Of course it can never be ruled out that conversions from conservative to revolutionary communities may occur, but this is not a 'natural' step, and it is not even a likely one. Value conservative Islam must not be considered a preliminary stage of radical Islamism, but instead as an alternative to it. The pressure the state exerts in this area affects precisely the conservative Islamic milieu which promises integration of young Muslims. The advantage of a policy that apparently aims at drying out the 'Islamistic swamp' seems to be at least doubtful.

While the advantage of this security policy is doubtful, some very clearly unintended results of the policy may be encountered which have negative consequences for the struggle against violent and revolutionary Islam. They all tend to undermine the plausibility of the conservative answer to the revolutionary spirit and may be summarized in four points.

Increasing pressure on the communities leads to an increasing distance towards German society. There always have been voices (primarily from the faithful of the first generation) in value conservative communities who saw them as islands in a sea of infidels. For some time, the second and third generations of the communities appeared to have overcome this view of the world, but experiences with security policy have reversed this process. At the moment, the advocates of the existence an unbridgeable gap between the Christian majority and the Islamic minority are again increasing in number. In terms of security policy, this is particularly problematic, since any factional dispute increases the pressure on loyalties. Reluctance to cooperate with security forces also grows with increasing distance to society.

This is aggravated by the experience of public humiliation through police actions. It is regularly reported that in raids, older community members must make an effort to calm down younger ones, to prevent them from seeking confrontation with the police. We know that the experience of (supposed or actual) state discrimination often has a more decisive effect than discrimination from the civil society and that it can be the cause of radicalisation.[17]

Acknowledgements

Here I would like to thank several people for their critical reading of, and very important comments on, this text. Especially to be mentioned are Julia Eckert, Reinhard Marx, Heiner Bielefeldt and Heiko Habbe.

---

17 We know, for example, from the biography of Abd Samad Moussaoui about his brother, who was involved in the attacks of 9/11 that racist behaviour of the French police was a drastic experience for him (2002: 86 ff.). A major factor in the emergence of racial unrest during the 1980s in Great Britain were, according to the information of the investigating commission there, the 'stop and search' practices of the British police (Banton 1982). It is no accident that the ignition spark for the unrest in the French suburbs in 2005 was the tragic end of a youth's flight from police controls.

References

Banton, M.B. (1982): 'Policies for Police-minority Relations'. In: C. Fried (ed.), *Minorities: Community and Identity*, Berlin and Heidelberg: Springer, pp. 299-314.

Bender, D. (2003): '"Verpolizeilichung" des Ausländerrechts? Die ausländerrechtlichen Maßnahmen des Gesetzgebers nach dem 11. September', *Kritische Justiz*, 36: 130-45.

Bigo, D. (2000): 'Liaison Officers in Europe. New Officers in the European Security Field'. In: J.W.E. Sheptycki (ed.), *Issues in Transnational Policing*, London: Routledge, pp 67-99.

Eckert, J. (2005): 'The Politics of Security', Working Paper 76, Halle/ Saale: Max Planck Institute for Social Anthropology, www.eth.mpg. de

Meng, F. (2004): *Islam(ist)ische Orientierungen und gesellschaftliche Integration in der zweiten Migrantengeneration – Eine Transparenzstudie*, Bremen: Akademie für Arbeit und Politik der Universität Bremen.

Moussaoui, A.S. (2002): *Zacarias Moussaoui. Mein Bruder*, Zürich: Pendo.

Puschnerat, T. (2006): 'Zur Bedeutung ideologischer und sozialer Faktoren in islamistischen Radikalisierungsprozessen – eine Skizze'. In: U. Kemmesies (ed.), *Terrorismus und Extremismus – der Zukunft auf der Spur*, München: Luchterhand Verlag, pp. 219-154.

Schiffauer, W. (2000): *Die Gottesmänner: Türkische Islamisten in Deutschland. Eine Studie zur Herstellung religiöser Evidenz*, Frankfurt am Main: Suhrkamp.

―――― (2004): 'Das Recht, anders zu sein', *Die Zeit* Nr. 48, 18 November 2004, p. 8.

Tietze, N. (2001): *Islamische Identitäten. Formen muslimischer Religiosität junger Männer in Deutschland und Frankreich*, Hamburg: Hamburger Edition HIS.

Political Rationalities, Counter-terrorism and Policies on Islam in the United Kingdom and France

FRANK PETER

Introduction

This article examines policies on Islam in France and the United Kingdom with a particular focus on their relation to and their embeddedness in strategies countering urban violence and terrorism. It is based on the assumption that policies concerning the incorporation, regulation and administration of Islamic institutions and Muslim practices are connected to counter-terrorism policies and a variety of policy measures directed against phenomena of urban violence and delinquency. Starting with a rethinking of our understanding of power in the context of European Islam, my principal aim is to outline an analytical framework for state policies which will replace the hitherto dominating analytical focus on national juridico-political orders with a Foucaldian perspective on the functioning of political rationalities in a governmentalized state. The application of the framework proposed here will bring into focus a type of counter-terrorism policy which is not based on mechanisms of surveillance and exclusion of suspected individuals or groups, but instead on targeting the milieu within which these individuals and groups supposedly operate through a policy which is partly conducted 'beyond the state', and notably by Muslims themselves. Fundamentally, this policy reconfigures its erstwhile object – the abstract category of Islam conceived as one 'religion' defined in law – as an Islamic milieu, an understanding of how social conditions in the long-term determine interrelated Muslim practices, beliefs and institutions. This policy is thus not based on a distorted legal framework, but on evaluations of feasibility and costs, prognostics of future developments in the Islamic milieu, and shifting standards of acceptable religious practices and beliefs by Muslim citizens.

My attempt to broaden our understanding of policies on Islam beyond an analysis of the national jurido-political order[1] – defined through citizenship legislation, state-religion regimes, and, more generally, national political cultures and underlying political theories – is motivated by two aims. First, by considering the juridico-political order as merely one of several mechanisms of power, I seek to foreground the questions of whether those state policies which deviate from this order are commanded by a specific rationality (and are not merely deviations) and how we can study this rationality in relation to the law. Second, the line of investigation pursued here aims at contributing to our understanding of discrimination against Muslims – a crucial topic in studies on Muslims in France and the U.K. – and possible remedies against it. The discursive rendering of the concept of power used here will lead us to study discrimination as being partly constitutive of Muslim understandings and practices of Islam, and not only as the enactment of constraints. This, in turn, will entail a different appraisal of remedies against it and help to illuminate the ways in which the latter are constrained by and possibly reiterate the conditions which enable discrimination in the first place.

My approach to the study of policies on Islam in France and the U.K. is grounded in Foucault's conceptualization of mechanisms of power and his reflections on those mechanisms specific to the exercise of bio-power in a governmentalized State (Burchell et al. 1991; Foucault 1997 and 2004). My point of departure is the assumption that the functioning of politics stems from three distinct rationalities of power which coexist, namely juridical and disciplinary rationality and, finally, what Foucault calls the security apparatus (*dispositif de sécurité*), which I want to elaborate here as 'anticipatory rationality'. In this article, I will limit myself to analysing the functioning of this specific political rationality, which has come increasingly, in the last decade or so, to underlie policies on Islam in France and the U.K.

In a first step, this rationality can be characterized by its object, the Islamic milieu within which racialized Muslims live, that is the group of those whose personal or inherited roots in Islamic countries have been naturalized and biologized and who now constitute the 'Muslim community' of France and the U.K., usually equated with immigrants (and descendants) from majority Muslim countries. Following Silverstein, I define racialisation here as 'the process through which any diacritic of social personhood – including, class, ethnicity, generation, kinship/affinity, positions within fields of power –

---

[1] For studies who seek to transcend this orientation in ways other than mine see for example Maussen (2004 and 2006).

comes to be essentialized, naturalized and/or biologized' (Silverstein 2005: 364). Anticipatory rationality can be characterized furthermore by its usage of an anticipatory – or prospective – analysis which aims to discern future risks of social or political conflicts arising from this part of the population which it conceives as part of an Islamic milieu. Finally, it can be characterized by its attempt to incorporate Muslims into the fight against 'radicalization'. As stated above, this anticipatory rationality will be considered one instantiation of a security apparatus. While this anticipatory rationality is closely intertwined with the legal order, it puts in operation a reconfiguration of the latter by adjusting the legal system – and the subject of law – to varying and indeed often conflicting knowledge claims about the social citizen, in this case the racialized Muslim conceived as part of an Islamic milieu. Put differently, this anticipatory rationality sets in motion a specific politicisation of difference inside the population which triggers variegated effects. While this movement of politicisation aims at the normalisation of Muslims, it does so by breaking up, at least momentarily, the universalism of law and political representation based on the relative subordination of particulars to the abstract 'we' of the universal community of the liberal state (Brown 1995).

In the following analysis, I will seek to identify the divergent policy consequences of this reordering of the uneasy balance between universalism and particularism and the concomitant shift in the combination of political rationalities and explore how we can study Islam both as an effect of this double movement of politicisation and normalisation and as its vehicle. More particularly, I will argue that the increased importance of a anticipatory rationality underlies the emergence of what I will call civil Islam, Islam understood as a set of discourses and practices which aim to 'sacralize the living-together of a specific collectivity' (Willaime 1993: 571) against the threat of 'radicalisation' of 'young Muslims' and, more generally, various forms of urban violence among the racialized Muslim population. The emergence of civil Islam – as policy aim and as specific remaking of the Islamic tradition by Muslims – implies, and this is the second argument advanced here, that the application of legal norms underlying policies on Islam and enabling or disabling Muslims practices is increasingly based on a specific non-legal rationality which induces various reconfigurations of concepts such as laïcité, Establishment, Republicanism or Multiculturalism. Finally, in a comparative perspective, I will argue that the heightened role of this anticipatory rationality is a major factor in the limited realignment of policies on Islam in France and Britain which we can observe during the last decade. Put another way, the study of this rationality provides one means to grasp the commonalities of European policies on Islam beyond national boundaries and nation-specific modes of regulating religion.

Political Rationalities

In his study 'Security, Territory, Population' (2004), Foucault distinguished between three mechanisms of power – juridical system, disciplinary system, security apparatus – all of which Foucault defines indirectly by contrasting them to each other. In 'Security, Territory, Population' he begins to do so by giving a simple and illuminating example, namely that of state policies concerning theft. In the context of a legal rationality, theft is to be punished simply according to the law which contains a number of prohibitions and specifies the respective punishments. The rise of disciplinary systems 'frames' the application of the law on the one hand by various practices of surveillance – which aim to detect the thief even before he passes to act – and on the other, by a complex of penitentiary practices which aim at the correction and transformation of the delinquent. Finally, inside a security apparatus, the functioning of both the legal and disciplinary systems are reordered in reference to a new series of questions concerning theft, such as statistical evidence on occurrence of theft; the impact of famine or any other social crises on the number of crimes committed; the costs incurred in the punishment of thieves; the cost and efficiency of re-educating criminals; and so forth. The rise of security mechanisms partially reconfigures the legal apparatus; while it enables a specific application of the law, no longer does this application follow directly from the binary code of prohibition vs. permission which underlies legal rationality. Instead, the security apparatus operates on the basis of a reasoning based on evaluations of what is socially and economically acceptable and feasible. In the course of the application of its policies, prior understandings of law are either suspended, even while continuing to determine the aims which these policies seek to actualize, or they are redefined – through new legislation and/or the application of laws – with reference to what is acceptable and feasible. The security apparatus is furthermore characterized by the fact that its matrix incorporates cost calculations as one of its constituent elements. Finally, specific phenomena are not considered in an isolated way, as in law or disciplinary institutions, but as part of a probable series of events; this is so since the security apparatus is fundamentally concerned with the problem of uncertainty. This problem of uncertainty is tackled to an important degree by relying on a reasoning in terms of what Foucault calls 'milieu': 'The specific space of security refers then to a series of possible events; it refers to the temporal and the uncertain which have to be inserted into a given space [which] […] one can call the milieu' (Foucault 2004: 22). Fundamentally, thinking in terms of milieus is an attempt to tackle the problem of uncertainty by understanding and calculating 'the action at a distance of one body on another' and, more generally, by grasping how, inside of a space conceived of as 'milieu', causes and effects loop. In brief, milieu designates a new 'space of intervention' for state power 'in which instead of affecting individuals as a set of legal subjects capable of voluntary action – which would be the case of sovereignty – and instead of affecting them as a multiplicity of organisms, of bodies capable of performances, and of required performances – as in discipline – one tries to affect precisely a population' (Foucault 2004: 23).

In the following analysis, I will study how policies on Islam in France and the U.K. have been reshaped, to different degrees, by a rationality which precisely is based on considerations of feasibility and acceptability, on calculations of costs, and on the notion of milieu, here Islamic milieu. Before examining the functioning of anticipatory rationality, one remark on the role of expert knowledge in this process is necessary, since the reliance on anticipatory analysis and the reasoning in terms of an Islamic milieu attribute a significant role to what I will refer to as expert knowledge on Islam.[2] This assertion raises the question of the scientific status of this expert knowledge. Now, it is clear that a lot of what is said today by the proliferating group of experts on Islam and what is referred to in public – by politicians, journalists, intellectuals, Church leaders, [...] – as expert knowledge is not considered scientific by scientists, whether they be from the social sciences or humanities. However, there is no need to enter into the debate on the question how we can classify the content of expert knowledge on Islam and, more generally, which factors – internal or external to science, scientific factors proper or social ones – make that specific artefact count as science. My point here is simply that a group of experts, a group which is larger than that of scientists, provides and/or legitimates a specific idiom for making reality amenable to deliberation and planning (as, e.g., in the case of the terms integration, radicalisation, 'young Muslims', etc.).[3] While the scientific status of this expert knowledge is often contested, this does not allow us to dismiss it as mere talk and irrelevant to a study of policies on Islam. These contestations are part of the political field which has been opened up by the increasingly prominent workings of anticipatory rationality. They co-determine the latter's functioning and thus need to be studied as such. Furthermore, expert knowledge not only serves to plan policies, but also, as I said, to make matters Islamic simply amenable to deliberation. Finally, importantly, expert knowledge on Islam – and not least the type of rationality which it enables and disseminates – is an important

---

2   The specific contribution of academic research on European Islam and immigration to expert knowledge cannot be dealt with here, but see, for the case of France, Peter (forthcoming), 'French Scholarship on Islam in the Republic', paper presented at Forum for Islamforskning-Workshop 'Research on Islam Repositioned', Copenhagen, May 2007.

3   I draw here on Rose and Miller's definition of political rationalities (Rose/Miller 1992: 179).

element in policies on Islam, since it directly reshapes the ways in which Muslims think of Islam and Islamic conduct in the context of France and the U.K. Put another way, expert knowledge on Islam is the primary vector through which state policies reconfigure what they target.

The Case of the United Kingdom

In the case of the United Kingdom, anticipatory rationality becomes significant for policies on Islam after 2001. As stated above, this rationality functions next to other mechanisms of power, some of which are politically narrowly defined (electoral tactics), others not (anti-discrimination politics and legislation; communitarian policies). The following analysis will touch only briefly upon them[4] and concentrate on the emergence and functioning of anticipatory rationality in relation to a legal rationality which notably underlies anti-discrimination policies. Anti-discrimination policies were formally introduced for the first time in 1965 following the restriction on immigration instituted in 1962, and were considerably extended in 1976 with the creation of the *Commission for Racial Equality* (CRE) which was authorized to conduct race relations audits of companies, government agencies, etc. (Anwar 1986: 17-20; Lester 1987: 22; Crowley 1992: 88 f.). These policies are first of all noteworthy for our discussion, since they institutionalize, from the 1960s on, the racial prism of British perception of the post-migratory reality. Society was divided into 'black' and 'white', the term 'Asians' being little used until the 1990s (Bensons 1996; Alexandre 2002; Modood 2005: 46 f.). As concerns Muslims, the limitation to racial groups, as has often been noted, excluded them from anti-discrimination measures and thus created a situation of inequality and furthermore directly contributed to redirecting the process of incorporation of Islam from the national to the local level (Lewis 1997; Rath et al. 2001: 227-29; Ansari 2004: 340-88).

I consider these policies as an outcome of a legal rationality not only because they largely – though not exclusively – work to ensure equality by legal means, but because the recognition of racial difference and discrimination by these policies aims at reaffirming equality of all citizens beyond these differences. Fundamentally, they consider difference as normalizable and they seek to normalize and neutralize it as a mere individual attribute that is irrelevant to national identity, through legal protection and measures of positive discrimination. Importantly, these policies are founded on the assumption of a stable identity, whether it is black, Asian or Muslim, which they themselves obviously contribute to stabilize. Both the emphasis placed on the normalisa-

---

4 For a more detailed study of these see Peter (2006c).

tion of difference on the one hand and the assumption of stable difference and identity on the other distinguish this rationality in contrast to anticipatory rationality, as we shall see. Policies on Islam, before 2001, have largely functioned in this framework which was slowly but not fully extended from racial groups to Muslims over the course of the 1990s, particularly after the Labour party came to power in 1997. While these policies are clearly not uniform, but inspired by various factors, notably electoral considerations responding to the increased articulation of British Muslim identities (see Peter 2006c), they rely on notions of a stable Muslim identity and they are also deeply concerned, in reaction to Muslim demands, with issues of legal equality and the normalisation of the Muslim presence through the latter's recognition. The central role in policies on Islam in the 1990s, of the equal treatment of Muslim confessional schools, realized by Labour, of debates on legislation against religious discrimination, of Muslim demands for amendment to the exclusively Anglican law on blasphemy and, later on, of the debate around the law against incitement to religious hatred (adopted in 2006) demonstrate this.

After 2001, under the impact of the riots in Northern English towns implicating young British Pakistanis, and September 11, this begins to change and anticipatory rationality becomes more important. The influence of this anticipatory rationality is visible already in the influential Cantle Report which contains the results of one of the government ordered enquiries made into the disturbances and its causes. The Cantle Report is important in two respects: first, because it makes a contribution to establishing the use of an anticipatory analysis in the elaboration of policies for governing 'modern multi-racial Britain' (Home Office 2002: 9); second, because it insists strongly on the normative dimension of the disturbances and the need for more 'cohesion'. The main message of the report, i.e. that it is necessary to define and to disseminate a common set of values in order to guarantee 'community cohesion', is precisely the result of an anticipatory analysis of Britain's multicultural society. According to the report, the absence of common values has strongly contributed to the disturbances in northern England. The entire report is thus basically an attempt to discern and to relate the diverse causes – political, social, cultural – underlying this absence of shared values in order to devise a strategy for preventing similar incidents in the future. Among the report's manifold recommendations, a substantial number thus relates to the need to enhance social cohesion through increased 'cross-cultural contacts'. This is reflected for example in the demands to confessional schools to take in more pupils from other confessions and the proposition to make funding of cultural, religious or ethnic associations dependent on their contribution to social cohesion (Home Office 2002).

While the report is relatively vague about many issues and deploys anticipatory rationality only in an incipient form, the latter soon becomes used more fully and more directly in relation to British Muslims. The reasons leading some British Muslims to join the Taliban in the fight against the allied forces in Afghanistan have been debated since 2001 in British media.[5] Very soon, the disaffection of Muslims towards British politics, a phenomenon which is regularly measured in opinion polls,[6] is also being debated in anticipation of a terrorist attack in England.[7] The perpetration of the first suicide attack by a Briton in Israel, in early 2003, contributes to nourishing these reflections.[8] In the course of these public debates, a variety of positions are defended. Generally speaking, we can discern two dominant positions which are to a large degree complementary. First, there are those who reason in terms of simple defence, notably through the police and military apparatuses, against the terrorist threat and, second, there are those who demand a more comprehensive and preventive approach to this threat. This latter approach is based on an anticipatory analysis. Government policies are informed by both approaches simultaneously.

The anti-terrorist strategy put into practice in 2002, *Contest*, aims not only at hunting terrorists and preparing how to deal with the aftermaths of future terrorist attacks, but also at reducing the number of individuals supporting terrorism or eventually becoming terrorists themselves (Intelligence and Security Committee 2006). On the one hand, the government thus introduces, in late 2001, a new anti-terror legislation (Bamford 2004: 747-49) and puts into practice a new police strategy which effectively discriminates against British citizens of Asian origin.[9] On the other hand, there are attempts to develop a more preventive approach to the terrorist threat and it is in this context that policies concerning the incorporation and administration of Islam enter. This second approach is based on the anticipatory analysis of the 'milieu' which allows disaffection and terrorism among Muslims to grow. Since 2001, the discussions in the public and among policy-makers are thus concerned with the relative impact which British foreign policy in the Middle East, discrimination and segregation and the activities of extremist Islamist groups have on the radicalisation of 'young Muslims' in order to devise an efficient policy to prevent this latter development in the future.

---

5   See for example 'Why Brits fight for the Taliban', The Observer, 4 November 2001.
6   See for example the opinion polls conducted for The Guardian at www: icmresearch.co.uk.
7   'Inside the Mind of a Terrorist', The Observer, 9 March 2003.
8   'Making of a Martyr: From Pacifism to Jihad', The Observer, 4 May 2003.
9   'Muslims face increased stop and search', The Guardian, 2 March 2005.

Fundamentally, this implies a shift in the configuration of political rationalities and, more precisely, the decline of the legal rationality. The latter's epistemology, presupposing the existence of relatively stable (ethnic or religious) communities, is strongly put under strain by the events of 2001 – indicating both the divergences between communities and their transformation – and the government's outlook, in the subsequent period, is certainly characterized by a stronger awareness not only of the internal plurality of religious and ethnic communities, but also of their constant evolution in relation to society. I would argue that in the post-2001 context, the government defines its task increasingly as controlling and guiding the range of processes which are continually shaping ethnic and religious identities inside the milieu circumscribed by immigration and ascribed Islamity. It is because of this new focus that expert knowledge begins to play a crucial role in policy-making and debates relating to it. Certainly, the question of equality has not simply been abandoned by British politicians. To the contrary, social, economic or legal equality is seen to varying degrees as a crucial factor – but insufficient on its own – to influence positively the development of the Muslim community. The Home Office's insistence in its 2005 programme on the need to strengthen equality and in turn community cohesion can be cited as one example here (Home Office 2005a).[10] However, today, this policy of equality and normalisation to a large degree is commanded by and embedded in an anticipatory rationality. This is no mean change to preceding times: in the context of such an anticipatory rationality, the principle of equal treatment of various religions, including Islam, can be suspended, openly or not, as a function of the results of such an analysis. The policies in favour of disseminating civil Islam are just one example of it.

What then are the effects of this development on policies on Islam and, more particularly, how does it relate to and lead to the government's support for civil Islam? In a first step, civil Islam can be defined here as a state policy aiming to refashion a certain number of institutions and practices among immigrants from Islamic background in order to reduce the risk of socio-political conflicts and terrorism in the future. In its attempt to identify the causes of the mentioned phenomena and adequate counter-policies, this state policy reasons in terms of an Islamic milieu. As introduction to the analysis of these policies, a reading of a series of leaked government documents, emanating essentially from the Home Office[11] and presenting reflections on the government's anti-terrorism strategy, provide one example of such a reasoning.[12]

---

10 The results of this policy cannot be evaluated in this article.
11 The role of the Foreign Commonwealth Office (FCO) in Islam policies in Britain is certainly of very limited importance. Nevertheless, it should be pointed out that the ministry is concerned with some aspects of this policy on a seemingly regular basis. For example, a FCO unit created in 2004 and in charge of

It should be noted first that the government's reasoning in matters of terrorism is in several ways incomplete. Policy-makers continue to struggle, for instance, with the question of whether there is an unambiguous correlation between terrorism and socio-economic deprivation.[13] Also, the precise trajectory of extremist Muslims[14] and terrorists is to a large degree unclear, apart from the fact that a certain number of extremist (non-violent) Islamic groups supposedly facilitate this process (Timesonline 2005). While these points are left in limbo, the Home Office report clearly identifies other causes and possible remedies to the radicalisation of young Muslims. The report relates the new British policies in the field of incorporation of Islam to three causal factors of radicalisation: the auto-segregation of Muslims; the absence of a strong rejection of extremism and terrorism by 'moderate' Muslims; weak or missing control by state authorities of Muslim activists, notably because of their transnational activities. What are the solutions proposed here? These consist in stimulating Muslim institutions and actors to interact more with majority society, notably via inter-religious dialogue; bringing 'moderate' Muslims who are to be supported by the state to reject and fight against extremism and terrorism; increasing the ratio of nationally rooted or trained activists in British Islam in order to facilitate its control and its adaptation to the British context.

This report also recognizes, as others have done,[15] that British foreign policy (in Palestine, Afghanistan, Iraq, [...]) is a factor of alienation of Muslims which is to be countered by a more efficient communication strategy with Muslims. This analysis has been strongly rejected by members of the British government, notably Prime Minister Blair. However, it would be wrong to take this rejection as indicating simply the limits of anticipatory rationality. Rather, it points more generally to the latter's profoundly ambivalent nature

---

    reinforcing contacts with the Islamic world is also assigned the task of promoting a positive image of British foreign policy among Muslims in order to reduce the risk of alienation (Home Office 2005c: 16).

12 The following remarks refer to an internal report, co-written by the FCO and HO for the Prime Minister, and leaked to the press after the bombings of 2005. In this report, written essentially in 2004, one finds an analysis of the different strategies applied or to be applied in the government's striving to keep 'young Muslims' from radicalisation and terrorism (Timesonline 2005).

13 While evidence is so far lacking to support this connection, this is, however, not seen as an argument against anti-discrimination policies. Given that the aim is to enlist support of 'moderate' Muslims in the fight against extremism (see below), the Home Office argues that Muslim leaders' perception that discrimination is a cause for the radicalisation would constitute in itself a reason to pursue such anti-discrimination policies.

14 See below on the Home Office's definition of 'extremism'.

15 See, e.g. 'Leak shows Blair told of Iraq war terror link', The Observer, 28 August 2005; 'Don't treat us like patsies, say Muslim MPs', The Guardian , 15 August 2006; Home Office 2005d.

which stems from the fact that the causal reasoning (in terms of milieu) is both a modality of power and a means for various persons and groups – including Muslims – to hold power accountable for the negative effects of policies, here those of British foreign policies on the 'radicalisation' of Muslims. Pointedly said, instead of seeing in this rejection by Blair and others the limits of anticipatory rationality, this rejection marks its presence in a specific form of opposition which it enables.[16]

Inter-religious Dialogue and the Imams

After 2001 and even more so after the bombings of July 2005, civil Islam is being institutionalized and this is done primarily via policies concerning inter-religious dialogue and imams.

First, the government decides upon giving more support to inter-religious networks (Home Office 2005a: 12; Inter Faith Network 2002, idem 2005 and cf. idem 2003 for the situation on the local level). While it is too early to evaluate the results of this attempt to insert Islam more firmly into the multi-religious landscape, it is reasonable to assume that this policy will, generally speaking, prove to be an accelerator of Islam's institutionalisation while at the same giving advantage to those Muslim actors, institutional or individual, who have the necessary profile, in terms of professional, social and cultural competencies, in order to fully participate in inter-religious activities.

The reasons for granting this support to interreligious groups are indicated without ambiguity by the Home Office whose position here illustrates well the changed political approach pointed to in the discussion of the Cantle Report. According to the ministry, 'a more cohesive society needs more than just equality of opportunities for all individuals' and also depends on 'certain social conditions' enabling citizens to get to know each other and to develop 'shared values' (Home Office 2005a: 11). Now, British policy is conceived precisely as an effort to create the conditions necessary for the dissemination of 'shared values'. Apart from measures such as funding for sport or artistic activities and the introduction of civic education in schools, inter-religious dialogue thus benefits from increased financial support. The justifications given for this support are to a certain degree distinct from the earlier objective, inspired by communitarian ideas (Bevir 2003; Smith 2004), to reinforce, on various levels, the consultation and cooperation with religious communities and to facilitate the access of these organisations to public funding (Home Office 2005b: 3-35). After 2001, the government's aim is not simply to sup-

---

16 For a discussion of this point see Peter (forthcoming), 'French Scholarship on Islam in the Republic', paper presented at Forum for Islamforskning-Workshop 'Research on Islam Repositioned', Copenhagen, May 2007.

port the activities of religious communities, but to orient them in their activities in order to turn them into forces of cohesion, and not factors of divisiveness. While the Anglican establishment – its 'minimal nature [...], its proven openness to other denominations and faiths seeking public space, and the fact that its very existence is an ongoing acknowledgement of the public character of religion' (Modood 1994: 73) – might have facilitated at various points in time the process of incorporation of Islam into the United Kingdom, we should be careful not to consider it as implying a specific view of religion by government or the latter's approval of the public character of religion. Rather, it opens up and legitimates a space for action between government agencies and Muslim (and other religious) groups which is commanded by varying rationalities and, after 2001, increasingly by an anticipatory one.

Second, the government starts to prepare, since 2001, a new policy aiming to reshape Islam as it is practised in Britain through a number of structural measures or measures directly focussed at specific groups or institutions. This policy, in England as elsewhere in Western Europe, is concerned primarily with mosques and imams (see Birt 2006 for a detailed study). In 2001, the Home Office announces that the conditions of immigration for religious ministers will be revised, the aim being to guarantee a sufficient knowledge of English. The rationale behind this move is illustrated by the example given in the Home Office's declaration where the importance of linguistic competencies for a 'religious leader' is highlighted for the case of interacting with other religious groups. In this respect, the Home Office also points to the events of the summer 2001 as a case where such interaction has been made impossible because of language problems. The Home Office also declares its preference as ministers for persons with residence in Britain or holders of British degrees. Apart from the fact that the professional qualifications of these persons are easier to validate, the Home Office considers that these persons are, because of their knowledge of society, 'better able to relate their particular faith to the context of the United Kingdom' (Home Office 2001: 46).

Put briefly, the function of an imam is conceived of here in the context of a policy of community cohesion. Given that the imam's mission is henceforth supplemented by the obligation to preach an Islam in conformity with 'British values', the criteria for judging his qualifications change. Since 2004, candidates for immigration into Britain as ministers of cult need to prove linguistic competencies whose standard has been raised considerably; other measures are being prepared in order to verify, after their entry into Britain, their knowledge of and engagement with British society (Home Office 2005b: 20 s.). This policy of closure towards foreign imams is continued, as shows Birt (2006), in the field of chaplaincy where new posts subsidized by the state are exclusively destined for candidates who hold a certificate from one of the two existing institutes in Britain preparing Muslim chaplains.

The State's Quest for 'Moderate' Muslims

The government's attempts to reshape British Islam are not limited to policies aiming at imams and chaplains, but also rely on a policy of support for specific Muslim groups. From the government's point of view, one of the principal aims of its policy is to reinforce 'moderate' Islam and to support it – and be supported itself – in the fight against extremism (see for example Home Office 2005c; for a survey of related government activities see Timesonline 2005 and Prime Minister 2006: 7). This raises of course the question of how the government goes about determining those Muslim groups which are 'extremist' and those which are suitable carriers of civil Islam?

In this respect, the government's reasoning is complex and does not simply reflect a division, which is supposedly that of the government, between 'good' and 'bad' Muslims (Bonnefoy 2003). The complexity of the decision by government agencies follows not only from difficulties in identifying correctly their Muslim interlocutors. In fact, the term 'moderate', as used by government agencies, comprises a broad range of groups with very divergent profiles in terms of resources and political outlook. Other criteria enter thus necessarily into the government's choice of its Muslim partners. In absence of other sources, the report by the Home Office, cited previously, provides us with some evidence for discerning these criteria. Following this report, extremism is defined as

'advocating or supporting views such as support for terrorist attacks against British or Western targets, including the 9/11 attacks, or for British Muslims fighting against British or allied forces abroad, arguing that it is not possible to be Muslim and British, calling on Muslims to reject engagement with British society and politics, and advocating the creation of an Islamic state in Britain' (Timesonline 2005).[17]

A reading of this report indicates that among those Muslim groups which are not 'extremist' government agencies make supplementary distinctions. The essential criterion in this respect is the influence which a specific group or actor wields inside the Muslim community and the simple acceptance to enter into contact with authorities. Put differently, the government does not limit relations with Muslims to those who are aligned on its policies. In fact, even the MCB, the main defender of an Islamic commitment for the 'common good' and for this reason and others regularly denigrated as 'a government creature' by other Muslims (Glynn 2002: 972 and, more recently, BBC News 2005), does not have, according to this report, satisfying relations with the govern-

---

17 See also Home Office (2005c: 1) for a similar definition.

ment. The government's aim, in fact, is rather to make and intensify contacts with a more important number of Muslim actors whose openness towards the government might vary, but who need to be influential. In a second step, the task is to convince them, 'in private', as the report underlines, to adopt a more intransigent position towards 'extremism' while at the same time developing their human and material capacities (Timesonline 2005). Put another way, the government recognizes differences with respect to how the various so-called moderate Muslim groups relate to its policies. However, these differences do not determine the decision of whether to cooperate with them or not, but reflect the government's ultimate policy aims regarding the transformation of Muslim groups. On the one hand, British policy towards Muslims is thus exclusionist, as for example in the case of the Muhajiroun (and successor organisations) or Hizb ut-Tahrir (Taji-Farouki 1996; Wiktorowicz 2005), and, more generally, legally discriminating against Muslims and/or British Asians; on the other hand, this policy is based on a more prospective approach which aims to prevent the radicalisation of British Muslims by transforming, in a mid-range perspective, the field's internal structure and relations between Muslims and the state. This latter policy has been challenged more recently following the reshuffle of the cabinet and the appointment of Ruth Kelly to the newly created Department for Communities and Local Government. While Kelly's counter-terrorism strategy does not depart from that of the preceding period (Department for Communities and Local Government 2007), she has questioned the MCB's commitment to Britain's 'shared values' and seems disinclined to continue cooperating with it. How this will affect the MCB's position in the long run and, more importantly, if this change signals the abandonment of a prospective approach in policies on Islam remains to be seen.

How then is the state support for civil Islam perceived by Muslim organisations? Civil Islam emerges from the partial convergence of government objectives and aims pursued by various Muslim organisations concerning the integration of immigrants of Islamic background and the strengthening of religious institutions. From the point of view of Muslim groups, the new government approach can be beneficial, since it directly leads to an acceleration of the incorporation of Islam. A comparison of propositions and demands in this field made by diverse Muslim personalities after the bombings of 2005 and government projects (concerning institutes for Islamic studies, the promotion of 'moderate' Islam or the role of imams) suggests that there is a partial convergence of aims between the two groups (Home Office 2005d). However, in the course of consultations about specific measures to be taken, divergences can emerge, as shown in the recent case of policies regarding mosques and places of worship in Britain. The government's projects were strongly criticized by the MCB as a simple attempt to control Muslims, whereas the

Muslim Council was asking for government support for its work. For Muslim organisations, the cooperation with the government in fact regularly raises important problems of legitimacy (Home Office 2005c; Muslim Council of Britain 2006). Another major divergence should be mentioned in this respect. While state policies clearly aim at ensuring the population's 'devotion to the unity of the social body' (Willaime 1993: 572), civil Islam, for many Muslim organisations, is part of a much broader (and older) tradition of understanding Islam as a public religion whose teachings certainly cannot be limited to the striving for social cohesion.[18] From the point of view of government, civil Islam can be considered a specific variation of the civil religion in Britain, a variation which is build upon combining the integrative function of religion with the idea of necessary reform of Islam.

As for Muslim associations, their commitment to civil Islam partly results from political and public pressure which has increased formidably since 2001 and which has contributed to reorienting the older civic engagement rooted, as for example in the case of the MCB and its constitutive members, in the tradition of Islamic movements (Birt 2005; McLoughlin 2005). In fact, the MCB has long since fought for facilitating social and political participation of British Muslims. After 2001, the Muslim Council reoriented its work to focus more on maintaining social peace. In statements made after that year, it thus recalls believers, notably the 'youth', their obligations as Muslim citizens and, addressing politicians and the broader public; it places increased emphasis on the role of mosques as social and educative centres and as means to prevent delinquency. More generally, the MCB is arguing in the interest of encouraging public authorities to cooperate with Muslim associations.[19] In 2004, after the bombings of Madrid, the MCB is taking a further step on this path and is explicitly asking Muslim leaders and activists to cooperate with security forces to prevent a terrorist attack (Muslim Council of Britain 2004).

The Case of France

The incorporation of Islam in metropolitan France is, for the first time, just as in the United Kingdom, taking place on the local level and it proceeds, broadly speaking, in the absence of any political strategy. Contrary to the U.K., this process started relatively late. The Muslim presence in France has for a long time been seen as temporary both by many immigrants – with the important exception of Franco-Algerians who left Algeria after independence

---

18 For this reason, I do not speak here of 'civic religion' (see Willaime 1993).
19 See for example 'Our Social Contract', The Common Good – The Newsletter of the Muslim Council of Britain, vol. 1, n°4: 4 and the press releases of the MCB from 15 July 2001 and 6 August 2001.

– and by the state. In fact, as is well known, the adoption of restrictive policies of immigration in Britain, in 1962, precedes by more than a decade similar measures taken in other European countries. This has led to a process of settlement which started much earlier in the United Kingdom than elsewhere and it also contributed to accelerating the creation of Muslim institutions (Nielsen 1992: 44).

In France, Islam is perceived, until the 1980s, as an essentially foreign phenomenon which is not, with two exceptions, a concern of French policymakers. First, there are, as pointed out, the 'French Muslims' (*Français Musulmans*) from Algeria whose needs, including religious needs, are taken into consideration by the state who creates a number of administrative organs whose task is to facilitate the insertion of these groups into French society, since 1977 (v. Krosigk 2000: 169-71). Second, the French state puts in motion, during the 1970s, a policy aiming to help bring about the 'return' of immigrants. From this policy follows a stronger awareness of 'cultural' needs, including religious needs, of immigrant groups in France which need to be taken care of in order to facilitate their reinsertion in the countries of origin (Kepel 1991: 139-45; v. Krosigk 2000: 186-89).

Apart from these points, however, Islam in France is administered basically according to three conditions: Muslims are seen as non-French; policy and/or administrative measures regarding Islam and Muslims are realized in cooperation with or simply by delegation to foreign friendly states in the Maghreb; 'French interests' are prioritized in decision-making in this policy field. The 'Mosquée de Paris', which is controlled by Algeria and which is the main interlocutor of the government in matters Islamic, is the symbolic expression of this approach (Kepel 1991; Boyer 1992). It is only during the 1980s that France wakes up to the reality of its ethnic and religious pluralism. The important national debates about the reform of citizenship legislation bear witness to the turmoil this recognition creates in politics and the broader public (Feldblum 1999; Weil 2004). As to Islam more precisely, its recognition as being somehow part of France is closely linked to the 'affaire du voile' of 1989 (and subsequent affairs) whose chronology does not need to be laid out here (Bauberot 1996). It is from this moment onwards, in a demographic context marked by the coming-of-age of new French-born generations of Muslims that the incorporation of Islam becomes politically important and Muslim identities politicized to a degree hitherto unknown.

Beyond Laïcité

As is well known, policies on Islam have been conflicted almost from their outset, i.e. since the late 1980s. A large number of studies have examined these conflicts and while these studies often do diverge considerably, it is certainly true to say that great emphasis has been placed by many of them on how different understandings of the appropriate policy relate to specific understandings of laïcité. More specifically, many studies have pointed to a fundamental opposition structuring these debates. Essentially, two different camps which seem to confront each other in the course of these debates are distinguished. On the one hand, there are the defenders of a 'new' or 'open' laïcité who demand that laïcité be adapted to a changed religious landscape and the sometimes new needs, in terms of religious practice and organisation, articulated by French Muslims. Furthermore, this process of adaptation, it is often argued, should be conducted in a way which reflects the peaceful relations between the state and religions today. On the other hand, there are those who defend an understanding of laïcité as being 'not negotiable' and who consider that its adaptation equals its dilution into supposedly Anglo-Saxon models of politics. As many studies have pointed out, these positions relate to often diametrically opposed policy proposals concerning Islam, as has been demonstrated notably with regard to the headscarf case.[20] While the approach just outlined has proven its utility in the analysis of French Islam policies, I will suggest here a different approach to their study. Basically, I will consider the elaboration of policies on Islam and conflicts around it as the outcome of two distinct rationalities which do not simply oppose each other, although they sometimes do, but in many respects also necessarily function in combination. Conflicts about the course of policies on Islam, to a large degree, concern the definition of the ways in which they should combine and the relative weight of each of them.

In terms of rationality, we can say that those who defend laïcité as non-negotiable give priority to an instance of a legal rationality which I will designate here as Republican. The Republican rationality can be characterized by an atomistic conception of its policy object, the citizen, and by its refusal to recognize particular identities (other than that particular identity configuration it proclaims in a given moment as universal). This rationality is justified by a discourse which makes social cohesion incumbent upon a type of normalisation subsumed in the principle of transcendance by citizenship (*la transcendance par la citoyenneté*) (Schnapper 2003). The principle of separation of state and religion is a central mechanism for enabling this practice of citizenship. Fundamentally, Republican rationality is based on the (obviously relatively contingent) application of law as mechanism for identifying difference and making it indifferent. Now, this rationality often combines with an instance of anticipatory rationality. This is so, since the outright refusal to recognize particular identities regularly conflicts with the state's fundamental

---

20 On this question see notably Amir-Moazami (2001); Rochefort (2002); Bouamama (2004); Tévanian (2005); Asad (2006).

aim of normalizing these identities, an objective which, furthermore, cannot be realized solely by enacting prohibitions. Anticipatory rationality, in the case of Islam and French Muslims, is based on an assessment of presently existing types of religious practice and religiosity. Furthermore, it inquires into their past evolution and future development as part of an Islamic milieu which is characterized notably by social and spatial exclusion, discrimination and the breakdown of social and religious authority. Whereas in the context of Republican rationality, the reference to legal norms is prioritized, anticipatory rationality takes as its starting point for determining its policy of normalisation an assessment of the relative distribution in the Islamic milieu of normal and deviant types of Muslim religiosity and an evaluation of the state's possibilities to change this state of affairs. To varying degrees, the application of law, broadly defined, and the (re)definition of normalcy are made dependent upon this process of evaluation. Also, law is applied by taking into account its effects on the milieu and, more generally, it is but one means within a broader policy which pursues normalisation with means other than that of prohibition.[21]

As I said, these two rationalities function in varying combinations. By combining, I mean that anticipatory rationality is either employed to realize in a mid-term perspective the ideals of Republicanism or it is employed on the assumption that the scope of application of Republican rationality is necessarily limited. In the first case, normalisation aims ultimately at the dissolution of particulars through policies restructuring their specific milieu, in the second the impossibility of realizing this aim fully is acknowledged and some particulars are thus declared as normal and normalizable while at the same time the Islamic milieu as a whole is targeted by various measures aiming at normalisation.

---

21 I cannot deal here with the headscarf law of 2004. While the proponents of the law (see for example the report of the Commission Stasi) study the practice of wearing headscarfs in the context of a specific milieu and regularly make use of prospective analysis, I consider the law by virtue of its enacting a prohibition an instance of Republican rationality whose primary justification for its proponents lies precisely in that it is 'an exercise in sovereign power' which confirms Republican sovereignty (Asad 2006). A comparison of the debates concerning this law in 2003/04 with previous discussions (in 1989 and 1994) demonstrates the degree to which anticipatory reasoning has become indispensable to French political debates on Islam including those participants wishing to reaffirm Republican sovereignty.

The Ethnicisation of the Republic[22]

As I said, it would be wrong to consider the Republican rationality in isolation. In fact, since the 1980s, the wilful denial of ethnicity and religion becomes increasingly difficult to maintain in France. The direct reason for this is the perceived failure of what is often called the Republican model of integration, i.e. a process of integration through state institutions which dissolves ethnic and other communities into the French nation. After the settlement of immigrants and as new generations of French-born Muslims come of age, France witnesses the 'birth of a religion' (Kepel 1991), namely Islam. The partly simultaneous emergence of Islamic institutions, notably since 1981,[23] and the coming of age of French-born Muslims, increasingly practicing their religion, was mostly seen as the opposite of a desirable course of integration. In this context, the question of how to regulate the practice of Islam arose with a new urgency and Muslim identity became politicized to a degree hitherto unknown.

This is in many respects a new and contested development as is illustrated in the introduction to the foundational study of French Islam, *'Les banlieues de l'Islam'*, published in 1987. The author, Gilles Kepel, a fervent defender of French laïcité, writes: 'According to some, it is illegitimate or inappropriate to study Islam in France. Such a project is in fact suspicious. It would only end up displacing the *tête de turc* from fairs of earlier times to the intellectual field, it would offer a specious description of immigrant populations and the cultural pretext for discriminating against them.' But, as Kepel points out with reference to the rise of the extreme right movement in France, 'the circumspection of some becomes aphasia and opens up the space for the noisy phantasms of the others'. And then 'only a thorough analysis of social phenomena without any concessions can break this vicious circle' (Kepel 1991: 10).

Beyond the specificity of this case, the argument made here is interesting, since it illustrates the general predicament of adherents to the Republican rationality and outlines the configurations of forces which make it necessary and profitable, from their point of view, to espouse a more ethnicized perspective on French society. By doing this, their aim remains, of course, to work for a society where ethnic and other particular identities can be abstracted. Nevertheless, the effects of their discourse are ambivalent: it contributes indirectly to legitimate a new conception of the French population, namely in terms of ethnic or religious groups, and thus also legitimates specific policies

---

22 See Geisser (1997).
23 After the victory of the socialists in the 1981 election, the law of associations is modified to allow foreigners to create associations. This strongly contributes to the rise in the number of Muslim associations during the 1980s. See Kepel (1991).

which, openly or not, are based on such a conception of France even when, which is the case, the policy-makers ultimately aim to create the conditions for successfully dissolving these communities. A variety of measures taken during the 1980s attest to this development. It is at that time that a wide-ranging system of 'positive discrimination' is created (Calvès 2004). This policy is directly related to and part of what will soon be designated as *'politique de la ville'*, a policy field which slowly emerges in reaction to the so-called crisis of the *banlieues*, prefigured in the disturbances of 1981 in Lyon's suburbs (Jobert/Damamme 1995). At the same time, the ministry of national education engages in similar measures and creates a complex system of priority education zones. In these zones, specific conditions regulate the functioning of schools in order to reduce the educational gap between the suburbs and other parts of France (van Zanten 2001). Finally, French policies, since the late 1990s, have made of the fight against discrimination, including discrimination based on ethnicity, an important objective (Fassin 2002).[24]

Without a doubt, these policies are discriminating, i.e. they recognize differences and apply differential treatments to citizens in function of them. While they are not doing so openly all the time, there is a recognizable trend towards doing this since the late 1980s. From the late 1980s until today, the perceived crisis of the Republican model of integration and the fear of Islam are being debated in a variety of subfields while scientific expertise on these topics continues to increase. The religiosity of immigrants from Islamic background and their relation to the French political and legal system, problems of security and delinquency in the suburbs, the rise of anti-semitism among Franco-Maghrebis in particular, gender-relations among immigrants from Islamic countries and, from a reversed perspective, the discrimination against them are the principal topics being debated, next to that of terrorism.

Independent of the aims of individual contributors to these debates, they have together collaborated in the production of a (problematic) social identity of 'Muslims' in France which is distinct of a juridical one based on abstract rights of citizenship. In fact, the government itself has been directly engaged, since 1989, in this process through the creation of institutions, such as the *Haut Conseil à l'Intégration* (HCI) in 1989 and the legal consecration of the *Commission Nationale Consultative des Droits de l'Homme* (CNCDH) in 1990, and through assigning various public bodies the task of analysing the socio-economic profile of the immigrated population and monitoring discrimination against them. In recent years, this development has clearly intensified (see Centre d'Analyse Stratégique 2006). While the standardized col-

---

24 See Fassin (2006) for a critical assessment of the policy turn in the question of ethnic discrimination.

lection of ethnic data for policy-making is still strongly criticized, the refusal of such policies is increasingly linked to the endorsement of more indirect ways of collecting ethnic data (for one example see Haut Conseil à l'Intégration 2007).

'Young Muslims' and Islam in France

The point I want to make here is not that a specific type of expert knowledge provides the blueprint for policies on Islam, but that various types of expert knowledge on Islam in France have reconfigured Islam as an object of policies (and, to a significant degree, as a discursive object for Muslims themselves). Today, Islam is not just one religion among several nor is it simply 'the Other', but Islam – as it manifests itself in modes of religiosity and practice – is *also* conceived as the outcome of an ensemble of interacting social factors which the state can and should to a certain degree influence in order to avert various threats ensuing from it. Put differently, the legal principles of equality of religions and separation of state and religion are partly suspended and policies are made dependent upon knowledge on Islam and Muslims. The effects of this development are, as in the case of the United Kingdom, ambivalent.

This reconfiguration of Islam as religion takes place by considering it as part of an Islamic milieu which is characterized notably by discrimination, i.e. the state's failure to realize the Republican promise of equality, and the breakdown of authority, both being supposedly crucial factors in processes of 'radicalisation'. Today, a surprisingly varied and large group of Muslim activists, experts on Islam and politicians insists on the effects of the breakdown of parental, religious and state authority when explaining the rise of 'radical' Islam: whether it is the alleged absence of religious authorities, the intergenerational breakdown or the weak authority of parents and the failure of socialisation in schools – all these elements have supposedly contributed to the radicalisation of 'young Muslims'. Underlying this view is the supposition that 'young Muslims' are essentially immature and in need of guidance (Peter 2006b). The effects of exclusion and discrimination which French Muslims suffer are also recognized by some as a factor alienating them from the Republic and possibly heightening the appeal of 'radical' trends in Islam. However, the importance of this factor is clearly valued differently. A significant number of actors agree upon the fact that exclusion and discrimination can be one cause for adopting 'fundamentalist' Islam and this has certainly added to the salience of anti-discrimination policies. However, the important role of Muslim actors – imams, preachers, associations, ... – in this process of 'radicalisation' is also widely agreed upon. In the context of such a reading of 'radical Islam', it is Muslim leaders who, to a large degree, decide if the experiences of discrimination by a believer lead to 'radical Islam' or not. In fact, given the limited possibilities for the state to put an end to discrimination, it is argued by some that Muslim associations fulfil a fundamentally important stabilizing role in society. One should add that the function of Muslim 'leaders' becomes even more important due to the fact that a large number of Muslims – together with the majority society – today hold that an effort to develop a specifically French reading of Islam is indispensable (Peter 2006a). In brief, in the context of the increasing importance of anticipatory rationality, policies concerning specific Muslim institutions and practices are debated by taking into account their role in processes of 'radicalisation' and their effects, direct or indirect, on the evolution of the Islamic milieu as a whole.

Civil Islam à la Française

The anticipatory analysis of Islam in France starts from the thesis that the breakdown of authority has strongly contributed to the rise of an *'Islam intégriste'* and it concludes from it the necessity to build solid structures of authority in French Islam. Hence the interest for Muslim federations and various individual actors to cooperate with the state, in spite of all difficulties – the construction of authority structures is central to French policies on Islam and this implies significant opportunities or threats to many Muslim activists (Peter 2006a). This analysis is intrinsically related to the identification of those Muslims whose message is adequate to the French context. While such an identification can be realized simply by evaluating the conformity of Muslim positions with so-called Republican values, my point here is that it has become increasingly common in French politics to abandon this type of reasoning in favour of a more complex thinking which is precisely anticipatory. The latter reasoning is based on the recognition that the state cannot regulate and/or directly refashion Islam in any desirable way without the cooperation of Muslim actors, including some of those often considered problematic. The inclusion of the *Union des Organisations Islamiques de France* (UOIF) – usually considered part of the Muslim Brotherhood – into the state-created representative body of French Muslims, the *Conseil Français du Culte Musulman*, illustrates this perfectly (Caeiro 2005). Such an approach is fundamentally argued in a mid-range perspective and it insists on the importance of realizing structural interventions in the Islamic milieu in order to initiate a progressive normalisation. Secondly, this approach is based, to varying degrees, on the idea that support to Islam, that is specific understandings of Islam, can be a useful tool in the management of immigrant populations, both in the fight against urban violence and delinquency on the one hand and against terrorism on the other. It is in this latter respect, that 'moderately Islamist' groups, such as the UOIF, are considered by some politicians particularly interesting partners to the state (Peter 2006a). A variety of policies can derive from this approach and no exhaustive picture can be drawn here. Some examples of primary fields of application, concerning the funding of mosques, Muslim associations and imams, will illustrate its relevance here. French policies concerning the construction of mosques have for a long time been a major obstacle in the establishment of community structures. Numerous mayors have been openly hostile to the construction of mosques. In 2004, while many problems persist (FASILD 2006), it is clear that the basic outlook of many mayors has changed: it is estimated that the majority of mayors grants subsidies to the construction of mosques.[25] Without doubt, these measures can partly be explained by electoral tactics. But this is clearly not the whole story. These measures also refer to the idea that the construction of 'decent' mosques (*mosquées dignes*) and/or the symbolic recognition of Islam reduces the appeal of radical tendencies in Islam (see e.g. Haut Conseil à l'Intégration 1995: 33; Debré 2003, vol. 1: 131). It should be emphasized that this idea is underlying the ongoing national debate about the public funding of mosques initiated by former minister of the interior Sarkozy.[26] In the course of these debates, Sarkozy's propositions have been and are certainly very much criticized to the point that Sarkozy has backed away from his proposal to modify the law of 1905 while maintaining his basic aim to put 'appropriate' places of worship at the disposal of Muslims.[27] While this clearly indicates the limited capacity of anticipatory rationality to effect legal change declared as such, it is important to note that many of his contradictors did not put into question the necessity to develop new readings of the law of 1905. These readings do not only displace the emphasis from the principle of separation of state and religion towards the legitimate means of intervention by the state in the religious domain, but they also understand these interventions as targeting a set of interrelated phenomena inside a variously conceived Islamic milieu.

The granting of direct or indirect subsidies to mosques and Muslim associations cannot be explained solely by a policy aiming to get rid of 'radical' Muslims. In fact, such an approach can also be based on a new conception of the educational role of associations, particularly religious associations, and its legitimate place in processes of socialisation and citizenship education in

---

25 Libération, 8 December 2004. Concerning the various possibilities to finance mosques see Al Istichara. Le Journal de la consultation des Musulmans de France (2 May 2000: 7f.). Since 2000, the ministry of the interior has called upon mayors to support the funding of mosques.
26 See e.g. L'Express, 18 September 2003. See also Kaltenbach/Tribalat (2002) and Machelon/Ministère de l'Intérieur (2006).
27 Libération, 5 April 2007.

France. Put differently, such an approach is grounded in an implied or explicit new understanding of what counts as acceptable belief and religious practice of French Muslims. Whether on the local or national level, there are a significant number of politicians who approve of the idea to involve Muslim associations, not only 'moderate' Muslims, in their policies of 'social appeasement' and inter-community harmony. Likewise, there is an abundant number of Muslim groups who are willing to support such a policy (Peter 2006a), a policy which the state today feels unable to realize itself (Khosrokhavar 1997: 295). The support granted to interreligious activities can be explained to a large degree by the same motivations (Lamine 2004). Finally, the political interest in matters related to imams and their training (Frégosi 1998) clearly reflects the perception by politicians that these persons are no simple *'ministres du culte'*, but also educators of 'young Muslims'. Benefiting from a legitimacy which perhaps state agencies are lacking, they are sometimes considered better placed, by politicians, to make the youth adhere to certain values considered essential for the living-together in France.

Conclusion

Drawing on Foucault's reflections on political rationalities, I have attempted to outline a new framework for understanding policies on Islam in the United Kingdom and France. By distinguishing legal rationality from that of a security apparatus, my aim was to bring into focus and analyse a different type of counter-terrorism policy which is played out in the incorporation, administration and regulation of Islamic institutions and practices. This perspective, I have argued, allows us to grasp not only the functioning of an important dimension of policies concerning Islam and Muslims. It also provides a way for understanding ongoing transformations in national juridico-political orders and, ultimately, a new starting point for an analysis of secularity in relation to European Islam.

The approach outlined here also leads us to a different understanding of the power configuration within which Muslims practice Islam. While this configuration needs in part to be examined as one subordinating Muslims, this study has shown how the state also exercises power through the reconfiguration of the category Islam as an Islamic milieu. Civil Islam as a specific understanding by Muslims of the Islamic tradition is largely enabled by this notion of Islam as part of an Islamic milieu. In a certain sense, civil Islam thus defined is a factor of empowerment, since it allows Muslims to hold the state and society accountable for various problems in the racialized Muslim community and to demand policy changes. At the same time, however, by institutionalizing Islam as a means for ensuring social peace and preventing radicalisation, and by adopting anticipatory rationality, civil Islam risks entrenching the perception of Islam as a potential threat. Finally, it certainly reinscribes the determination of 'acceptable' Islamic practices and beliefs through expert assessment of the milieu in which they are embedded as well as prognostics of its future development.

Acknowledgements

This chapter is based on material presented in Peter 2006c and develops further the argument made there. Research for this study has been made possible by fellowships from the German Historical Institute in London (2004) and the Centre d'Études et de Recherches Internationales at the Université de Montréal (2005). I would like to thank both institutions and the Centre Canadien d'Études Européennes et Allemandes at the Université de Montréal for supporting my research and I gratefully acknowledge the opportunity they have given me to present the initial results of this project. My thanks also go to Elena Arigita, Alexandre Caeiro, Ruth Mas, Werner Schiffauer and Barbara Thériault for comments on earlier versions of this text.

References

Alexandre, C. (2002): 'Beyond Black. Re-thinking the Colour/Culture Divide', *Ethnic and Racial Studies*, 25(1): 552-71.
Amir-Moazami, S. (2001): 'Hybridity and Anti-hybridity: the Islamic Headscarf and its Opponents in the French Public Sphere'. In: A. Salvatore (ed.), *Muslim Traditions and Modern Techniques of Po-wer*, Hamburg/New Brunswick: Lit/Transaction, pp. 309-29.
Ansari, H. (2004): *'The Infidel within'. Muslims in Britain since 1800*, London: Hurst & Company.
Anwar, M. (1986): *Race and Politics. Ethnic Minorities and the British Political System*, London: Tavistock.
Asad, T. (2006): 'French Secularism and the "Islamic Veil Affair"', *The Hedgehog Review*, 8(1/2): 93-106.
Bamford, B. (2004): 'The United Kingdom's "War against Terrorism"', *Terrorism and Political Violence*, 16(4): 737-56.
Baubérot, J. (1996): 'L'Affaire des Foulards et la Laïcité à la Française', *L'Hom-me et la Société*, 120: 9-16.
BBC News (2005): 'Protesters Disrupt Muslim Event', 19 April 2005.
Bensons, S. (1996): 'Asians Have Culture, West Indians Have Problems. Discourses of "Race" and Ethnicity in and out of Anthropology'. In: T.O.

Ranger/Y. Samad/O.W. Stuart (eds), *Culture, Identity and Politics. Ethnic Minorities in Britain*, Aldershot: Avebury, pp. 47-56.
Bevir, M. (2003): 'Narrating the British State. An Interpretive Critique of New Labour's Institutionalism', *International Political Economy*, 10(3): 455-80.
Birt, J. (2005): 'Lobbying and Marching: British Muslims and the State'. In: T. Abbas (ed.), *Muslim Britain. Communities under Pressure*, London: Zed, pp. 92-106.
—— (2006): 'Good Imam, Bad Imam. Civic Religion and National Integration in Britain post-9/11', *Muslim World*, 96(4): 687-705.
Bonnefoy, L. (2003): 'Public Institutions and Islam. A New Stigmatization?' *ISIM Newsletter*, 13: 22-23.
Bouamama, S. (2004): *L'Affaire du Foulard Islamique. La Production d'un Racisme Respectable*, Roubaix: Editions Le Geai Bleu.
Boyer, A. (1992): *L'Institut Musulman de la Mosquée de Paris*, Paris: CHEAM.
Brown, W. (1995): *States of Injury. Power and Freedom in Late Modernity*, Princeton: Princeton University Press.
Burchell, G./Gordon, C./Miller, P. eds (1991): *The Foucault Effect. Studies in Governmentality*, Chicago: University of Chicago Press.
Caeiro, A. (2005): 'Religious Authorities or Political Actors? The Muslim Leaders of the French Representative Body of Islam'. In: J. Césari/S. McLoughlin (eds), *European Muslims and the Secular Sta-te*, Aldershot: Ashgate, pp. 71-84.
Calvès, G. (2004): *La Discrimination Positive*, Paris: Presses Universitaires de France.
Centre d'Analyse Stratégique (2006): *Statistiques 'Ethniques': Eléments de Cadrage*, Paris, La Documentation Française.
Crowley, J. (1992): 'Consensus et Conflits dans la Politique de l'Immi-gration et des Relations Raciales du Royaume-Uni'. In: J. Costa-Las-coux/P. Weil (eds), *Logiques d'Etats et Immigrations*, Paris: Kimé, pp. 73-118.
Debré, J.-L. (2003): *La Laïcité à l'Ecole. Un Principe Républicain à Réaffirmer*. (Rapport N° 1275, 2 vol.; Rapport fait au nom de la mission d'information sur la question du port des signes religieux à l'école), Paris: Assemblée Nationale.
Department for Communities and Local Government (2007): *Preventing Violent Extremism – Winning Hearts and Minds*.
FASILD (Fonds d'Action et de Soutien pour l'Intégration et la Lutte contre les Discriminations) (2006): *L'Exercice du Culte Musulman en France. Lieux de Prière et Lieux d'Inhumation*, Paris, La Documentation Française.

Fassin, D. (2002): 'L'Invention Française de la Discrimination', *Revue Française de Science Politique*, 52(4): 403-23.
—— (2006): 'Aveugles à la Race ou au Racisme? Une Approche Stratégique'. In: D. Fassin/E. Fassin (eds), *De la Question Sociale à la Question Raciale? Représenter la Société Française*, Paris: La Découverte, pp. 106-30.
Feldblum, M. (1999): *Reconstructing Citizenship. The Politics of Nationality Reform and Immigration in Contemporary France*, Albany: State University of New York Press.
Foucault, M. (1997): *'Il Faut Défendre la Société'. Cours au Collège de France (1976)*, Paris: Seuil/Gallimard.
—— (2004): *Sécurité, Territoire, Population. Cours au Collège de France (1977-1978)*, Paris: Seuil/Gallimard.
Frégosi, F. (1998): *La Formation des Cadres Religieux Musulmans en France. Approches Socio-juridiques*, Paris: L'Harmattan.
Geisser, V. (1997): *Ethnicité Républicaine. Les Elites d'Origine Maghrébine dans le Système Politique Français*, Paris: Presses de la Fondation Nationale des Sciences Politiques.
Glynn, S. (2002): 'Bengali Muslims: the New East End Radicals?' *Ethnic and Racial Studies*, 25(6): 969-88.
Haut Conseil à l'Intégration (1995): *Liens Culturels et Intégration*, Paris, La Documentation Française.
—— (2007): *Les Indicateurs de l'Intégration. Statistiques Ethniques, Enquêtes sur les Patronymes, Mesure de la Diversité, Baromètre de l'Intégration*.
Home Office (2001): *Secure Borders, Safe Havens: Integration with Diversity in Modern Britain*.
—— (2002): *Community Cohesion. A Report of the Independent Review Team Chaired by Ted Cantle*.
—— (2005a): *Improving Opportunity, Strengthening Society. The Government's Strategy to Increase Race Equality and Community Cohesion*.
—— (2005b): *Working together. Co-operation between Government and Faith Communities – Progress Report*.
—— (2005c): *Preventing Extremism together: Places of Worship*.
—— (2005d): *Preventing Extremism together: Working Groups August-October 2005*.
Intelligence and Security Committee (2006): *Report into the London Terrorist Attacks 7 July 2005*.
Inter Faith Network for the UK (2002): *Community Cohesion: a New Agenda for Inter Faith Relations?*
—— (2003): *Local Inter Faith Activity in the UK: a Survey*, London.
—— (2005): *2004- 2005 Annual Review*.

Jobert, B./Damamme, D. (1995): 'La Politique de la Ville ou l'Injonction Con-tradictoire en Politique', *Revue Française de Science Politique*, 45(1): 3-30.

Juhem, P. (2000): '"Civiliser" la Banlieue. Logiques et Conditions d'Efficacité des Dispositifs Etatiques de Régulation de la Violence dans les Quartiers Populaires', *Revue Française de Science Politique*, 50(1): 53-72.

Kaltenbach, J.-H./Tribalat, M. (2002): *La République et l'Islam. Entre Crainte et Aveuglement*, Paris: Gallimard.

Kepel, G. (1991): *Les Banlieues de l'Islam. Naissance d'une Religion en France*, Paris: Éditions du Seuil, second edition.

Khosrokhavar, F. (1997): *L'Islam des Jeunes*, Paris: Flammarion.

Krosigk, C. v. (2000): *Der Islam in Frankreich. Laizistische Religionspolitik von 1974 bis 1999*, Hamburg: Dr. Kovač.

Lamine, A.S. (2004): *La Cohabitation des Dieux. Pluralité Religieuse et Laïcité*, Paris: Presses Universitaires de France.

Lester, A. (1987): 'Anti-discrimination Legislation in Great Britain', *New Community*, 14(1/2): 21-31.

Lewis, P. (1997): 'Arenas of Ethnic Negotiation: Cooperation and Conflict in Bradford'. In: T. Modood/P. Werbner (eds), *The Politics of Multiculturalism in the New Europe. Racism, Identity and Community*, London: Zed, pp. 126-46.

Machelon, J.-P./Ministére de l'Intérieur (2006): *Les Relations des Cultes avec les Pouvoirs Publics*, Paris, La Documentation Française.

Maussen, M. (2004): 'Policy Discourses on Mosques in the Netherlands 1980-2002. Contested Constructions', *Ethical Theory and Moral Practice*, 7(2): 147-62.

—— (2006): *Ruimte voor de Islam? Stedelijk Beleid, Voorzieningen, Organisaties*, Amsterdam: Het Spinhuis.

McLoughlin, S. (2005): 'The State, New Muslim Leadership and Islam as a Resource for Public Engagement in Britain'. In: J. Cesari/S. McLoughlin (eds), *European Muslims and the Secular State*, Ashgate: Aldershot, pp. 55-69.

Modood, T. (1994): 'Establishment, Multiculturalism and British Citizenship', *Political Quarterly*, 65(1): 53-73.

—— (2005): *Multicultural Politics. Racism, Ethnicity, and Muslims in Britain*, Minneapolis: University of Minnesota Press.

Muslim Council of Britain (2004): '[Letter] to: Imams, Ulema, Chairs & Secretaries of Mosques, Islamic Organisations and Institutions', 31 March 2004.

—— (2006): *Voices from the Minaret. MCB Study of UK Imams and Mosques*.

Nielsen, J. (1992): *Muslims in Western Europe*, Edinburgh: Edinburgh University Press.
Peter, F. (2006a): 'Leading the Community of the Middle Way: a Study of the Muslim Field in France', *Muslim World*, 96(4): 707-36.
—— (2006b): 'L'Islam de France: une Religion Civile en Quête d'Autorités Religieuses', *Confluences Méditerranée*, 57: 69-81.
—— (2006c): 'Rationalités du Pouvoir et Incorporation de l'Islam. Une Comparaison Anglo-française', *Sociologie & Sociétés*, 38(1): 183-212.
—— (forthcoming): 'French Scholarship on Islam in the Republic', paper presented at Forum for Islamforskning-Workshop 'Research on Islam Repositioned', Copenhagen, May 2007.
Prime Minister (2006): *Government's Response to the Intelligence and Security Committee's Report into the London Terrorist Attacks 7 July 2005*.
Rath, J./Penninx, R./Groenendijk, K./Meijer, A. (2001): *Western Europe and its Islam*, Leiden: Brill.
Rochefort, F. (2002): 'Foulard, Genre et Laïcité en 1989', *Vingtième Siècle*, 75: 145-56.
Rose, N./Miller, P. (1992): 'Political Power beyond the State: Problematics of Government', *The British Journal of Sociology*, 43(2): 173-205.
Schnapper, D. (2003): *La Communauté des Citoyens. Sur l'Idée Moderne de Nation*, Paris: Gallimard, second edition.
Silverstein, P. (2005): 'Immigrant Racialization and the New Savage Slot. Race, Migration, and Immigration in the New Europe', *Annual Review of Anthropology*, 34: 363-84.
Smith, G. (2004): 'Faith in Community and Communities of Faith? Government Rhetoric and Religious Identity in Urban Britain', *Journal of Contemporary Religion*, 19(2): 185-204.
Taji-Farouki, S. (1996): *A Fundamental Quest. Hizb al-Tahrir and the Search for the Islamic Caliphate*, London: Grey Seal.
Tévanian, P. (2005): *Le Voile Médiatique. Un Faux Débat: 'L'Affaire du Foulard Islamique'*, Paris: Raisons d'Agir.
Timesonline (2005): *Leaked No 10 Dossier Reveals Al-Qaeda's British Recruits, 10 July 2005*, at: http://www.timesonline.co.uk (accessed 21 October 2005).
Van Zanten, A. (2001): *L'Ecole de la Périphérie. Scolarité et Ségrégation en Banlieue*, Paris: Presses Universitaires de France.
Weil, P. (2004): *La France et ses Etrangers. L'Aventure d'une Politique de l'Immigration de 1938 à nos Jours*, Paris: Gallimard, second revised edition.
Wiktorowicz, Q. (2005): *Radical Islam Rising. Muslim Extremism in the West*, London: Rowman & Littlefield.

Willaime, J.-P. (1993): 'La Religion Civile à la Française et ses Métamorphoses', *Social Compass*, 40(4): 571-80.

Documents, Security and Suspicion: the Social Production of Ignorance

TOBIAS KELLY

In April 2005 Kamel Bourgass, described by the media as being of 'North African origin', was found guilty of the murder of a British police officer and for plotting to 'spread poisons'. Bourgass was implicated in a plot that, it was claimed, would have poisoned thousands of Londoners by spreading ricin, a toxin reportedly 6,000 times more deadly than cyanide, on car door handles across north London. Although the case against eight other suspects collapsed, Bourgass was sentence to life in prison. Two of the other defendants were convicted of possessing false passports. During the trial it emerged that Bourgass had arrived in the U.K. on false papers which he had destroyed shortly before claiming asylum in January 2000 under the name of Nadir Habra. Habra was refused asylum in August 2001 and his appeal against the decision was dismissed in October 2001, when he became liable to be arrested and deported. In July 2002 he was arrested for shoplifting, but escaped detection as he used the name Bourgass rather than Habra. When he was finally arrested he was found with several fake IDs and he is believed to have had up to four different documented identities. There was considerably confusion over whether he was Tunisian or Algerian, and indeed whether his real name was Bourgass at all.

The conviction of Bourgass came just before the U.K. general election and amidst widespread fears over what was widely seen the threat from 'Islamic terror'. In this climate, the opposition Conservative party claimed that the Bourgass case showed the government had no idea who was in the country despite the 'terrorist threat' and that all people who arrived in the U.K.

with 'suspect documents' should be detained immediately.[1] The governing Labour party's response was to announce the electronic tagging of some and the fingerprinting of all asylum applicants to prevent 'changes in identity' and the issuing of ID cards to all visitors planning to stay in the U.K. for more than three months. Ian Blair, the most senior police officer in the U.K., waded into the debate, saying that 'we have to go to a place where we do know who people are' and called for the introduction of biometric identity cards.[2] He went on to argue that it was a 'danger to the state [...] that the government did not know who some people were'. The U.K. government then announced plans to introduce biometric identity cards. A lengthy debate followed with proponents arguing that if people 'had done nothing wrong they had nothing to fear' from the new identity cards. According to the British Home Office, biometric identity cards would create a universal form of citizenship, free from racial and class distinctions, by showing 'that everyone belongs to our society whether they were born here, have chosen to make their home here or are just staying for a while to study or work' (Home Office 2003). Opponents, on the other hand, called biometric identity cards a fundamental invasion of privacy that heralded the rise of an all knowing surveillance state. People marched through London with supermarket bar codes tattooed into their bodies, protesting at what they saw as the Orwellian future promised by the new cards. According to some, the new system of identity cards and databases would create a 'total life history of every individual, to be retained even after death'.[3]

The plan to introduce identity cards is the first attempt to do so in the U.K. since the Second World War. For the past sixty years, and most of the years before that, British citizens and residents have not been forced to carry identity documents. Indeed, under British law there is no stand alone obligation to identify yourself to those acting in the name of the state. The spectre of a universal, or near universal, system of identity cards introduced in the name of security therefore raises important questions about the forms of knowledge produced by identity cards and how they transform the relationship between citizens-subjects and the state. In the absence of a history of identity cards, much of the debate in the U.K. about their implications has necessarily remained speculative. In sharp contrast, everyday life in Israel/Palestine, where I have been carrying out research for the last ten years, is marked by a proliferation of identity documents that are constantly checked and rechecked

---

1 Daily Telegraph, 'Milburn apology for Policeman's death', 15 April 2005.
2 Public Service Review, 'Britain's senior policeman backs ID cards', 18 April 2005.
3 See the website of the anti-identity card group No2id, available at: http://www.no2id.net/IDSchemes/NO2IDSummaryBriefingMay2005.pdf (last accessed 17 January 2007).

(Kelly 2006, 2006a). In a context where not only are security threats seen as travelling across borders, but also the techniques and methods of security control are passed from state to state, a comparative approach to identification practices allows us to explore how seemingly technical forms of governance can be shot through with particular political and cultural assumptions.

Fears over terror and migration have resulted in ever increasing attempts by states to produce knowledge about their citizen/subjects. The threat from 'terror' is seen as clandestine and covert (see Eckert this volume), forcing security forces to come up with new ways of uncovering dangers. Identity cards play a crucial role in this 'securitisation of citizenship', as states try and distinguish between friend and foe. Through a comparison of Israel/Palestine and the U.K., this paper asks what types of knowledge do identity documents produce, and what are the implications for contemporary forms of citizenship? I argue that identity documents are an unstable and opaque method of producing knowledge about their holders, as whilst attempting to create 'legible' persons, they also hide people behind papers that are always potential forgeries. Rather than creating an all knowing state, documents create what might be called 'known unknowns', and thereby produce new grounds for uncertainty and suspicion. Precisely because identity cards do not tell the state every thing they want to know, state officials are forced to resort to reading bodies for marks of suspicion, feeding into racialized notions of danger. Far from promoting the universal rights of citizenship, identity cards therefore promote cultural notions of belonging.

Security, Knowledge and Techniques of Identification

The implicit logic of the global 'war on terror' sees the principle threat as originating outside Euro-American culture in a malevolent form of radical Islam. As a result, security practices have often focused on attempts to control movement across borders in order to keep out dangerous persons and ideas. At the same time this threat is often also perceived as being clandestine and invisible. Traditional crime control methods based on detection and prosecution can not work in a situation where the threat is seen as being very real but largely unknown. The result is the promotion of preventative forms of security based around perceived risks. As Eckert argues in this volume, particularly when an enemy is perceived to be elusive the state takes preventative measures that involve the categorisation of whole populations. The default position becomes suspicion, and people have to prove their innocence. In this context, control over movement becomes an issue of security, and identity cards are used to sort out potential friends from enemies. The constant checking and rechecking of identity documents by officials over the world must therefore be understood as an attempt to make people more 'legible' (Scott 1998; see also Torpey 2000) in order to determine the potential threat that they pose. In the face of large and largely unknown populations that are constantly moving, identity documents help states 'fix' people in place. In this process Torpey argues that there has been move from identifying people's rights and responsibilities from their physical appearance or social relationships, to a determination of status through documents (2000).[4] Identity documents seemingly offer a way of knowing who should be in particular places at particular times, and of separating citizens who need to be protected from those who would do them harm.

It is an open question, however, as to what types of knowledge the checking of identity documents actually produces. To begin to answer this question it is important to note that identity documents look in two directions. The first direction is towards legal status in order to establish entitlements and rights. The second direction is towards actual bodies in order to establish physical presence and individuality. However, in both directions the forms of knowledge produced are marked by gaps and breaks. In practice, legal status is often far from self-evident, being made up of numerous contradictions and fissures. Following EU enlargement for example, residency have become increasingly complex, with uncertainties about the rights of Eastern Europeans to live work and claim benefit in Western Europe. Identity documents also only provide a partial form of knowledge about what these rights and responsibilities might be, forcing low level officials to make numerous discretionary judgements (Calavita 2001). Furthermore, the production of identity documents can also hide actual bodies behind layers of administration and piles of paper, leading people to have both a physical and a legal presence. A migrant, for example, may 'look like a Somali' to the border guard, but his passport says that he is Finnish and therefore has rights of entry to the U.K. The result is that documents become objects to be manipulated as part of broader political and economic strategies (Ong 1999; Caplan/Torpey 2001; Lyon 2001). People such as Bourgass can collect identity documents as a means of avoiding police detection. Finally, and perhaps most importantly, in a context of mass migration where fears are often expressed in cultural and racial terms,

---

4 Identity documents become an essential prerequisite for recognition by state authorities, even to the extent that new born babies are required to have a passport complete with photograph in order to move across borders. Without documents, states often do not know who they are dealing with. The difficulties that states have in dealing with people who do not have documents can perhaps most clearly be seen in the case of immigrants who destroy their documents on arrival in a new state. Without proof of citizenship in another country, the receiving state has great difficulties in returning these people.

separating citizens from non-citizens does not necessarily distinguish between potential threats and responsible citizens who need to be protected. The mapping of nation, territory and citizenship, does not hold, if it ever has done. The soul searching in the British media that was caused by the fact that the perpetrators of the bombs in London on 7 July 2005 were British citizens is testament to the awkward relationship between formal citizenship and perceptions of security and threat. Against this background, identity documents do not help officials sort friend from foe, and may even confuse the issue.

Given the seeming gap between the documented and the social person, it has been common to see identity documents as reifications or representations that distort or hide complex social relationships (cf. Gordillo 2006). However, such a view is open to two criticisms. First, identity documents are not designed to identify the 'whole person', but are instrumental devices intended to uncover particular aspects of personhood in order to establish rights and entitlements in particular contexts. Whether it is for reasons of welfare or security, identity documents are a form of instrumental knowledge (Riles 2004). When an official at an airport checks your documents they are not interested in knowing about your complete social and cultural history, they are merely using the document to check whether you have the right to be in that place at that time, and whether they might represent threat or not. Second, documents are not removed from social and cultural processes, but rather are embedded within them. Instead of distorting social relationship, it is only through holding particular documents that people can act as agents, produce particular forms of knowledge and maintain social relationships (Serres 1982; Gell 1998; Barry 2002; Coles 2007). Identity documents are not distorted representations of some already existing form of personhood, but produce particular forms of agency and knowledge (compare Keane 2005). After all, Bourgass was able to avoid police and immigration detection because of the documents he held, not despite of them.

However, the forms of knowledge and action produced by identity documents are never complete or smooth, but filled with fissures and gaps. Instead of stabilizing, they can destabilize social relationships (Latour 1987; Ecks 2003). Rather than creating an all knowing surveillance state, the very presence of identity documents creates its own forms of ignorance. Whilst attempting to fix people in place and make them legible, documents simultaneously make this fixity impossible, creating new forms of illegibility.[5] Not only are documents based on an assumption of deception, in that people such as Bourgass might not really be who they say they are, but they also create

---

5   All attempts at fixity and stability arguably produce their own forms of instability (Bauman 1993). The instability of identity documents is linked specifically to the tensions between legal and cultural notions of community.

their own possibilities for fraud. Far from creating a stable form of identification, documents are therefore always a partial form of knowledge, obscuring as much as they reveal. David Lyon has famously argued that identity documents are 'tokens of trust' when we do not know who it is we are dealing with (2001). However, identity documents are perhaps best understood as artefacts of suspicion. In doing so they help to produce a shift towards cultural notions of belonging, where some groups are seen as being more suspicious than others, resulting in security practices that produce their own forms of insecurity.

Documents, Suspicion and the Limits of the Legal Person

From the moment you step foot in Israel/Palestine you are confronted with an array of document checks and questions. Indeed, amongst the many 'internationals' that live and work in the Palestinian Territories, the experience of security checks at Ben-Gurion airport are a constant topic of conversation. Everyone has their own story to tell and they get wheeled out regularly whenever the conversation lags at a diner party or over drinks in a café or bar. If a Palestinian is present whilst these stories of passing through Ben-Gurion are recounted, they usually listen quietly, with a wry smile on their face. Since the late 1990s, as part of the wider restrictions that the Israeli state has placed on the movement of Palestinians in the name of 'security' (Kelly 2006, 2006a), Palestinians have been effectively forbidden from flying in and out of Ben-Gurion airport. If they want to leave or enter the West Bank or Gaza Strip they must travel overland to Egypt or Jordan. This does not mean, however, that Palestinians do not travel through the airport.

Some Palestinians have accumulated forms of legal documentation that have enabled them to pass through Ben-Gurion despite the formal restrictions. Many West Bank Palestinians hold foreign passports, especially from South America, and Colombia, Brazil and Venezuela, in particular. Palestinians who emigrated to South America in the 1920s and 1950s, returned in the 1970s due to the economic boom caused by the Israeli occupation. These people often hold foreign passports and use these to pass through checkpoints, border controls and fly through Ben-Gurion airport. Such people are amongst the richest in the West Bank, and they have used their passports to set up businesses in Israel or important goods and labour between the West Bank and Israel. Dozens of people in the West Bank village in which I lived from 2000 to 2002 held Venezuelan passports, and would fly out of Ben-Gurion airport, usually to Cyprus, every three months in order to renew their visas. Walid, one such person, used to joke to me that after these trips, usually just a few days long, he would chat and with the immigration control people who had begun to recognize him. The fun of the trip was only added to by the fact that for many Palestinians a flight to Cyprus was associated with illicit dalliances, as it was to Cyprus that many people went to arrange the civil marriages that are unavailable in Israel/Palestine.

My land lord, in the same West Bank village, held a British passport after he married a British volunteer on the kibbutz on which he worked as a labourer during the 1980s. He had returned to the West Bank shortly after the start of the second *intifada*, hoping that his British passport would allow him to circumvent the restrictions that the Israeli military had placed on the movement of Palestinian identity card holders, and enable him to set up a small business importing roasted sunflower seeds. There were even more people in the village where I lived who had managed to obtain Israeli identity cards, usually through marriage to a Palestinian citizen of Israel, and these people would also travel through Ben-Gurion. Indeed, Nazmi, the man who picked me up from Ben-Gurion airport whenever I needed a lift, was born, brought up and continued to live in a West Bank Palestinian village. He had gained an Israeli identity card after marrying a Palestinian citizen of Israel, and had eventually found a job driving a taxi out of the airport. Whenever I make my way out the arrival lounge, I can usually guarantee to see his smiling face greeting me.

Given the advantages that holding Israelis identity cards or foreign passports give, West Bank Palestinians have attempted to accumulate and manipulate multiple forms of legal identification to enable them to travel through places such as Ben-Gurion, with all that implies to access to cultural and financial resources (compare Ong 1999). I also made use of this ability to manipulate documents, having two British passports, one which I used for going into Israel, and another that I used for entering Arab countries. As people with stamps from Israel are banned from entering Syria and Lebanon, and can expect a great deal of questioning at other borders in the Middle East, many people who travel in the region have two identical passports that they swap around. As Susan Coutin has argued, documents are formally seen as merely representing an already pre-existing legal status, but in practice documents can have a 'life of their own' creating their own forms of rights and responsibilities (2000: 54). The social life of identity documents allows them to be used and manipulated as people attempt to pass through international borders or internal checkpoints.

It would be extremely naïve, however, to think that Israeli security officials, and officials elsewhere in the world, are not aware of such attempts to hide bodies behind documents. Indeed, an internal Israeli military investigation concluded that the use of checkpoints and identity cards could not prevent Palestinians from infiltrating into Israel. Rather than bypassing checkpoints and identity checks, most Palestinian 'infiltrators' into Israel pass straight through them. Furthermore, following the start of the second *intifada* in September 2000 Israeli soldiers were under explicit orders to be on the look out for Palestinians who were attempting to use foreign passports in order to pass. The fear that documents can be forged is a particularly persistent theme. The former Israeli cabinet minister Meir Shetreet has estimated that up to 400,000 forged Israeli identity cards are in circulation.[6] As in the debates that followed the conviction of Bourgass, the suspicion of possible fake identity documents is found at border crossing and checkpoints around the world. I am often called upon to write so called 'expert witness report' for the U.K. Immigration tribunal on whether the documents presented by a particular asylum seeker are 'genuine'. The basic assumption of the Home Office officials seems to be that the documents presented by asylum applicants are in some way forged. Indeed, writing in the context of the U.S.-Mexican border, Heyman has argued that immigration inspectors see one of their principle tasks as the uncovering forged identity documents (1995: 272). Similarly, in August 2006 all U.K. ports and airports were warned by the British Home Office to be on the look out for people trying to enter the U.K. on false visas following the theft of the stickers that house the visas from a London printing plant. There were also reports that failed asylum seekers were using faked passports in order leave the U.K. before they were deported to their country of 'origin'. Over 200 were reportedly sent back to the U.K. from France for trying to travel on such documents.[7] In order to combat the perceived widespread use of forged documents, the U.K. government has created a new offence of holding false documents. Under this law, a person can be charged merely for holding forged forms of identification, irrespective of whether they try and use them.

In the context of suspicion over fraud produced by documents, Israeli security officials never take the documents that they are presented with at face value. Every time my landlord Juma flew into Ben-Gurion, with his wife and two young children, security officials questioned him about his British passport, asking him he also had a Palestinian identity card as well. As Palestinians, since the late 1990s, have been effectively forbidden from travelling through Ben-Gurion airport, this would have meant that he was unable to enter Israel and return to his home in the West Bank. Israeli security officers can see from his passport that he was born in the West Bank, and therefore might hold a Palestinian identity card. On one occasion, his wife, nervous and tired after flying all night, admitted that Juma had a West Bank identity card. As a result Juma was forbidden from entering Israel via Ben-Gurion and had 'From

---

6   Ha'aretz, 'Immigrations smash forgery ring', 23 September 2002.
7   In another case a Brazilian football player was accused of trying to enter the U.K. on forged Brazilian passport that his agent had apparently provided for him.

the Territories' stamped in his British passport, preventing him from trying to use Ben-Gurion again. He had to return to the U.K. and fly to Jordan, entering the West Bank over land.

The possibility of fraud, and hence suspicion, is inherent in identity documents. The extensive use of documentary practices by modern states to control, coordinate and stabilize, simultaneously produces possibilities for the forged and the fraudulent.[8] The sense of fraud has two elements. The first is that the documents are counterfeit. The second, and perhaps more important, is that although the document may be genuine, it does not really tell you who the holder is, as legal notions of citizenship run up alongside cultural notions of belonging. Although Juma was a British citizen, for the Israeli security officers this merely obscured his more important Palestinianness. For this reason, documentary forms of governance are never entirely trusted either by state officials or those subjected to their force.[9] There is a pervasive sense that the world is made up by 'more than the play of documents' (Coutin/Maurer/Yngvesson 2002) and that there is a self that 'exceeds its documentation' (Coutin/Yngvesson 2006: 179). This means that although documents may appear to have a social life of there own, there is always a referral to a seemingly more stable form of knowledge that stands beyond the documents. The inclusion of place of birth on passports for example, points to this sense of a more stable presence that exists elsewhere (Yngvesson/Mahoney 2000). My landlord Juma may have been a British citizen and held a British passport, but his passport also said that he was born in the West Bank, alluding to a seemingly less transient origin, rooted in birth, that the Israeli security official picked up on. The desire of the British media to find out if Bourgass was 'really' Algerian or Tunisian is also testament to this search for a seemingly more stable source of origin. Whilst identity documents may have been introduced in order to identify and fix in place in the face of a mass of seemingly changing and unknowable bodies (Torpey 2000), the instability of documents means that officials continue to look beyond the documents they are given, onto the bodies of the people that hold them.

---

8 States can be complicit in the forgery of their own practices. As Calavita has argued, for example, U.S. immigration law in the 1980s required employers to request paper documents from immigrants, but did require employers to verify the authenticity of these documents (1990). The contradictions between political pressures to regulate illegal immigration demands from employers for cheap Mexican labour crated a situation where a blind eye was turned by immigration inspectors to all but the most obviously counterfeit immigration documents.

9 Longman describes how during the Rwandan genocide people did not trust official identity cards that distinguished Hutu from Tutsi, but sought to research into family histories and used phonotypical markers instead (2001).

Biometrics, Documents and Bodies

In the face of the ever present possibility of fraud, biometric identity cards seem to offer the promise of binding transient documents to seemingly more stable bodies.[10] Indeed senior British Police officers have only supported identity cards on the grounds that they will contain biometric information, claiming that as otherwise they are actually an obstacle to countering potential terrorist threats.[11] According to their proponents biometric identity cards 'make counterfeiting virtually impossible' as a 'criminal may steal your card, but your unique biometric data cannot be taken from you'.[12] The creation of a direct link between physical bodies and the documents that they hold, in the shape of information about physiological traits, creates the promise of increased 'legibility'.[13]

The Israeli state has been at the forefront of attempts to introduce biometric technology. Since 2002 several terminals have been installed at Ben-Gurion airport that seek to match hand prints to information stored on a card to a central database. Israeli citizens and international businessmen who frequently fly in and out of Ben-Gurion can apply for the scheme and then have background checks carried out. If they are passed by the Israeli security services, they then have their personal details and hand print recorded and join the estimated 250,000 other people on the scheme. The Dallas based producer of the system boasts that the system 'eradicates human error' and is 'foolproof' (EDS 2004). Similar technology has been used at some checkpoints used by Palestinians. In 2002 the Israeli military started to install a new biometric scanning device at Erez, the largest checkpoint between Israel and the Gaza Strip, which on some years has seen tens of thousands of Palestinians passing through on a daily basis in order to work in the Israeli economy. As the Palestinian enters the checkpoint a gate closes behind him and he has to swipe his card through the reader and have his palm and face read by a scan-

---

10 The demand for biometric technology has grown so fast in the past few years that the industry has grown from being worth around $1bn to $4.5bn between 2000 and 2004 (Guardian, 'Biometrics – great hope for world security or triumph of big brother', 18 June 2004).
11 They argue that the possibilities for fraud inherent in non-biotitic identity documents will actually hinder rather than help police work.
12 See the website of the U.K. Identity and Passport Service, available at: http://www.identitycards.gov.uk/benefits-society-idtheft.asp (last accessed 30 January 2007).
13 Biometric systems work by attempting to create a match between information held on a card and the unique physiological traits, such as fingerprints or iris patterns, of the card holder. They do so either by matching information on an ID card with physical traits read off a body – known as verification – or matching an ID card, with physical traits on a body and a central data based – known as identification. Identification is a much more complicated and costly procedure.

ners. If a central database verifies that the information read off the card and the body match and that the card holder has the right to enter Israel, a gate to left opens. However, if the biometric data does not match or the computer refuses the card holder entry, a gate to the right is opened up, where further interrogation can take place. The Israeli security forces boasts that the system, known as *Basel*, can eradicate the 'need for human intervention' (Israeli Ministry of Public Security 2003). The use of biometric cards was included in the 1999 agreement between the government of Israel and the PLO, designed to facilitate safe passage between the West Bank and Gaza. Although this agreement has effectively become moribund, there are eventual plans as the Wall, which the Israeli military is building across the West Bank, is completed, to roll out the technology across the region. The checkpoint at Beitunia to the west of Ramallah for example, which is reserved for businessmen, has required biometric identity cards since 2005. Several thousand Palestinians from the north of the West Bank have also reportedly been issued with similar cards. A new checkpoint unit was created within the IDF in 2004 whose members were specially trained in the use of biometric technology.

Israel is far from being alone in the introduction of biometric identity documents. The International Civil Aviation Organisation (ICAO) has set new standards that require the inclusion of a biometric facial image in all new passports. Most EU states are moving towards the incorporating of fingerprint and facial biometrics in passports. The EU also increasingly requires fingerprint and facial biometrics for residence permits and visas for visitors from outside the European Economic Area. Similarly, the 9/11 commission in the U.S. recommended the introduction of biometric identity cards as a means of 'strengthening security' (National Commission on Terrorist Attacks upon the United States 2004). The U.S. military has also started collecting biometric data on people detained in Iraq, Afghanistan and elsewhere. U.S. immigration now requires the routine face-scanning and finger printing of visitors from most states in the world. The U.S.-Visit (U.S. Visitor and Immigrant Status Indicator Technology) security system is meant to identify travelers who have violated immigration controls, have criminal records or belong to groups listed as terrorist organisations by the U.S. Visitors are also required to have a biometric passport or face more stringent security checks. In the past few years, biometrics, in the shape of a fingerprint, have also been included in the identity cards issued to U.S. residents who are non-citizens.

In the U.K., after a heated debate in parliament and the press, new biometric passports and identity cards are due to be introduced from 2008. Biometric technology is already used on identity documents for asylum applicants and visa applications from citizens of specific states. The new U.K. passports will have fingerprint and facial biometrics, whilst the identity card will also carry iris biometrics. The biometric information recorded will then be registered on a central National Identification Registry. Registration will be a mandatory for all U.K. residents. It will not however be compulsory to carry a card and there will be no new powers for the police to demand the card. The Home Office has claimed that biometrics represented a 'cutting edge' solution to identity fraud, arguing that recent advances in technology meant that a 'truly effective and secure scheme is now possible' providing a 'hi-tech form of security for every citizen'[14]. The new Identity and Passport Service set up to administer the new cards has claimed that they will 'help the security services in their investigations into organized crime and terrorist activities' and help protect the U.K. against threats to 'national security', as well as 'help to identify people who try to work here illegally and could deter potential illegal immigrants from coming to the U.K'.[15] Biometric identity cards are being sold has a 'hi-tech' solution to security problems that would bind physical bodies to documents and therefore make the population more 'legible'. Bodies are treated as a source of biologically based information that can be broken down and read by electronic equipment in order to identify distinct aspects of a person (Ericson/Haggerty 2001: 613). The uncertainty of legal documents is seemingly overcome by the certainty of technology, creating new forms of what might be called 'biosociality' (Rabinow 1996; Rose/Novas 2005).

The Limits of Biometrics

Despite the claims of cutting edge technology, it remains an open question as to how revolutionary the introduction of biometric technology actually is in the processes of identification and knowledge production. After all, and despite the more extreme fears of some of its critics, biometrics is not the storing of a part of a physical person in a card, but rather is the storing of an electronic representation of a physiological trait. In this sense, biometric markers have long been common on identity documents, in the shape of photographs. The 'traditional' nature of biometric technology means that, in many ways, it is as open to manipulation and problems as 'old style' identity cards. Indeed, according to the inventor of the algorithm used in most iris biometrics, all biometrics are vulnerable to fraud.[16] Fingerprints can be faked with latex, faces can be altered through plastic surgery, and irises can be disguised with

---

14 See http://www.identitycards.gov.uk/scheme-now.asp (last accessed 20 Ja-nuary 2007).
15 See http://www.identitycards.gov.uk/benefits-society-immigration.asp (last accessed 24 January 2007).
16 BBC, 'Facing a biometric future', 13 January 2004, available at: http://news.bbc.co.uk/1/hi/technology/3389209.stm (last accessed 24 January 2007).

contact lenses. For the effective working of biometric technology, data on the physiological characteristics must be easily recordable. However, trials have found for example, that it is more difficult to take fingerprints from manual labourers. Contact lenses and eye conditions also mean that one in a thousand can not give iris scans, with a higher recognition rate for white and Asian participants than those who are black (House of Commons Science and Technology Committee 2006). No biometric system records a complete picture of the physiological characteristics, but creates a template containing key points. Small variations in the way this template is taken, such as angle, light or heat, can effect the recorded information.

Even once biometric information has been gathered, the techniques for matching stored biometric information with physical bodies are far from one hundred percent reliable. Identification systems must be balanced between a high false acceptance rate – allowing more people to pass than should – and a high false rejection rate – rejecting genuine people. Fingerprints only achieve about a 98 percent accurate match rate. Facial recognition technology is between 95 percent and 60 percent accurate (Kong et al. 2005).[17] Hand-shapes, another biometric in common use, are not unique in large populations and therefore potentially have a very high false acceptance rate. Human bodies also change over time. People grow beards, or put on weight, fingerprints change with age. This means that flexibility has to be built into the system, creating further space for error. At an airport such as Heathrow, with more than sixty million people travelling through each year, even a system with 99.99 percent accuracy could still fail to recognize tens of thousands of people a year. Furthermore, the facial biometrics put into new passports around the world are not designed to be checked against a central database, but still require a visual check from an immigration officer. They are therefore only as accurate as non-digital photographs. Indeed, a study by the Israeli military concluded that no single biometric technique provides an 'acceptable' measure of accuracy and that biometrics could not be relied on as a fail safe means of identification (Croft 2001). Despite the promise of a bright new 'biosocial' future, bodies can not be so easily read.

Whilst biometric identity documents do not necessity represent a revolution in the accuracy of matching an identity document to the holder, they are a significant development in the ways in which that information is stored. Physiological data, rather than being simple stored in a photograph or a thumb print is encrypted into an electronic chip and in some cases, such as the U.K. identity card, on a central database, raising important questions about the management of information. At a global level however not all states will use

---

17 See also: 'UK National Physical Laboratory test report', available at: http://www.cl.cam.ac.uk/~jgd1000/NPLsummary.pdf (last accessed 18 January 2007).

same databases, and access will depend on fluctuating alliances and influence. Furthermore, any encryption system is only as reliable as the initial registration. The best that any system can provide is a compelling connection with some *previous* verification of identity. The entire system is therefore reliant on the initial point of entry, when the person is registered. This in turn has to rely on other documents and personal statements that can be more easily forged. It is worth remembering that Bourgass came into the U.K. on forged documents. Biometrics, rather than creating a fail safe linkage between bodies and documents merely reproduce the same problems of fraud, forgery and deception in new forms. The more profound sense of possible fraud – that documents might not tell you who some one really is and that cultural notions of belonging are more powerful than legal forms of citizenship – remains.

Incomplete Knowledge and Reading off Bodies

As a form of knowledge, identity cards, whether biometric or not, are inherently incomplete, and must therefore be accompanied with additional forms of knowledge. Despite all the biometric technology and the constantly checking and rechecking of documents, any passage through Ben-Gurion is also marked by incessant and often repeated questions by young airport security staff. Where have you been? Where are you going? Who did you stay with? Did you meet any locals? Who paid for your trip? Can I see your notes? These questions are often asked again and again as you are passed from one official to the next. In order to understand why these questions are asked alongside the checking of documents, it is important to remember that identity documents are not designed to identify every aspect of a person's life history, but rather are created for specific purposes – they are a means to and end. In a climate dominated by fears over terrorism, these ends are primarily, although not exclusively, those of security. Identity cards are used therefore to identify whether somebody represents a particular threat. However, in very few cases can identity cards be used to reveal particular threats represented by known individuals. Even when Kamel Bourgass was arrested, it was not because police knew where he would be, but rather because they came across him in the course of a raid. To use identity cards to target specific individuals requires knowing that such and such a person was planning on doing such and such, and all too often this type of knowledge is not available. Identity cards therefore are primarily used to identify dangerous categories of person rather than known individuals. It is here that bodies re-enter the picture once again, as attempts are made to identify possibly suspicious persons.

Immigration officers and security officials have to make on the spot decisions about whether or not to let somebody pass, and the documentary evidence they have is often incomplete or inconclusive, or not entirely trusted. According to Raphael Ron, the former head of security at Ben-Gurion airport, security staff are therefore trained to detect suspicious behaviour, in a technique known as 'behaviour pattern recognition' or BPR (Croft 2001). According to Ron, officials would question a person buttoned up in a trench coat on a 100-degree day, or a person with no baggage buying a ticket at the international travel counter. Questioning patterns are designed to reveal inconsistencies in stories and suspicious forms of behaviour. Similarly, in her ethnography of Israeli security practices, Juliana Ochs describes how Israeli civil guards are trained to read 'bodily signs of suspicion' that can include 'being a youngster who is trying to blend but do not belong to that group', 'running suspiciously' or 'wearing unsuitable clothes' (Ochs 2006). Such reading off bodies is not as crude as straightforward racial profiling. Indeed any security system would be naive to do so, as it would create new opportunities to pass as non-threatening. However, a context where fears often take a cultural and racialized form, some bodies are more suspicious than others. As Josiah Heyman argues, when faced with such situations, officials at U.S. border crossings use markers often read off bodies or clothes, based on overt national stereotypes, in order to decide whether someone represents a threat, whether they really are who they say they are, and whether they should be allowed to pass (2001; see also Gilboy 1991).

Perceptions of legitimate presence or suspicion will of course depend on specific local histories. Markers of dangerousness and the populations that they are seen as referring to change over time and space. In the U.K., after the London bombs in July 2005, people carrying heavy rucksacks on the underground were often viewed suspiciously. In Israel, on the other hand, wearing heavy winter coats in summer arouses suspicion, due to the tendency of suicide bombers to hide their bombs under thick jackets. More generally styles of dress or physical characteristic are often associated with particularly dangerous groups. As Ochs (2006) argues, Israeli security officials pay close attentions to clothes and appearance, as well as try in engage people in conversion in order to 'listen to their accents to determine whether they are Jewish Israeli, Palestinian or foreign and ascertain their degree of suspicion' (see also Paine 1992; Liebes/Blum-Kulka 1994; Helman 1997; Ben-Ari 1998). This is not to say that Israeli security officials necessarily have clear idea of what they were defending, or of who is the enemy. Indeed these notions are probably very fractured and contradictory. As Virginia Dominguez (1989: 166) has argued you cannot assume 'too neat and clear cut a separation between self (Israeli and Jewish) and other (epitomized by, but not restricted to, Arabs)'. For Dominguez, the references are neither fixed nor determinate, as there are 'uncertainties and indeterminacies at the boundaries of the collective self' (Dominguez 1989: 174). This means that for Israeli security officials bodies can not be easily read for culturally based notions of danger. Many Israelis and Palestinians are physically, socially and culturally difficult to tell part. Nearly 20 percent of the Israeli population are Palestinian Arabs. Furthermore, many Jewish Israelis are descended from the Jewish populations of other Middle Eastern countries, and speak Arabic fluently. Many of the Palestinian residents of the West Bank have worked in Israel for years and therefore not only speak Hebrew, but also dress and cut their hair in ways that make them indistinguishable from many Israeli citizens. In such a context it can be difficult to 'tell' an Israeli citizen who needs to be protected from a Palestinian threat.[18] Arguably however, the difficulties in telling Israeli from Palestinian only increases the fear and suspicions of security officials, as they constantly look between confusing documents and bodies in order to determine possible dangers.

Similar racially and culturally based conceptions of threat are also present in the U.K. Dangers to the security of the British state and individual citizens are increasingly viewed as originating in particular forms of Islamic belief and practice, often seen as stemming from outside the U.K., both culturally and territorially. However, friend and foe can only be problematically mapped onto citizens and non-citizen, due to the large U.K. born Muslim population that is increasingly seen as a potentially dangerous presence. The result is that suspicion is inherently racialized. This can be seen most obviously in the 2006 decision to bar two British students of Pakistani origin from a flight from Spain to Manchester on the grounds that they were behaving suspiciously. Their suspicious behaviour included speaking a language that sounded like Arabic (actually Urdu) and wearing beards. More tragically, such a process can also be found in the shooting of Jean Charles de Menezes, the Brazilian who was mistaken for suspicious person of Arab descent by the British police.

In this context, the very demand for identification becomes racialized. Under U.K. law there is no stand alone legal requirement to prove your identity in public spaces. Police officers can 'stop and search' as well as demand personal details only if they have 'reasonable grounds for suspicion' that a person is in the possession of stolen or prohibited items.[19] Home Office fig-

---

18 I have one South African friend who has worked in Israel for many years as a building contractor. He is of Afrikaans origin, nearly two metres tall, with a big bushy moustache and a former semi-professional rugby player. In the 1990s he worked in Sudan and converted to Islam, changing his name to Mohammed Abdallah. Whenever he would fly through Tel Aviv's Ben-Gurion airport he would always cause confusion for the border guards who were uncertain how to deal with him.
19 Police and Criminal Evidence Act 1984. Furthermore, senior officers can give authorization for stop and searches in a given locality, without individual suspicion, if they believe that a violent incident may take place, or a person is carry-

ures reveal that between 2001/2002 and 2002/2003 the number of recorded stop and searches rose by 17 percent for white people, but by 36 percent for Asian people and 38 percent for black people (LSE 2006). There is considerable controversy over the reliability of these statistics and the U.K. NGO State Watch has claimed that between 2001/2002 and 2004/2005, stop and searches have increased by 66 percent for black people and by 75 percent for Asians compared to less than 4 percent for white people. Furthermore, between 2001/2002 and 2002/2003, police stop and searches under terrorism legislation rose by 302 percent for Asian people, by 230 percent for black people and by 118 percent for white people. Such statistics have caused widespread arguments over whether they show widespread institutional racism within the U.K. police forces. Defenders of the police have argued that crime and terrorism are not equally distributed amongst the British population, and therefore it makes sense to target 'stop and search'. Whether this is true or not, it ignores a context where racial and cultural markers can implicitly become grounds for suspicion. The point is that rather than create a universal form of identification where 'if you have nothing to hide you have nothing to fear', some people clearly seem more suspicious than others.

Conclusion

In the face of security threats that are widely seen as clandestine and hidden, identity cards are increasingly used by states as they try to make their citizens/subjects more 'legible'. The question remains however as to what forms of knowledge are produced by identity cards and how this transforms the relationship between states and the populations they seek to control. The claims that identity cards produce transparent and secure forms of knowledge, or that they create an all knowing Orwellian state, are equally misplaced. Rather than simply create legibility and knowledge, identity cards also produce their own forms of illegibility and ignorance. After all, Bourgass was able to remain undetected not despite of identity documents but because he was able to manipulate them. He was able to do so because documents create a separation between the physical and the legal aspect of personhood, hiding bodies behind

---

ing 'dangerous instruments' without 'good reason' (s60 of the Criminal Justice and Public Order Act 1994). Finally, police are also entitled to stop and search for articles that could be used for terrorism in specific areas that have been authorized by senior officers (s44 of the Terrorism Act 2000). London has been continuously designated as such a zone since February 2001. Although they have fewer powers than police officers, immigration officials can also question people to determine their immigration status where there is a 'reasonable suspicion' that a person is an immigration offender.

layers of always potentially forged paper. Despite the promise of a bright technological future, biometric identity cards do not radically alter the situation, as they still rely on a form of representation that rather than bind bodies to documents, creates spaces for misrepresentation, manipulation and potential subterfuge. Furthermore, and perhaps more importantly, in a context where legal forms of citizenship and culturally based notions of belonging exist in an uneasy tension, the more powerful sense of fraud, that someone might not be who their documents say they are, remains.

Rather than create security through knowledge, identity documents create their own particular types of suspicion, ignorance or 'known unknowns', and therefore produce new forms of racialized suspicion and insecurity. Precisely because identity cards do not tell the state every thing they want to know, state officials are forced to resort to reading bodies for marks of suspicion, feeding into racialized notions of danger. Yet bodies too only offer a confusing surface from which to read possible threats. Facial characteristic, skin colour and styles of clothes can only tell you so much in a world where bodies, ideas and objects are constantly crossing borders. As people try and separate friend from foe there is therefore a constant movement between confusing bodies and unclear documents, neither of which are entirely trusted. The result is a racialized form of citizenship, where bodies, documents and legal status merge. The rights and obligations of citizenship are therefore not the product of a stable mapping of documents and legal status or straightforward racial stereotypes, but rather emerge through the gaps and fissures created by an unstable technique of governance. As a result, the forms of knowledge created by identity cards therefore create their own forms of insecurity. The crucial question of course, is who is made to bear the burden of these new forms of uncertainty.

Acknowledgements

I would like to thank the participants at the Law and Governance conference at the Max Planck Institute for Social Anthropology, and in particular Julia Eckert, for their insightful comments on an earlier version of this paper. The wider research upon which this chapter is based was supported by an ESRC Postgraduate studentship and an Emslie Horniman Award from the RAI.

References

Barry, A. (2002): 'The Anti-Political Economy', *Economy and Society*, 31(2): 268-84.
Bauman, Z. (1993): *Modernity and Ambivalence*, London: Routledge.
Ben-Ari, E. (1998): *Mastering Soldiers: Conflict, Emotions, and the Enemy in an Israeli Military Unit*, New York: Berghahn Books.
Calavita, K. (1990): 'Employer Sanctions Violations: towards a Dialectical Model of White-Collar Crime', *Law and Society Review*, 24(4): 1041-70.
—— (2001): 'Chinese Exclusion and the Open Door with China: Structural Contradictions and the 'Chaos' of Law, 1882-1910', *Social and Legal Studies*, 10(2): 203-26.
Caplan, J./Torpey, J. eds (2001): *Documenting Individual Identity: the Development of State Practices in the Modern World*, Princeton: Princeton University Press.
Coles, K. (2007): *Democratic Designs: International Interventions and Electoral Practices in Postwar Bosnia-Herzegovina*, Ann Arbor: University of Michigan Press.
Coutin, S. (2000): *Legalizing Moves: Salvadoran Immigrant's Struggles for U.S. Residency*, Ann Arbor: University of Michigan Press.
Coutin, S., with Maurer, B./Yngvesson, B. (2002): 'In the Mirror: the Legitimation Work of Globalization', *Law and Social Inquiry*, 27(4): 801-43.
Coutin, S./Yngvesson, B. (2006): 'Backed by Papers: Undoing Persons, Histories, and Return', *American Ethnologist*, 33(2): 177-90.
Croft, J. (2001): 'Israeli Security Experts: Technology not the Answer', *Aviation Week and Space Technology*, 26 November 2001.
Dominguez, V. (1989): *People as Subject, People as Object: Selfhood and Peoplehood in Contemporary Israel*, Madison: University of Wisconsin Press.
Ecks, S. (2003): 'Is India on Prozac? Sociotropic Effects of Pharmaceuticals in a Global Perspective', *Curare*, 26(1&2): 95-107.
EDS (2004): *Case Study: Ben-Gurion Airport Authority*. Available at: http://www.eds.com/services/casestudies/downloads/bgaa.pdf (last accessed 19 January 2007).
Ericson, R./Haggerty; K. (2001): 'The Surveillant Assemblage', *British Journal of Sociology*, 51(4): 605-22.
Gell, A. (1998): *Art and Agency: an Anthropological Theory*, Oxford: Oxford University Press.
Gilboy, J. (1991): 'Deciding who Gets in: Decision Making by Immigration Inspectors', *Law and Society Review*, 25(3): 571-600.
Gordillo, G. (2006): 'The Crucible of Citizenship: ID-Paper Fetishism in the Argentinean Chaco', *American Ethnologist*, 33(2): 162-76.

Helman, S. (1997): 'Militarism and the Construction of Community', *Journal of Political and Military Sociology*, 25(2): 305-32.

Heyman, J. (1995): 'Putting Power in the Anthropology of Bureaucracy: the Immigration and Naturalization Service at the Mexico-United States Border', *Cultural Anthropology*, 36(2): 261-87.

—— (2001): 'Class and Classification on the U.S.-Mexico Border', *Human Organization*, 60(2): 128-40.

Home Office (2003): *Identity Cards: Next Steps*, London.

House of Commons Science and Technology Committee (2006): *Identity Card Technologies: Scientific Advice, Risk and Evidence. Sixth Report of Session 2005-06*, London: The Stationary Office.

Israeli Ministry of Public Security (2003): *Deploying the Basel Smart Card at Border Check Points*. Available at: http://www.mops.gov.il/BPEng/InformationCenter/TechnologynEquipment (last accessed 18 January 2007).

Keane, W. (2005): 'Signs are not the Garb of Meaning: on the Social Analysis of Material Things'. In: D. Miller (ed.), *Materiality*, Durham, NC: Duke University Press, pp. 182-205.

Kelly, T. (2006): *Law, Violence and Sovereignty among West Bank Palestinians*, Cambridge: Cambridge University Press.

—— (2006a): 'Documented Lives: Fear and the Uncertainties of Law during the Second Palestinian Intifada', *Journal of the Royal Anthropological Institute*, 12(1): 87-107.

Kong, S./Heo, J./Abidi, B./Paik, J./Abidi, M. (2005): 'Recent Advances in Visual and Infrared Face Recognition – a Review', *Computer Vision and Image Understanding*, 97(1): 103-35.

Latour, B. (1987): *Science in Action: how to Follow Scientists and Engineers through Society*, Cambridge, MA: Harvard University Press.

Liebes, T./Blum-Kulka, S. (1994): 'Managing Moral Dilemmas: Israeli Soldiers in the Intifada', *Armed Forces and Society*, 21(1): 45-68.

Longman, T. (2001): 'Identity Cards, Ethnic Self-Perception, and Genocide in Rwanda'. In: J. Caplan/J. Torpey (eds), *Documenting Indivi-dual Identity: the Development of State Practices in the Modern World*, Princeton: Princeton University Press, pp. 245-357.

LSE (2006): *The Identity Project: an Assessment of the UK Identity Cards Bill and its Implications*, London: London School of Econo-mics.

Lyon, D. (2001): 'Under my Skin: from Identification Papers to Body Surveillance'. In: J. Caplan/J. Torpey (eds), *Documenting Individual Identity: the Development of State Practices in the Modern World*, Princeton: Princeton University Press, pp. 291-310.

National Commission on Terrorist Attacks upon the U.S. (2004): *The 9/11 Commission Report*, Washington, DC.

Ochs, J. (2006): 'Security and Subjectivity: the Everyday Life of Jewish Israelis during the Second Intifada', Unpublished PhD Thesis, University of Cambridge.
Ong, A. (1999): *Flexible Citizenship: the Cultural Logics of Transnationality*, Durham: Duke University Press.
Paine, R. (1992): 'Anthropology beyond Routine: Cultural Alternatives for the Handling of the Unexpected', *International Journal of Moral and Social Studies*, 7(3): 183-203.
Rabinow, P. (1996): *Essays in the Anthropology of Reason*, Princeton: Princeton University Press.
Riles, A. (2004): 'Property as Legal Knowledge: Means and Ends', *Journal of the Royal Anthropological Institute*, 10(4): 775-95.
Rose, N./Novas, C. (2005): 'Biological Citizenship'. In: A. Ong/S. Collier (eds), *Global Assemblages: Technology, Politics and Ethics as Anthropological Problems*, Oxford: Blackwell, pp. 439-63.
Scott, J. (1998): *Seeing like a State: how Certain Schemes to Improve the Human Condition Have Failed*, New Haven: Yale University Press.
Serres, M. (1982): *The Parasite*, Baltimore, MD: Johns Hopkins University Press.
Torpey, J. (2000): *The Invention of the Passport: Surveillance, Citizen-ship and the State*, Cambridge: Cambridge University Press.
Yngvesson, B./Mahoney, M. (2000): ''As One Should, Ought, and Wants to Be'': Belonging and Authenticity in Identity Narratives', *Theory, Culture and Society*, 17(6): 77-110.

The Danger of 'Undergoverned' Spaces: the 'War on Terror' and its Effects on the Sahel Region

JAN BACHMANN

Introduction

This article aims at a reconstruction of how the Sahel region of Africa has been integrated into the 'war on terror' by security experts and an analysis of the various social implications of the discourse and intervention practices. Applying the arguments of critical geopolitics and the securitisation framework, this contribution will show how the U.S. government operates with a spatial terminology in problematizing the Sahel as an 'undergoverned' space, where terrorist activities, smuggling and illegal migration constitute a threat to international security. It will be asked how these discursive manifestations came to be the dominant interpretation of social reality in the Sahel. The article outlines perceptions and assessments, in short: the political rationality which made the military programme 'Pan-Sahel Initiative' and its broader successor, the 'Trans-Saharan Counter-Terrorism Partnership', possible. It is an investigation into the question of how dominant representations of and actions in the region are embedded within the U.S. global strategy of pre-emptive action against perceived threats. An analytical lens on space aims at highlighting the entire apparatus that has securitized the Sahel over the last few years. In a remarkably open public policy, U.S. security professionals have made powerful geographical statements about the Sahel region, supported by the use of illustrative maps, reiterating the dangerousness of this area. It will be argued that by generating knowledge about the 'poorly policed Sahel', the U.S. military experts play a decisive role in transmitting the propositions of the global discourse of the 'war on terror' into practices and, thus, create the field of their own operations.

However, the subsequent interventions have unintended consequences as they aim at strengthening state authorities in a region where distrust against state institutions prevails. It is not the intention of this article to prove which part of the intervention 'caused' which effect on the ground. However, the case will be made that the representation of the region and the subsequent interventions have impacts on how different local actors perceive their role in this power relation. They have done so in a variety of ways. The 'targets' of the interventions, be it governments and their local officials or communities, are able to translate, appropriate or challenge the discourse and its policies. As a consequence, state-society relations and community relations have changed, with ambiguous effects.

Representations of the 'Third World'

Problematisations of geographical or social spaces by hegemonic political players are a common instrument for creating urgency and legitimizing interventions in these spaces. It is part of the geopolitical tradition of Western actors to categorize spaces in the 'Third World' in order to make them manageable. Northern actors construct the problem and, at the same time, offer strategies for its solution. Thus, the production of geographical knowledge can be seen as a political act.

During the Cold War the two superpowers accumulated knowledge about non-European regions in order to help create strong states capable of transforming their 'backward' societies. States in which the assumed modernisation project did not meet the expectations were categorized as 'weak'.[1] After the end of the Cold War the discussion of deficiencies of states in the South was significantly expanded into security politics. During the 1990s two of the

---

1 For the interplay between knowledge-production and space-production in the Anglophone social sciences see Agnew (1998) and Bilgin/Morton (2002). In the 1950s and 1960s, observation and statistics became the primary means of empiricist knowledge-gathering. The Gross Domestic Product appeared to be the new indicator of development. This was complemented by anthropological studies of cultural habits in the 'Third World'. According to Bilgin and Morton the logic of abstracting the state from its society, from its historical formation and the international context persists to date. Within this logic, large parts of the social sciences keep focussing on observable data on the capacities of agencies. Thus, 'the architecture of modernisation and development theory, including consequent representations of the post-colonial state, has undergone minor modifications and shifts of emphasis, adapting to new conditions and circumstances, while remaining relatively unchanged' (Bilgin/Morton 2002: 65).

most prominent representations of spaces by Western foreign policy actors with regard to the Non-Western World were those of the 'failed' and the 'rogue' state. However, while the main deficiency of the former is most of all seen in the incapability of state authorities to provide basic services or to effectively control their territory, which was interpreted as having mainly internal effects, the latter was believed to pose a direct threat to the international state system by supporting terrorism, violating human rights or through the proliferation of weapons of mass destruction (Bilgin/Morton 2004: 170).[2] After the 9/11 attacks one characteristic originally assigned to rogue states, namely the accusation of harbouring terrorists, was now attributed to states perceived as weak or failed. The U.S. National Security Strategy, announced in 2002, officially marked the shift towards pre-emptive action within U.S. foreign policy and drew the attention to weak states:

'The events of September 11, 2001, taught us that weak states, like Afghanistan, can pose as great a danger to our national interests as strong states. Poverty does not make poor people into terrorists and murderers. Yet poverty, weak institutions, and corruption can make weak states vulnerable to terrorist networks and drug cartels within their borders' (White House 2002: ii).

'America is now threatened less by conquering states than by failing ones' (White House 2002: 1).

The perceived threat makes it mandatory for Western states to engage in weak states as in times of terror no one can afford to ignore these spaces. In a speech at the West Point Military Academy George W. Bush is explicit about the new danger and the steps that need to be taken: 'We must take the battle to the enemy, disrupt his plans and confront the worst threats before they emerge. In the world we have entered, the only path to safety is the path of action. And this nation will act.' (Bush 2002) It is remarkable that since 9/11, the new threat apparently roots in somewhat diversified geographical spaces as the terms 'weak states', 'failed states' and 'undergoverned regions' are used interchangeably in key policy documents. It has become common sense for Western government authorities to stress the link between such regions, which are perceived as insufficiently governed, and the possibility that they might become a breeding ground for terrorism (among others EU 2003: 8-9; OECD/DAC 2003: 16; USAID/Department of State 2003: 10; White House

---

2   At the same time, however, 'rogue' or 'failed' states have functional aspects for the West: Their existence makes the justification for action – in order to 'end' the alleged threat – easier. To call states 'weak' or 'failed', on the other hand, allows one to blame internal factors for their deficiencies rather than to take aspects of the global economic structure into account (Jacoby 2005).

2003: 23; Department of Defense 2006: 12). In contrast to the 1990s, when the individual's security in the South rather than state security was the primary addressee of Western policy interventions, it is now the security of the population in the homeland that is at stake when promising to deal with 'troubled' areas:

'German interests are being defended [...] at the Hindukush' (the former German minister of defence, Peter Struck, 4 December 2002).

'Canadians cannot be safe in an unstable world, or healthy in a sick world; nor can we expect to remain prosperous in a poor world' (CIDA 2005: 1).

'[T]urning a blind eye to the breakdown of order in any part of the world, however distant, invites direct threat to our national security and wellbeing. [...] For as well as bringing mass murder to the heart of Manhattan, state failure has brought terror and misery to larges swathes of the African continent, as it did in the Balkans in the early 1990s. And at home it has long brought drugs, violence and crime to Britain's streets' (Straw 2002: 1).

Recently the ambitious characterisations of deviant statehood by Western players (such as weak, rogue, failing, failed, collapsed, problematic, dissolving, anaemic, captured, aborted, shadow states and those under stress, etc.) have given way to a more amorphous conceptualisation of 'dangerous places'. External and internal security are seen as inherently linked and the challenges have to be addressed by the 'whole-of-government'-phalanx of Western security, foreign policy and development actors.[3]

Consequently, not only foreign policy agendas had to be adjusted. Different policy fields have since been expected to act in a 'coherent' way towards states perceived as 'fragile'. An illustrative example is the modification of Western development policies. In a process which started in the 1990s with an integration of conflict prevention, all major development agencies in the Western world have since incorporated security-related aspects (Duffield 2001; Hönke 2005; Beall et al. 2006; Klingebiel 2006). In order to secure funding by their governments they now even designed concepts on how development assistance can support the fight against terrorism (USAID 2002; AusAid 2003; U.S. Department of State/USAID 2003; Danish Ministry of Foreign Affairs 2004; CIDA 2005; DFID 2005).

By reiterating that the 'undergoverned' spaces of the Sahel are exploited by terrorists, the U.S. military creates urgency for a regulating intervention. Taking problematisations of geographical and social spaces into account

---

3 Inter-agency and inter-department efforts, labelled whole-of-government-approaches, were especially developed for dealing with 'fragile states'. This concept is advanced by the Australian government, the U.S. government and by the OECD/DAC.

when analysing the integration of Africa into the 'war on terror', allows a broader insight into the political rationalities which motivate foreign policies towards these spaces.

The Spatialisation of Danger

In critical social theory there are two interlinked frameworks which help to understand the political implications of the notions of space. Building upon a broad range of materialist and poststructuralist works (as e.g., Harvey 1989; Soja 1989; Lefebvre 1991), critical geopolitics scholars argue that geographical knowledge constitutes a political category (Agnew/Corbridge 1995; Dalby/Ó Tuathail 1998). In this context, the various perspectives of securitisation have shown how social phenomena – which allow the inclusion of spaces – can be declared a serious threat. Both approaches imply that spaces are socially produced. For a long time, however, the notion of space was identified with the territorial state. This equation was foundational for the discipline of International Relations. And, in turn, states claimed authority to be the main narrator of space and territory (Ó Tuathail 1996). The expansion of social order from the sixteenth century onwards was linked to the fabrication of spatial order. During the time of evolving statistics, statehood and conquest, the 'blank spaces on the globe succumbed to the sovereign authority of governmental institutions and imperial science, the surface of the globe appeared for the first time as a system of "closed space", an almost completely occupied and fully charted geographical order' (Ó Tuathail 1996: 15). The key questions within classical geopolitics, that is, the spatializing of global politics, were: 'Who does this space belong to' and 'In what way is "their" space different from "ours"' (ibid. 16). In order to understand the focus on territoriality, the aspect of control is crucial. According to Sack, territoriality involves a form of classification by area; it furthermore contains a form of communication (to establish the boundary, e.g., by setting up a sign stating a possession or exclusion); and finally, territoriality involves an attempt at enforcing control over access to the area and to the things within it, i.e., that transgression will be punished (Sack 1986: 21 ff.). Territory therefore inherently includes a relation of violence in so far as the monopolisation of the use of force within a designated territory is part of Max Weber's famous definition of the state (Neocleous 2003: 102). The reluctance in mainstream International Relations Theories to go analytically beyond the imagination of a compartmentalized, state-centred world provoked Agnew to argue that it finds itself in a 'territorial trap'. He accused the mainstream approaches of being ahistorical and of taking for granted the state-territorial spaces as fixed units of secure sovereign space. Furthermore he refused to accept the territorial state as existing prior to and as a container of society (Agnew/Corbridge 1995: 83 f.).

In the 1990s critical political geographers started to analyse the functioning of geographical knowledge 'as an ensemble of technologies of power concerned with the governmental production and management of territorial space', termed 'geo-power' by Ó Tuathail (1996: 7). They shifted the focus from fixed and given spaces towards representations of space, that is, the system of classification and meaning of spaces conceptualized by experts, including scientists and urban planners.[4] Focusing critically on the production of geographical knowledge by experts and institutions is a politicizing act as it questions the often familiar and unchallenged assumptions of such manifestations. Critical political geographers build upon Foucault's works on the interplay of power and knowledge and on his concept of governmentality (Foucault 1980: 119, 2006a, 2006b). Foucault analysed the broad range of the 'arts of government', which include more than regulating efforts by the state. These strategies are more broadly understood as structuring the field of actions of the subjects (Foucault 2000: 341). Based on political rationalities, they are made possible by problematisations and expertise of a certain phenomenon, which are then being 'translated' into political programmes (Rose/Miller 1992: 177-83). Governmentality constitutes:

'a discursive field, within which the exercise of power is being 'rationalized'. This happens through the elaboration of terms and concepts, the specification of objects and boundaries, through the supply of arguments and rationales, etc. A political rationality thus allows to propose a problem and offers particular strategies for the treatment and the solution of this problem. [...] These programmes not only express wishes and intentions, but define an implicit knowledge' (Lemke 1997: 147).[5]

Thus, it is the strategies of government which render such political programmes operable (Rose/Miller 1992: 183).

Critical political geographers aim at replacing essentialist notions of space with a focus on practices and representations. In contrast to the explanatory

---

4   Critical geopolitics scholars refer specifically to the works of the French philosopher Henri Lefebvre (1991[1974]) who was one of the first to argue that space is a social product.
5   My translation. Original quotation in German: '[Regierung bezeichnet] ein diskursives Feld, innerhalb dessen die Ausübung der Macht "rationalisiert" wird. Dies geschieht durch die Erarbeitung von Begriffen und Konzepten, der Spezifizierung von Gegenständen und Grenzen, durch die Bereitstellung von Argumenten und Begründungen etc. Eine politische Rationalität erlaubt also, ein Problem zu stellen und bietet bestimmte Lösungs- und Bearbeitungsstrategien an. [...] Diese Programme drücken nicht nur Wünsche und Absichten aus, sondern definieren ein implizites Wissen.'

problem-solving tradition they work genealogically. They challenge the sayings of 'wise statesmen' and draw attention to broader culturally embedded expressions in administration, the academia and popular culture (Dalby/Ó Tuathail 1998: 1-14). Drawing from Dodds, Allen illustratively points out that 'in this vein, the practice of foreign policy making, for instance, appears as primarily a collection of scripts which combine various coded geographical assumptions and descriptions about "faraway" places which are then used to narrate geopolitical events and legitimize a particular course of action' (Allen 2003: 102).

Foreign policy makers do not simply accumulate 'objective' knowledge about particular regions. They have used this to declare these spaces dangerous in order to create the urgency to take action. This process was termed securitisation. The dealing of U.S. government authorities with the whole Sahelian region during the past years is a striking example. Applying this perspective, categorizing regions as 'failed states' or a 'breeding ground for terrorism' has proved to be a securitizing practice insofar as it has allowed for the establishment of interventions into theses spaces in order to regulate them. Based on a constructivist approach, the concept of securitisation assumes that the term security does not necessarily need a referent object but is socially constructed. Securitisation is therefore a political decision to conceptualize an issue in a particular, security-centred, way. Participants of such a discourse problematize a certain issue and consequently assign 'existential threats to a referent object, [generating] endorsement of emergency measures beyond rules that would otherwise apply' (Buzan et al. 1998: 5). This notion has been criticized for its focus on existential threats and exceptional measures (Abrahamsen 2005).[6] In contrast to that, Didier Bigo stressed that the securitizing process works continuously in everyday (discursive and non-discursive) practices in the field of security agencies. Linking external and internal security, transnational experts create a 'continuum of threats and general unease' as they semantically relate different phenomena such as migration, drug trafficking and terrorism (Bigo 2002: 63 ff.). In this vein the process of securitisation involves the capacity of security professionals to claim what security is and to establish a code of practice for a regulation of the issue. In short, it is a technology of government (Bigo 2000: 194 ff.).

Although heavily discussed in the field of securitisation, critical scholars in International Relations Theory have shown the interplay between the construction of danger and the politics of identity (Dillon 1996; Campbell 1998).[7]

---

6   For further critical accounts see McSweeney (1996); Huysmans (1998) and, from a materialist perspective, Neocleous (2000).
7   Critics accused Buzan et al. of their half-hearted constructivism, as they would treat the results of a social construction (such as identity) as an objectively given and thus retain an objectivist and realist view (McSweeney 1998).

Through the mobilizing politics of securitisation the object (dangerous people or places) is clearly identified, homogenized and certain characteristics, values and behaviours are assigned to it. This labelling is of central importance to the discursive construction of threat. The process of securing provokes the question of who is being secured and who remains 'outside'. Insecurity can thus be seen as the necessary condition for security. Calls for security have to refer to the danger which threatens this security (Neocleous 2000). Through politics of identification, securitisation includes a moral agenda. It aims at legitimizing the actions taken to eliminate the threat. By doing so, it closes the ranks in the 'homeland' and mobilizes public support for – like in our case – the 'war on terrorism' (Abrahamsen 2005: 65). At the same time it draws a line between *our* place and *their* spaces. Since *they* are presented as posing an external threat, the spaces on the 'dark side of globalisation'[8] cannot be ignored. These spaces therefore have to be engaged by different strategies, such as inclusion of the willing and containment of the ones considered as the most problematic (Rose 1999: 240 ff.; Abrahamsen 2005: 70; Hönke 2005). Africa's integration into the 'war on terror' is a showcase illustration of the engagement of such 'problematic' spaces.

Africa's Integration into the 'War on Terror'

After a brief episode in the early 1990s during which the continent was more or less ignored, Northern policies towards Africa began to focus on the resolution and prevention of violent conflicts (Duffield 2001). While at this time weak or failed statehood was still mainly described as a problem for the population in the affected regions, these spaces were soon integrated into the global discourse of the 'war on terror'. The terrorist attacks in East Africa in 1998 and 2002 as well as the proximity of the 'failed' state Somalia to the Arabian Peninsula alerted the U.S. to re-engage on the continent. At the same time it became known that the reliance of the U.S. on African oil was increasing. Today 15 percent of the oil imported by the United States comes from Africa. Some years from now every fifth imported barrel is expected to originate in Africa (Goldwyn 2005).[9]

Therefore, in order to prevent an influx of terrorists into Africa, an international 'Combined Joint Task Force – Horn of Africa' was established in

---

8 Label used for 'weak states' in a USAID document (USAID 2005: v).
9 Klare and Volman compare the attention the continent has recently attracted in Washington with the developments in the Caspian region in the 1990s. In the Caspian region as well as in (West) Africa they identify a 'trajectory of ever-expanding U.S. military involvement' where oil reserves and an alleged terrorist threat form the key determinants for the U.S. engagement (Klare/Volman 2006).

Djibouti in 2002. Along with French, Spanish and German troops, 1,700 American soldiers are monitoring the Red Sea and the Somali borders. However, the effectiveness of this force was doubted from the very beginning, as weapons continue to reach Somalia. In reaction to the second severe terrorist attack on the Paradise hotel near the Kenyan coastal city of Mombasa in November 2002, U.S. President George W. Bush set up the 'Eastern Africa Counter-Terrorism Initiative', funded by the State Department with U.S.$ 100 million over five years.

Engaging the Sahel Region

Around the same time the U.S. European Command of the U.S. Armed Forces (Eucom) was trying to persuade the Department of State that a similar counter-terrorism initiative is needed in another part of Africa as well. A region that was actually recovering from instability and that had no known links to international terrorism: the Sahel. The political rationality of the 'Pan Sahel Initiative' and its reproduction by the media constitute an illustrative example of how security experts problematized a whole geographical region in order to pave the way for an expansion of influence and control. Within several months this diverse region was represented as a space where terrorists, arms dealers and human traffickers roam freely and where, therefore, 'this nation has to act', to paraphrase U.S. president Bush's justification for pre-emptive action. It was thus securitized. Jeremy Keenan estimates that around 3,000 journalistic articles were published in the twelve months after the hostage-taking of thirty-two European tourists in 2003, reproducing the narrative of the Sahel as Africa's lawless and dangerous 'Wild West' (Keenan 2005: 622; *San Francisco Chronicle*, 27 December 2005).

Based on the few deviant voices, I will trace the rationalities of this discourse and its transformation into concrete interventions. These strategies have severe ramifications within the region insofar as they have enabled political actors in the region to appropriate, to instrumentalize and even to shape the discourse and interventionist policies to a certain extent. The militarisation of the region, which aimed at strengthening the capabilities of the governments in regions where state authorities have only limited influence, threatens to have unintended effects.

The official trigger for the engagement of the U.S. in the Sahel region may be seen in the hostage-taking of thirty-two European tourists in Southern Algeria by the 'Groupe Salafiste pour la Prédication et le Combat' (GSPC) in 2003, an action that Eucom's then Deputy Commander Charles Wald considered a 'blessing in disguise' (Village Voice, 31 January 2006). As after the end of the Cold War most of the conflicts Eucom was dealing with simply faded away, Eucom had to find new challenges in order to justify the resources

it is being allocated. That is why a State Department official once called Eucom's new activities in Africa 'a hammer looking for a nail' (ibid.).
In 2002, the year before the hostage-taking, a conflict between Eucom and the State Department over the appropriate U.S. policy towards the Sahel region was developing. The State Department had reservations against Eucom's aggressive military strategy, and particularly against the proposed aerial bombings against militants in northern Mali. The U.S. embassy in Mali strongly warned against the radicalizing effects those strikes against what were believed Arab nomads rather than terrorists would have (ibid.). The plans were dropped, but after the hostage-taking in spring of 2003 a slightly altered counter-terrorism programme, the Pan-Sahel Initiative, could take off. The main goal of this operation was to enable the militaries of Mauritania, Mali, Niger and Chad to effectively control their whole state territory and to prevent cross border movements of 'illicit arms, drugs, goods and people' (Eucom Interview 2005). Eucom acted as an agenda-setter in 'putting the Sahara on the map as a new front in the war on terror' (*BBC World Service*, 8 and 15 August 2005).[10] And despite the fact that the Department of State officially established the PSI, it was Eucom's public policy machinery which was able to mobilize the media by reproducing the argument of 'an ungoverned Sahara as a breeding ground for terrorists':

'They're there for a purpose, whether it's looking for real estate or recruiting or looking for arms, whatever it is, we know there's a preserve. It may be small but it's a bad indicator. [...] It's an area we think is becoming appealing potentially for terrorist organisations or individuals to operate with semi-impunity. [...] It has a lot of expanses of open area that are conducive to terrorist operations or sanctuary' (Eucom's former Deputy Commander, General Charles Wald in Associated Press 2004).

In the West, one can receive attention for Africa – beyond humanitarian issues – particularly by referring to security interests. While security issues always were part of the Northern engagement with the South, 9/11 changed the weighting of phenomena such as migration, arms proliferation, disease, and terrorism. They are now represented as interconnected problems on the same scale of 'risks of open borders', which therefore, so the implication, have to be addressed by the same means of intervention. Within the predominant 'war on terror' the military – as we can see not only in Eucom's engagement with the Sahel – has a special role to play.

---

10 Eucom is responsible for the coordination of the U.S. forces in Europe, large parts of the former Soviet Union and Africa, with the exception of East Africa, the Horn, Egypt and Sudan.

Through an extraordinary public relations policy Eucom disseminated their authoritative knowledge about the terrorist threat originating in the Sahel and the military way to its solution. The perpetual rhetoric of the uncontrolled Sahel and the action needed to counter this supposed threat was escorted by an extensive use of maps, aiming at illustrating the dimensions of the problem. These maps are indicative manifestations of the political rationality within U.S. security circles. They categorize and simplify whole regions and create urgency to take action.

Mapping the Threat

It is commonly expected that maps provide guidance and orientation in representing geographical areas. They have long been considered as adequately describing territories, as 'mirroring' spaces. However, geographers early on acknowledged that maps are simplifying devices – as indeed they have to be since they face the challenge to collapse three-dimensional spaces into a two-dimensional form. Such simplifications necessarily have political implications. As Harley puts it: 'Maps are too important to be left to cartographers alone' (2001b: 149). Maps constitute value-laden images and are deeply involved in the relations of power and knowledge. Harley reminds his readers to look '[...] not through the map at the world it depicts but inwards or backwards to its maker and outwards or forwards to its readers' (quoted in Andrews 2001: 6).

In fact, cartography has played an important role in state-making from the seventeenth century onwards. Rulers of the emerging states after the Peace of Westphalia needed to negotiate and mark their territories. During the Imperial Age maps became powerful tools in establishing borders, claiming ownership of various territories across the globe. As Mark Neocleous put it: The map as an illustration for identity, sovereignty, and legitimacy within a demarcated space 'became the perfect symbol of the state' (Neocleous 2003: 119). The map in its political functionality creates and constructs a reality rather than representing it, using the techniques of selection, omission, simplification, classification, creation of hierarchies, and symbolisation (Harley 2001b: 163; Neocleous 2003: 120). Maps serve the project of the modern state in collecting information about space and transforming it into an object of political knowledge by classifying and generalizing landscapes – similar to the role statistics have in gathering data on the state population. Neocleous has pointed to the mystifying effects of maps. By omitting authorship and interest and by pretending accuracy and actual facts, the map is naturalizing: Borders become accepted, violence is obliterated and – through the reiteration of the own map – emotions towards the homeland are activated (Neocleous 2003: 123).

In our context, the mechanisms of silencing constitute the most important feature as empty spaces on maps are deliberate positivist statements (Harley, summarized by Andrews 2001: 13). Harley identified various ways of silencing in maps: A space can be described as empty and information can deliberately be withheld. Here he refers to the omission for certain reasons like 'x has [...] properties that render it unsuitable for inclusion in this map' (ibid. 14). Neocleous reminded us that the Oxford English Dictionary describes 'off the map', as something 'obsolete' and even 'out of existence' (Neocleous 2003: 121).

Therefore, maps are political and at the same time '[de-socialising] the territory they present. They foster the notion of a socially empty space' (Harley 2001a: 81). However, in deconstructing the map, Harley identified possibilities to challenge the hegemonic representations: 'By dismantling [a text, a map] we build' (Harley 2001b: 168). In his conclusion he stresses the need for alternative actions: 'If we can accept intertextuality then we can start to read our maps for alternative and sometimes competing discourses' (ibid.).[11]

The securitisation of the Sahel region by U.S. military experts was accompanied by the extensive use of visual aids. The selected maps below were applied at Eucom-workshops to illustrate the urgency of the Pan Sahel Initiative.[12]

---

11 The need for a 'cognitive mapping' in order to stay capable of political action in a capitalist system was famously raised by Jameson (1984: 83 ff.)
12 The shown maps were used at Eucom workshops within the programme of the Africa Clearing House, which is a discussion forum on security issues in Africa. Map 1 was created by The Economist but was used by Eucom.

Map 1: Africa's key problems

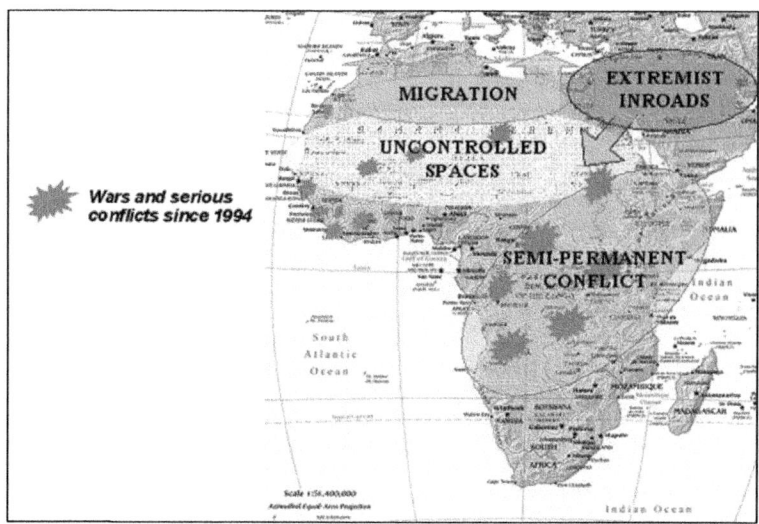

Source: Eucom

Map 1 gives a simplified overview of Africa's presumed key problems. Almost the whole continent seems to be under severe stress and is dominated by four features: conflict, uncontrolled spaces, extremism and migration into Europe. According to Eucom, U.S. operations in Iraq and Afghanistan 'squeezed' terrorists out of these regions into Africa as the 'extremist inroads' from the Arab peninsula show. This 'squeeze-theory' was used on a regular basis by the U.S. military to claim a link between terrorism in the Middle East and Africa.[13] A 'semi-permanent' conflict belt stretches from Somalia in the northeast across Central Africa to Angola in the southwest. Interestingly it includes relatively peaceful regions like Tanzania and Kenya. The whole Sahel area consists of 'uncontrolled spaces', from which there is a massive flow of migration across North Africa into Europe. During the last three years Eucom officials have been very active in the public realm to share their characterisation of the region. They continually depicted the Trans-Sahara region as 'vast empty spaces', 'remote expanses', as 'ungoverned', 'under-governed' or 'poorly policed' regions. The first two characteristics strengthen our perception of the Sahara as a blank space on the globe, a mysterious region we have insufficient knowledge about. It is a region which is not yet classified. However, the latter descriptions applied by Eucom have somewhat clearer implications. These are normative attributions smoothing the way for an active – and

---

13 See for example Stars and Stripes, 11 January 2004 or Washington File, 23 March 2004.

military – engagement, regardless of the actual presence of internationally operating terrorists in the region. This pattern of levelling and homogenizing the diverse space of the Sahelian Sahara, supported by the illustrating maps below, deliver an easy-to-grasp classification of the proposed area of operation.

Map 2: The terrorist corridor in the Sahel region

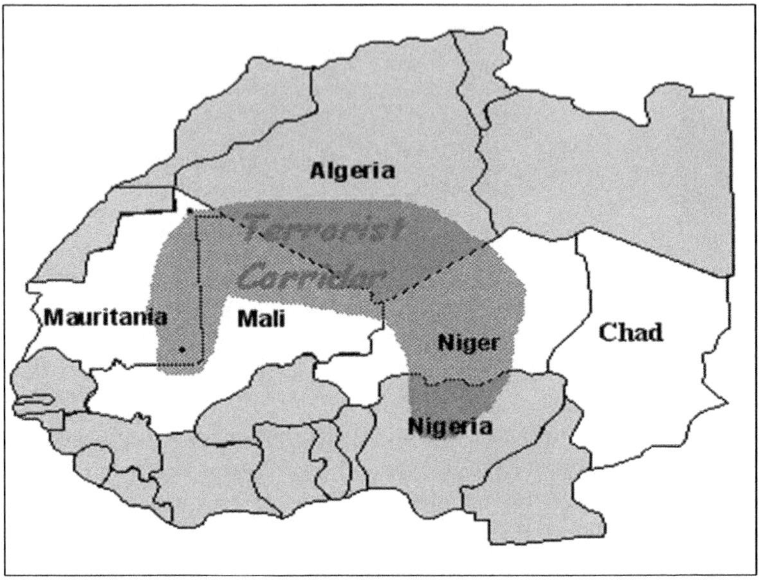

Source: Eucom

On map 2 the whole Sahel region is not only uncontrolled, but forms a terrorist belt reaching from Mauritania across Mali, southern Algeria and Niger into northern Nigeria. In map 3 this belt is expanded even further to the shores of the Mediterranean Sea in the northwest. Remarkably – with the exception of Senegal, but including Libya – safe havens for extremists can be found in all the countries the successor of the PSI, the Trans-Sahara Counter-Terrorist Initiative, will later operate in. According to this map, terrorists are now believed to 'operate throughout the Sahel'. This strategic manifestation of an increased threat is needed to justify the broadening of the counter-terrorism initiatives. In map 3 geopolitical arguments are applied to illustrate a situation that illustrates urgency: 'Interiors are too large to enforce laws' or 'borders are unable to be regulated or patrolled due to enormous size'. Again, geographical size is self-explanatorily related to an absence of order and to terrorist activity. With the expansion of the PSI, Eucom offers another solution to the 'problematic' of the Sahel. The illustration tells us that the fight against terrorism demands cross-border operations, whereas the goal of the Trans-Saharan Counter-

Terrorism Initiative is to reinforce national borders and to control movements on the ground. The solution for the transnational problem is – at least publicly – still seen in the effective nation-state.

Map 3: The expanded terrorist area

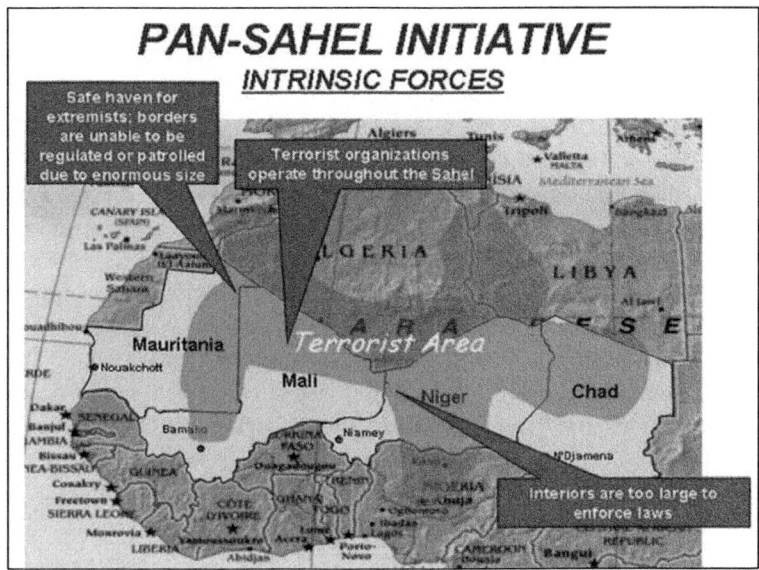

Source: Eucom

Broadening the Intervention

The Trans-Sahara Counter-Terrorism Partnership (TSCTP), as the initiative is being called after the most recent renaming, is an inter-agency programme, formally led by the Department of State. Apart from the State Department, it involves the Military, the Treasury Department, the Justice Department and the development agency USAID (*New York Times*, 10 June 2005). A certain part of its budget will be managed by USAID. As part of the U.S. State Department USAID has always been an integral pillar of the U.S. foreign policy. Since the 9/11 attacks, however, the convergence of development and security politics has been intensified. Applying the 'whole-of-government'-approach within the counter-terrorism initiative TSCTP, USAID's goal is to 'create a "line" past which the spread of Islamic extremism stops from entering into sub-Saharan West Africa' (USAID 2006). USAID focuses on supporting local governance and on the establishment of a conflict early warning system. Aware of the reservations against an American presence in the Sahel region,

USAID has additionally set up a TSCTP-programme to support marginalized parts of the population in Mauritania, Chad and Niger.

Despite its repeated denial to establish permanent bases in Africa, U.S. president Bush announced in February 2007 the establishment of a 'unified combatant command for Africa' (Africom), a step that reflects the growing strategic interest and the preventive policy approach of the U.S. in Africa.[14] However, U.S. officials were quick to stress that the new command is more than a pure military affair. It is rather seen as a showcase for the now fashionable inter-agency approach and will deal with 'humanitarian assistance', 'disaster relief' but will 'have the responsibility to do whatever military operations that the secretary of defense and the president direct' (DoD 2007). The aim of Africom, according to Pentagon officials, is to 'prevent problems from becoming crises and crises from becoming catastrophes' in light of 'poor governance, wars and population pressures' and 'natural threats' (American Forces Press Service 2006). At the same time, however, the Pentagon insists that the establishment of Africom does not mean an expansion in numbers of combat troops permanently based on the continent (DoD 2007).

'The long war' as the 'war on terror' has been dubbed, rather requires rapid (re-)actions in different parts of the world. To meet the challenges of 'irregular' warfare by non-state actors, the U.S. prefers to aim for temporary basing rights. Often, 'bare-bone facilities' (Klare/Volman 2006: 302) like airstrips or warehouses are sufficient for use in a prompt time frame. In the Trans-Sahara region the U.S. Department of Defence has access to airfields or ports in Algeria, Mali, Senegal, Gabon, Morocco and Tunisia (ibid. 303).

How can this form of intervention be conceptualized while integrating a spatial perspective? From a transnational lens, PSI and TSCTP can be described as flexible types of 'transterritorial deployments' (Latham 2001: 72). As Latham has illustratively shown, such transterritorial deployments differ from other forms of transboundary formations such as arenas and networks. Transterritorial deployments can be defined as purposeful placements of an external entity (unit, representative, organisation) into a local context in which they keep their external identity by retaining strong links to the context from which they are deployed (ibid. 75 ff.). Following Latham, these deployments differ in scope and time, that is, they can include a broad or a narrow agenda (annexation of a territory vs. an expedition or a humanitarian relief operation), and they can be temporary or permanent (military campaign vs. religious missions). As shown above, with the expansion of the PSI into the TSCTI/TSCTP the scope of the deployment was broadened. On the one hand, this reflects a

---

14 Africom will then be responsible for the whole continent with the exception of Egypt, which will remain under the responsibility of the U.S. Central Command. Africom is supposed to be fully operational by September 2008.

more comprehensive notion of security among policy-makers after 9/11, which requires action of the full-range of government. On the other hand, an intensified engagement influences the social impact in the particular region. Short and narrow deployments such as the Pan Sahel Initiative have the greatest 'situational power', as Latham calls it. They focus on a narrow area of concern, a situation such as a famine, a refugee crisis or, as in our case, a perceived security threat by terrorists in the Trans-Sahel. By doing so, people, discourses and resources are drawn into this concrete situation and power emerges from the delimited focus of the operation: 'It is the power not to have to take on responsibility entailed by these powers over and within society. It is the power to enter and withdraw relatively flexible from situations' (ibid. 82). This reflects to a certain extent the military strategies within the 'long war'.

For many people in the Sahel the biggest concern is the militarisation of the region by the U.S., who aims at expanding often autocratic state structures. The presence of foreign or national military is encountered with distrust, as state actions were considered the source of violence and arbitrariness in the past. Publicly branded as a 'hot spot for terrorism', people fear that the economic marginalisation will aggravate as long as their region is dealt with as a security problem.

It can only be speculated why exactly the PSI expanded into the Trans-Sahara Counter-Terrorism Partnership, which also includes economic and development policies. To broaden the agenda of a transterritorial deployment usually means less flexibility, more responsibility for the local context and more interaction with people on the ground. Following the goal of the U.S. government, which is to prevent the spread of extremist thoughts into the region, gaining trust of the local people seems to be a necessary condition. 'Winning the hearts and minds' may, however, be feared to result in the imperial endeavour of a permanent management of these societies, a direction that is being discussed as 'trusteeship'. It is defined as the governance of territories by a mixture of transnational actors, including strong states, multilateral organisation, non-governmental organisations and domestic authorities (Fearon/Laitin 2004: 7 ff.)

Troublemakers in the Sahel?

It is beyond the scope of this contribution to assess the actual terrorist threat by Islamists in the Sahel. In fact, there are confusing and divergent statements coming from the region. Even reports resulting from long field works did not come to a decisive conclusion (ICG 2005a; Mc Govern in *BBC World Service*, 8 and 15 August 2005). Suffice it to say that in the beginning of the 1990s, the region was in a state of recovery: The brutal civil war in Algeria and the Tuareg rebellions in Mali and Chad came to an end, extremist groups were dispersed and tourists started to rediscover the region. The overall level of security in the countries improved. However, according to Keenan's analysis, this period came to an end shortly after with the advent of the Pan-Sahel Initiative (Keenan 2006: 270 ff.). For the U.S. government the kidnapping of the European tourists in Southern Algeria in 2003 was proof of the presence of Islamist terrorists in the Sahel, namely the GSPC, a splinter group of the Algerian Groupe Islamique Armé (GIA). However, several organisations, journalists and experts articulated doubts about the alleged acuteness of this threat. Keenan is convinced that the Algerian military intelligence services lured the Americans into the region by infiltrating the GSPC in order to rid the country of the international pariah status it had had in the 1990s and to attract foreign investments and military equipment: 'Probably 90 percent of the Saharan population, as far as I can make it out, just know that the word GSPC now is a name for the Algerian intelligent services. And there is a lot of truth in that' (Keenan in *BBC World Service*, 8 and 15 August 2005).[15] The Algerian military service Département du Renseignement et de la Sécurité (DRS) has some experience in manipulating different groups. Former Algerian militaries made allegations that during the civil war the infiltration of armed rebel groups was a deliberate strategy of escalation of the DRS in order to undermine popular support for the Islamists (AI 2006: 8).

Since the hostage-taking of the European tourists in 2003 Algerian authorities and Eucom officials have been quick to stress this link between armed groups operating in the Sahel and al Qaeda, a claim that remains questionable until today.[16] In 2004 the U.S. State Department added the GSPC to its 'Terrorist Exclusion List'. However, at the same time the then U.S. ambassador to Mali, Vicki Huddleston, said that the Algerian GSPC did not constitute a threat in the region any longer (Faath 2005: 8). Yet, General Wald rated the risk of terrorism in the Sahel at '100 percent. They have already had terrorism in the Sahel region. It is a matter of how bad it could get' (Wald in *BBC World Service*, 8 and 15 August 2005). U.S. officials are unclear about whether terrorism already 'breeds' or 'could breed' in the region. Even Eucom admits that there is a dispute on whether the Sahel is a breeding ground or could become one (Eucom interview 2005). Within the paradigm of 'preemptive action' within U.S. foreign policy, the level of threat needs to be sustained in order to justify interventions and tough security measures. The secu-

---

15 In the same line see Le Monde diplomatique, February 2005.
16 For the ongoing dispute even amongst academics see the various articles in the special issue of the *Journal of Contemporary African Studies* 2007, 25 (1). Despite GSPC's self-proclaimed and widely reported merger with al-Qaeda, its character and role in Algeria remain ambiguous. See *Washington Post,* 5 October 2006.

ritisation of the Sahel and its persistent representation as a region characterized by the lack of governance, illegitimate cross-border trade and rising extremism gives a striking example. Thus, it does not matter whether terrorists are active in the region or whether 'roaming' people are affiliated to al Qaeda. It is sufficient to refer to the pure probability in the future, that is, to claim that the threat 'may materialize'. As Charles Wald put it: 'They are not necessarily al Qaeda but they'd like to be with al Qaeda and they have to be addressed' (Wald in *BBC World Service*, 8 and 15 August 2005).

Militarisation, Marginalisation and Discontent in the Sahel Region

Despite the relatively narrow scope of the U.S. counter-terrorism initiatives in Northern Africa, they deeply affect local settings. Conceptualizing spaces as empty or undergoverned are, as critical cartographers have shown, strong manifestations of political rationalities. They delimit spaces and assign certain characteristics to a territory. On the maps discussed above, the whole area of the Sahelian Sahara region is shown as an 'uncontrolled space', which is at the same time translated into instability and a threat to global security. The labelling of people of the Sahara as susceptible to terrorist activities constitutes an influential knowledge about this space which allowed for the counter-terrorism initiatives to be established. Yet, according to critical scholars, it was these interventions – aiming at fostering security – which have resulted in an increased instability within the affected countries:

'[…] far from furthering political stability, security and democracy, Washington's ill-conceived policy has taken North Africa and much of the Sahel – a region which is considerably larger than the entire USA – into a dangerous spiral of increased authoritarianism and repression, increased regional instability and insecurity, increased popular resentment of both Washington (anti-Americanism) and their own regimes and the increased threat of militant extremism' (Keenan 2006: 271).

There is no doubt about the fact that certain actors in the region, foremost state authorities, welcome the international counter-terrorism engagement as they profit in various ways from its presence. In a report, indicatively entitled *Islamic Terrorism in the Sahel – Fact or Fiction?*, the International Crisis Group, states: 'It is […] apparent that actors on the ground in these four countries [Mauritania, Mali, Niger, Chad – J.B.] are poised to use American fears of an Islamist threat to benefit financially and/or politically in ways that recall the manipulation of Cold War politics by many African governments' (ICG 2005a: 2).

Mauritania's government adapted to the discourse of the 'war on terror' most avowedly. Its performances aimed at confirming the perception of the Islamist threat that has dominated U.S. foreign policy since 9/11 (Jourde 2007: 87 ff.). The government of former President Maaouya Ould Taya construed the coup attempts of 2003 and 2004 as evidence for the existence of international terrorism within his country, although the plotters came from Mauritania and to a certain extent even from within the Mauritanian military. He overstated the internal Islamist threat and played down internal political cleavages (ICG 2005b). In April 2005 the government carried out a crackdown on Muslim leaders and in June it declared to have found evidence related to the GSPC. The U.S. government agreed with the assessment of the government of Taya in underlining that the biggest threat to Mauritania allegedly came from outside forces (*Associated Press*, 25 June 2005). The government quickly blamed Muslim fundamentalists for an attack on a Mauritanian border post near Lemgheyti in June 2005, where twenty-four people lost their lives.

However, opposition media and international experts claimed that several important questions remain unanswered.[17] Firstly, it is unrealistic that the GSPC would launch such a large scale attack just a few days before the beginning of the region's largest military manoeuvre, the United States-led Operation Flintlock, in which 4,000 troops including 1,000 U.S. soldiers took part. Secondly, why were over twenty vehicles, which the rebels allegedly used for the attack, not spotted by plane or satellite surveillance? Thirdly, why did the first soldiers at the scene, the Algerians, offer no assistance to the wounded? And finally, why did the government deny access to the wounded in the hospital? Additionally, experts on the ground doubt that the GSPC even has the capacity to carry out such a large attack. However, the most important question is what should be the reason for GSPC to attack Mauritania, as members of the group took refuge and received medical treatment in Mauritania earlier on? It rather seems to be the case that it was convenient for the government to blame the GSPC. At that time, human rights violations, widespread corruption, a growing inequality and frustration, particularly among people from the south who did not feel sufficiently represented in the state apparatus, was soaring in Mauritania. Several scholars are convinced that Ould Taya's tactics of securing support by constantly stressing an external terrorist threat to the country, proved to be successful for a considerable time (Jourde 2007: 77-78). The International Crisis Group argued that 'the Ould Taya government's anti-terrorist rhetoric accompanied by repressive actions appears to be primarily a convenient device for not tackling acute political problems' (ICG 2005a: 16 and 2005b).

---

17 See for the following BBC World Service, 8 and 15 August 2005.

Ould Taya's reign was ended by a coup d'état on 3 August 2005. Parts of the Mauritanian military under the former head of national security, Colonel Eli Ould Mohamed Vall, seized power while the president was abroad. Having known Ould Taya's rule, the international community remained largely silent in their reactions to the coup – despite their initial support of his politics. In a referendum in June 2006 the elaboration of a new constitution and the schedule for the transfer of power back to civilian rule were approved by an overwhelming majority of the Mauritanians. With the parliamentary and presidential elections held in November 2006 and March 2007, respectively, the military so far stuck to its promise.[18]

Temporarily, the coup had a subduing effect on the counter-terrorism initiatives in Mauritania. The U.S., who had trained Mauritanian soldiers in the PSI and in Operation Flintlock under the old government, put the training on hold and reassessed the political development. Today, however, the U.S. have arranged the reintegration of Mauritania into their 'International Military Education and Training Program' in 2007.

The main profiteer of closer ties to the U.S. seems to be Algeria. Due to the brutal massacres of the Algerian army in the civil war following the annulment of the 1992 elections, which the Islamist party FIS would have won, the country became an international outcast. The Army, the Military Security DRS and various militias committed large scale human rights violations in the name of 'fighting terrorists'. It was not until the Bush administration gained power that the economic and political relationship between the U.S. and Algeria under Abdelaziz Bouteflika as president were revived. Since 9/11 this relationship also involves the military and intelligence sectors (Faath 2005: 5). The Bouteflika government managed to convince the Bush administration that the two countries were fighting against the same extremist enemies and, therefore, should foster a symbiotic relationship. Since then, U.S. authorities have acknowledged the Algerian 'experience' in fighting terrorists. As members of the U.S. military stated, the United States can learn a lot from Algeria about fighting enemies in sparsely populated desert areas (Eucom interview 2005). Reversely, on a visit to Algeria, then U.S. defence secretary Donald Rumsfeld said that 'they need some things and we have things we can help with' (*New York Times*, 13 February 2006). In 2002 the Maghrebian countries were included in the U.S. Anti-Terror Assistance programme.

---

18 In March 2007 Sidi Mohamed Ould Cheikh Abdallahi, a former minister under Taya who lived in exile, was elected new president of Mauritania. At this stage, it is too early to predict Mauritania's future foreign policy. However, the fact that Abdallahi was seen as a 'consensus' candidate and that he was backed by the army makes a certain continuity in the relationship with the West highly probable.

Since then, the U.S. have multiplied their military and non-military aid to Algeria. Despite the still opaque role of the Algerian DRS[19] within the intra-Algerian conflict and the ongoing human rights violations, in the two years of 2005 and 2006 Algeria was permitted to buy military equipment from U.S. companies ('commercial sales') for more than U.S.$ 500 millions (Volman 2006; Department of State/USAID 2007: 734). Additionally, the European Union made Algeria one of the priority countries in their counter-terrorism assistance (Council of the EU 2005). Still, the dependency seems to be mutual. Keenan believes that the Americans rely on Algerian intelligence in the region, as they themselves lack capacities on the ground (Keean in *BBC World Service*, 8 and 15 August 2005). Some sources even claim that Algerian and U.S. military are jointly carrying out anti-terror operations across the Sahel, which is, however, constantly denied by the U.S. military (ibid. Eucom interview 2005). The close military relationship between Algeria and the U.S. is expected to have strengthened the notorious security establishment in Algeria. Despite the decrease in violent acts, a culture of impunity and torture still holds reign in the country. Keenan summarizes that the militarisation of the region has reinforced 'cleavages between ruling elites, protected by their security establishments, and the "unrepresented many"' (Keenan 2006: 271). Local Tuareg in the southern part of Algeria complained that since the Algerian government won the U.S. as their partner, the local state authorities – including the police and the DRS – act even more repressive against members of the opposition and civil society. This led to a widespread violent outbreak in the southern city of Tamanrasset in July 2005. There are allegations that state agents provoked these riots in order to prove 'extremist activity' in the region (Keenan 2005: 635).

In Mali an instrumentalisation of the 'war on terror' by the government was not performed as blantantly as in Mauritania. However, the extended counter-terrorism initiative has become a symbol for fostering the North-South divide in the country. While the government profits from both the international funding and the partnership with the West, Northern leaders are suspicious of a strengthened central government at a time when decentralisation is supposed to gain ground.

According to some scholars, the widely circulated and reiterated representation of Northern Mali as 'ungoverned' and the subsequent materialisation of the counter-terrorist rhetoric, undermines a trust-building co-operation between the government and the population in Northern Mali and is more likely to facilitate a destabilisation of the region (Gutelius 2007: 66 ff.). The U.S. military states that Mali is one of the most difficult cases within the TSCTP.

---

19 To date, no public information is available about the mandate and the organisation of the DRS (AI 2006: 7 ff.).

Eucom admits that they do not have an answer as yet to question of how to improve the security situation without destabilizing the region (Eucom interview 2005). Although the 1990s rebellions of the Tuareg in northern Mali were settled in 1996, there is still a high level of frustration amongst the Tuareg. The peace accord included the integration of former rebels into the Malian Army and investment in northern infrastructure (Klute/von Trotha 2000). However, the distrust against the national government persists. Local sources estimate that up to 90 percent of the Tuareg in towns like Kidal are unemployed and do not feel they can participate in development and investment programmes, despite the efforts made by the government to include the northern regions (*BBC World Service*, 8 and 15 August 2005). In fact, marginalisation continues to thrive as poverty remains the most challenging problem (*IRIN*, 14 October 2004, ICG 2005a: 20). Local Muslim leaders fear that hopeless youths could follow everyone who promises an opportunity, and that the dissatisfaction could make people susceptible to join fundamentalist groups who are present in northern Mali.

For many young people the cross-border trade constitutes the only possibility for social advancement. Northern Mali's livelihood depends on the trade across the Sahara. Virtually all products which can be found on the markets in Kidal come from Algeria. On the border there are hardly any customs posts, large parts of the traded goods remain undocumented. Cigarette smuggling is a lucrative business. It is particularly this uncontrolled cross-border movement of goods which worries the U.S. government the most. They fear that smuggling activities contribute to supporting terrorist operations. The primary goal of the U.S. counter-terrorism initiatives is to help the Malian government to effectively control their national borders and to cut-off cross-border smuggling. However, strengthening state structures and reinserting the presence of the Malian Army in the north is a sensitive issue.

Economically, the region has for a long time been a self-help system. In the 1990s, due to the privatisation policy of the World Bank, neglect of the region by the Malian government and corruption of formal markets, Islamic NGOs, coming from Saudi Arabia and Libya, introduced new economic possibilities into the area and made new resources accessible. They established development projects and provided services in areas that Western donors and the government neglected (Gutelius 2006). As there is no alternative for ensuring subsistence, a disruption of informal trade would deepen desperation and frustration. International experts compare this policy with the destruction of the poppy fields in Afghanistan. If one destroys the lifeblood of a region without offering an alternative, then the people may turn towards more extremist thoughts (Mc Govern in *BBC World Service*, 8 and 15 August 2005).[20] These informal networks offer possibilities for acquiring different kinds of capital for many young people. As David Gutelius put it:

'What the U.S. and its allies have failed to recognize is the multivariate nature of these struggles, which comprise in any case more than cigarette smuggling or other goods thought to fund al-Qaeda. Informal marketing activities are social mechanisms by which communities not only cope with serious environmental degradation and deep social change, but also the shifting formal sector markets over which they have little control and to which they have little access' (Gutelius 2006: 39).

Due to these developments, experts fear a new Tuareg rebellion.[21] An incident in May 2006 gave proof of the volatility of the region. On 23 May, several Tuaregs under the leadership of the former rebellion leader Hassan Fagaga attacked three military bases in Kidal and Menaka and took arms and ammunition. Six people were reported to have died during this action. Afterwards, the attackers demanded increased efforts for the development of the north and a more effective integration of Tuareg into the Malian Army.

Conclusion

The article critically analysed the integration of the Sahel into the 'war on terror' by the various practices of 'problematizing' the region. A spatial perspective on this process shows which kinds of images were assigned to these geographical spaces in order to create the sense of urgency which has legitimized the interventions in the Sahel. After demonstrating the range of techniques used by the U.S. government, the article sought to show how the rhetoric and the subsequent counter-terrorism initiatives affect the social relations in the countries on different levels. The discourse of the 'war on terror', which works rather like a global template, has opened various ways for governments to use its rhetoric to meet their own ends. As critical voices have shown, it is not unlikely that the counter-terrorism initiatives have become a cash cow for governments who know that using the T-word will certainly raise awareness in Washington. Such tactics threaten to render a profound dealing with internal conflicts, such as the marginalisation and exclusion of the population in

---

20 In November 2006 Mali's application for funding under the U.S. Millennium Challenge Account was approved. The country signed a 'development Compact' and will receive 461 million U.S. $ for irrigation and infrastructure projects by the U.S. government over the next five years.
21 As the Malian professor Aboubacrim Ag Hindi put it: 'The biggest danger in this region is not al-Qaida. It is famine. If the development of these zones is not undertaken, we may see more rebellion there' (IRIN, 14 October 2004).

the remote areas of the Sahel countries, impossible. So far, the expanded security policies in parts of Algeria, Mali and Mauritania have revealed their repressive effects and have resulted in growing frustration which, in turn, may lead to resistance or disengagement among the excluded groups. Finally, a Western policy focusing solely on expanding government control into areas where distrust against the central state prevails, where internal conflicts may flare up again, where the ecological and economic vulnerability is high and, not least, oil resources were recently discovered[22], is on the verge of promoting unintended consequences. However, such a policy reflects the persistence of state-centred views in the North despite the operation of other modes of social control and governance in many postcolonial settings.

With regard to epistemology and methodology, pioneering research aiming at a full understanding of the 'social life of the war on terror' needs to focus on different levels: a thorough textual analysis helps to identify the rationalities of political actors and security professionals about the problematic of 'undergoverned' spaces and populations; a study of knowledge production makes obvious the conditions of its translation and dissemination from the global into the local. Additionally, future research must examine the mechanisms of appropriation of the discourse and its conversion into security practices in the region. Finally, an ethnographic analysis explores the reactions of the problematized groups to the exclusionary policies which deeply affect the social fabric. There is no doubt that hegemonic discourses and subsequent interventions are to different extents translated, internalized or challenged on the ground. An interdisciplinary approach that combines a multi-sited ethnographic with a political-sociological approach, sharing an interest in the analysis of the global topography of security (on a macro level), of the conditions of knowledge production (on a medium level) and of the everyday security practices and reactions to them (on a micro level) can yield a heuristic value in revealing the multifaceted apparatus of the 'war on terror'.

---

22 There are offshore fields in Mauritania and oil fields in the Tuareg areas in northern Mali and at the border to Niger. Additionally, neighbouring Nigeria is the 5th biggest oil provider for the U.S. Africa will come up for 25 percent of the U.S. oil consumption within the next years. U.S. energy companies have invested 45 billion $ in exploring oil fields, 50 billion $ are due to be invested (ICG 2005a: 26). The former acting assistant secretary of state for African Affairs, Charles Snyder, said: 'It used to be a kind of cruel joke twenty years ago when some of us tried to pretend Africa might rise to the level of a strategic interest, but thanks to the oil deposits we're finding every day in and near Africa, I can say with a straight face 30 percent of our oil will come from there, and I promise you it is a strategic interest' (ICG 2005a: 25).

References

Abrahamsen, R. (2005): 'Blair's Africa: The Politics of Securitization and Fear', *Alternatives*, 30(1): 55-80.
Agnew, J. (1998): *Geopolitics*, London: Routledge.
Agnew, J./Corbridge, S. (1995): *Mastering Space: Hegemony, Territory and International Political Economy*, London: Routledge.
Allen, J. (2003): 'Power'. In: J. Agnew/K. Mitchell/G. Ó Tuathail (eds), *A Companion to Political Geography*, Oxford: Blackwell, pp. 95-108.
Amnesty International (2006): *Unrestrained Powers. Torture by Algeria's Military Security*, AI index: MDE 28/004/2006. July 2006.
Andrews, J.H. (2001): 'Introduction: Meaning, Knowledge, and Power in the Map Philosophy of J.B. Harley'. In: J.B. Harley (ed.), *The New Nature of Maps*, Baltimore: The Johns Hopkins University Press, pp. 1-32.
Beall, J./Goodfellow, T./Putzel, J. (2006): 'Introductory Article: on the Discourse of Terrorism, Security and Development', *Journal of International Development*, 18(1): 51-67.
Bigo, D. (2000): 'When two Become one. Internal and External Securitisations in Europe'. In: M. Kelstrup/M. Williams (eds), *International Relations Theory and the Politics of European Integration: Power, Security and Community*, London: Routledge, pp. 171-204.
—— 2002. 'Security and Immigration: towards a Critique of the Governmentality of Unease', *Alternatives*, 27 (Special Issue): 63-92.
Bilgin, P./Morton, A.D. (2002): 'Historicising Representations of 'Failed States': beyond the Cold War Annexation of the Social Sciences?' *Third World Quarterly*, 23(1): 55-80.
—— (2004): 'From Rogue to Failed States? The Fallacy of Short-termism', *Politics*, 24(3): 169-80.
Buzan, B./de Wilde, J./Wæver, O. (1998): *Security: a New Framework for Analysis*, Boulder: Lynne Rienner.
Campbell D. (1998): *Writing Security. United States Foreign Policy and the Politics of Identity*, revised edition, Minneapolis: University of Minnesota Press.
Dalby, S./Ó Tuathail, G. (1998): 'Introduction' In: S. Dalby/G. Ó Tuthail (eds), *Rethinking Geopolitics*, London, New York: Routledge, pp. 1-15.
Dillon, M. (1996): *Politics of Security: towards a Political Philosophy of Continental Thought*, London: Routledge.
Duffield, M. (2001): *Global Governance and the New Wars*, London: Zed Press.
Faath, S. (2005): 'US-Engagement im Sahelraum: Terrorismusbekämpfung als Vorwand oder Notwendigkeit', *DOI Fokus*, 18 January 2005 (Deutsches Orient-Institut Hamburg).

Fearon, J.D./Laitin, D.D. (2004): 'Neotrustreeship and the Problem of Weak States', *International Security*, 28(4): 5-43.

Foucault, M. (1980): *Power/Knowledge: Selected Interviews and other Writings 1972- 1977*, ed. C. Gordon, Brighton: Harvester.

—— (2000): 'The Subject and Power'. In: J.D. Faubion (ed.), *Essential Works of Foucault 1954-1984. Vol. 3: Power*, London: Penguin, pp. 326-48.

—— (2006a): *Sicherheit, Territorium, Bevölkerung. Geschichte der Gouvernementalität 1. Vorlesungen am Collège de France 1977-1978*, Frankfurt/Main: Suhrkamp.

—— (2006b): *Die Geburt der Biopolitik. Geschichte der Gouvernementalität 2. Vorlesungen am Collège de France 1978-1979*, Frankfurt/Main: Suhrkamp.

Goldwyn, D. (2005): 'Africa's Petroleum Industry', Paper presented at the Symposium *Africa: Vital to U.S. Security?* National Defense University, Washington, D.C., 15 November 2005.

Gutelius, D. (2006): 'War on Terror and Social Networks in Mali', *ISIM Review*, 17 (Spring 2006): 38-39.

—— (2007): 'Islam in Northern Mali and the War on Terror', *Journal of Contemporary African Studies*, 25(1): 59-76.

Harley, J.B. (2001a): 'Maps, Knowledge, Power'. In: J.B. Harley (ed.), *The New Nature of Maps*, Baltimore: Johns Hopkins University Press, pp. 51-81.

—— (2001b): 'Deconstructing the Map'. In: J.B. Harley, (ed.), *The New Nature of Maps*, Baltimore: Johns Hopkins University Press, pp. 149-68.

Harvey, D. (1989): *The Condition of Postmodernity. An Enquiry into the Origins of Cultural Change*, Oxford: Blackwell.

Hönke, J. (2005): 'Fragile Staatlichkeit und der Wandel der Afrikapolitik nach 1990', *University of Leipzig Papers on Africa. Politics and Economics Series, no 77*.

Huysmans, J. (1998): 'Revisiting Copenhagen or about the Creative Development of a Security Studies Agenda in Europe', *European Journal of International Relations*, 4(4): 488-506.

International Crisis Group (2005a): *Terror in the Sahara – Fact or Fiction?* Africa Report 92, 31 March 2005.

—— (2005b): *L'Islamisme dans l'Afrique du Nord IV: Contestation Islamiste en Mauritanie: Menace ou Bouc Emissaire?* Rapport Moyenne-Orient/Afrique du Nord Nr. 41, 11 May 2005.

Jacoby, T. (2005): 'Cultural Determinism, Western Hegemony and the Efficacy of Defective States', *Review of African Political Economy*, 32(104/105): 215-33.

Jameson, F. (1984): 'Postmodernism or the Cultural Logic of Late Capitalism', *New Left Review*, I(146), (July/August 1984): 53-92.

Jourde, C. (2007): 'Constructing Representations of the 'Global War on Terror' in the Islamic Republic of Mauritania', *Journal of Contemporary African Studies*, 25(1): 77-100.

Keenan, J. (2004a): 'Terror in the Sahara: the Implications of U.S. Imperialism for North & West Africa', *Review of African Political Economy*, 101(31): 475-96.

—— (2004b): 'Political Destabilisation and Blowback in the Sahel', *Review of African Political Economy*, 31(102): 691-98.

—— (2005): 'Waging War on Terror: Implications of America's 'New Imperialism' for Saharan Peoples', *Journal of North African Studies*, 10(3-4): 619-47.

—— (2006): 'Security and Insecurity in North Africa', *Review of African Political Economy*, 33(108): 269-96.

Klare, M./Volman, D. (2006): 'America, China and the Scramble for Africa's Oil', *Review of African Political Economy*, 33(108): 297-309.

Klingebiel, S. ed. (2006): *New Interfaces between Security and Development*, Bonn: Deutsche Stiftung für Internationale Entwicklung.

Klute, G./von Trotha, T. (2000): 'Wege zum Frieden. Vom Kleinkrieg zum parastaatlichen Frieden im Norden von Mali', *Sociologus*, 50(1): 1-36.

Lefebvre, H. ([1974] 1991): *The Production of Space*, Oxford: Blackwell.

Latham, R. (2001): 'Identifying the Contours of Transboundary Political Life'. In: T. Callaghy/R. Kasimir/R. Latham (eds), *Intervention and Transnationalism in Africa*, Cambridge: Cambridge University Press, pp. 69-92.

Lemke, T. (1997): *Kritik der politischen Vernunft: Foucaults Analysen der modernen Gouvernementalität*, Hamburg, Berlin: Argument.

McSweeney, B. (1996): 'Identity and Security: Buzan and the Copenhagen School', *Review of International Studies*, 22(1): 81-93.

—— (1998): 'Durkheim and the Copenhagen School: a Response to Buzan and Wæver', *Review of International Studies*, 24(1): 137-40.

Neocleous, M. (2000): 'Against Security', *Radical Philosophy*, 100 (March/April 2000): 7-15.

—— (2003): *Imagining the State*, Maidenhead: Open University Press.

Ó Tuathail, G. (1996): *Critical Geopolitics*, London: Routledge.

—— (1998): 'Postmodern Geopolitics? The Modern Geopolitical Imagination and beyond'. In: S. Dalby/G. Ó Tuathail (eds), *Rethinking Geopolitics*, London, New York: Routledge, 16-38.

Rose, N. (1999): *Powers of Freedom: Reframing Political Thought*, Cambridge: Cambridge University Press.

Rose, N./Miller, P. (1992): 'Political Power beyond the State: Problema-

tics of Government', *British Journal of Sociology*, 43(2): 173-205.
Sack, R.D. (1986): *Human Territoriality: its Theory and History*, Cambridge: Cambridge University Press.
Soja, E. (1989): *Postmodern Geographies. The Reassertation of Space in Critical Social Theory*, London: Verso.
Volman, D. (2006): *U.S. Military Programmes in Sub-Saharan Africa 2005-2007*, Washington, D.C. (Association of Concerned Africa Scholars) http://www.prairienet.org/acas/military/military06.html (accessed November 2006).

Official Documents, Reports and Speeches

American Forces Press Service (2006): *Officials Weigh Need for Africa Command*, 6 December 2006. Washington, D.C. http://www defenselink.mil/news/NewsArticle.aspx?ID=2327 (accessed 7 February 2007).
AusAID (Australian Agency for International Development) (2003): *Counterterrorism and Australian Aid*, Canberra.
CIDA (Canadian International Development Agency) (2005): *Canada's International Policy Statement: Development*, Gatineau.
Bush, George W. (2002): *Speech Given at the U.S. Military Academy West Point*. 1 June 2002. http://www.whitehouse/gov/news/releases//2002/06/20020601-3.html (accessed July 2006).
Council of the EU (2005): *Report on the Implementation of the Action Plan to Combat Terrorism. Document 15704/05*. December 2005. http://ec.europa.eu/justice_home/fsj/terrorism/strategies/fsj_terrorism_stra tegies_counter_en.htm (accessed October 2006).
Danish Ministry of Foreign Affairs (2004): *Principles Governing Danish Development Assistance for the Fight against the New Terrorism*. http://www.um.dk/en/menu/DevelopmentPolicy/DanishDevelopmentPolic y/FightagainsttheNewTerrorism/ (accessed January 2007).
Department of Defense (2006): *Quadrennial Defense Review Report*, Washington, D.C.
—— (2007): *News Briefing with Ryan Henry, Principal Deputy Undersecretary of Defense for Policy and Army Lt. Gen. Walter L. Sharp, Director, Joint Staff*. Washington, D.C. 7 February 2007. http://www.defenselink.mil/Transcripts/Transcript.aspx?TranscriptID=3882 (accessed 7 February 2007).
DFID (Department for International Development) (2005): *Why We Need to Work More Effectively in Fragile States*, London.

Department of State and USAID (2003): *Security, Democracy, Prospe-rity: Strategic Plan 2004-2009*, Washington, D.C.
—— (2007): *Congressional Budget Justification Foreign Operations 2008*, Washington, D.C.
European Union (2003): *A Secure Europe in a Better World. The European Security Strategy*, Brussels.
OECD/Development Assistance Committee (2003): *A Development Cooperation Lens on Terrorism Prevention. Key Entry Points for Action*, Paris.
Straw, J. (2002): 'Failing and Failed States', Speech Given at the University of Birmingham, 6 September 2002.
USAID (U.S. Agency for International Development) (2002): *Foreign Aid in the National Interest: Promoting Freedom, Security and Opportunity*, Washington, D.C.
—— (2005): *Fragile States Strategy*, Washington, D.C.
—— (2006): Congressional Budget Justification 2007. West Africa Regional Program. http://www.usaid.gov/policy/budget/cbj200/afr/warp.html (accessed October 2006).
White House (2002): *The U.S. National Security Strategy*, Washington, D.C.
—— (2003): *The National Strategy for Combating Terrorism*, Washington, D.C.

Interviews

Interview at the European Command Headquarters, Stuttgart, 25 August 2005.

Media

Associated Press. *Mauritania Debates Anti-Terror Campaign*, 25 June 2005.
——. *U.S. General: al-Qaida Eyeing Africa*, 5 April 2004.
BBC. *Secret in the Sands*, Broadcasted by BBC World Service on 8 August 2005 (part one) and on 15 August 2005 (part two).
IRIN. *Mauritania: Junter Leader Vows to Fight Terrorism, Confirms Ties with Israel*, 11 October 2005.
—— *West Africa: Famine not Fanaticism Poses Greatest Terrorist Threat in Sahel*, 14 October 2004.
Le Monde diplomatiqe. *El Para, the Maghreb's bin Laden*, February 2005.
New York Times. *Rumsfeld's Algeria: Arms Sales and Closer Ties*, 13 February 2006.

New York Times. *As Africans Join Iraqi Insurgency, U.S. Counters with Military Training in their Lands*, 10 June 2005.

San Francisco Chronicle. *U.S. Takes Terror Fight to 'Africa's Wild West'*, 27 December 2005.

Stars and Stripes. *Eucom Slated to Step up Role in Africa*, European Edition, 11 January 2004.

Village Voice. *Pursuing Terrorists in the Great Desert. The U.S. Military's $500 Million Gamble to Prevent the Next Afghanistan*, 31 January 2006.

Washington File (U.S. Department of State). *US-African Partnership Helps Counter Terrorists in Sahel Region*, 23 March 2004.

Washington Post. *Al-Qaeda's Far-Reaching New Partner*, 5 October 2006.

Islamic Activism and Anti-terrorism Legislation in Morocco

BERTRAM TURNER

Introduction

The aim of this paper is to analyse different aspects of the socio-legal transformation which the integration of the Moroccan state into the international war on terror unleashed in the country after a period of intense exposure to transnational Islamic activism. It will be argued that this transformation opened up new vistas for actors with divergent interests, leading to a readjustment of their agencies under the conditions of changed interdependencies that permeate through scales and frames. The interactions between global, national and local scales are approached here as scalar arrangements. These are socially constructed through political-legal interaction and are dependent on the socio-political and juridical agendas of those actors who are empowered by those arrangements.[1] The focus on scalar arrangements draws attention to the dynamics in power relations between actors at different scales.

Focusing on these scalar interdependencies, the state's response to terrorism and Islamic activism in Morocco is analysed in conjunction with the reaction of the rural population in southwestern Morocco both to activities of the prominent Islamic movement in this rural area, the Salafiyya, and to the effects of anti-terror legislation. The period of time to be examined in this respect is that between the emergence of Islamic activism in one rural area in the southwest of Morocco in 1999 and the end of the year 2006. Turning

---

1   Cf. Purcel/Brown (2005) for environmental issues and Tsing (2005) for an integration of the concept of scale in the anthropology of globalisation; cf. Herod/Wright (2002) for a wider theoretical frame.

points or key dates structuring this time frame are the terrorist attacks of 11 September 2001 in New York and of 16 May 2003 in Casablanca. The reactions to these events on state level as well as in a remote rural area will be analysed as an interconnected and globally embedded process. While focusing on the consequences the adoption of an anti-terror legislation had at a local scale, these will not be considered as independent of particular social conditions the preceding Salafi impact had created.

The context of law and terror has found increasing resonance in recent times – with reference to a quite limited and upscale empirical basis, however.[2] If one looks at the empirical lowlands where legal practice is generated, it becomes obvious, so my argument, that the intertwining of Islamic activism and anti-terror legislation triggers a series of interactions between locales, the state and a global environment. For this context, the analysis necessitates reference to rather different types of data. Sets of empirical data and information collected and extracted from oral transmissions in the form of hearsay, gossip, rumours and narratives, are included into the analysis just as are official statements and the reaction to Islamic activism in the public debate and the media in Morocco. Therefore, my argumentation is based on a balance between empirical facts and the analysis of oral transmissions. Using these different sources it becomes apparent that the concerns involved are divergent, but clearly interdependent. While at a national public level, security concerns and the defence of civil liberties against the range of options the new legislation provides state agents with are controversially debated, the local discourse is about social coherence and solidarity, targeting the problem of how to come to an arrangement with Islamic activists and whether to integrate them into or ostracize them from the local community. This reveals, firstly, that local cohesion is challenged by both the Salafiyya activities and the state intervention in local affairs. I will argue that in the resulting struggle, local people seem to be successful in restricting the external control over local affairs which both Islamic activism and anti-terror legislation have tried to exercise. This process, the argument continues, led to an expanded local agency with regard to state officials without a weakening of the state.

I will argue further that this process did not prevent an adaptation of the new legal tool in local repertoires of legal practice, a process which, in turn, cannot be seen independently of its being embedded in a wider context. So, the fact that local people make use of Moroccan anti-terror legislation for their own purposes implicitly keeps it operative and this way establishes new dimensions of interdependency throughout scales. The argument is subdivided into four successive lines. Firstly, resolute state intervention in local affairs with respect to the new anti-terror law reinforced the local people's pol-

---

2 Cf. e.g. Dickinson (2005); Mazrui (2006).

icy of keeping away state agents from their local affairs. At the same time, the external threat enhanced the local process of reconstructing social cohesion and of reintegrating religiously deviant members of the community. Secondly, the continuing process of political liberalisation under the umbrella of the anti-terror law, combined with the new emphasis state authorities put on local tradition and values as remedies against Islamic activism, created a state of conflicting priorities. This incertitude paved the way for a strategic proceeding of local actors and contributed to the successful local management of the process of local reconciliation. Thirdly, and parallel to that process, an alternative instrumentalisation of anti-terror legislation beyond the narrower local framework of the village by the same local actors who successfully thwarted the states' application of the law in their villages took place. This was partly motivated by the possibility to take advantage of the new law by denouncing opponents to state agents in local conflicts. Reference to anti-terror laws was also employed against propagators of Salafi ideology without a local background because local people felt betrayed by the movement and unwillingly connected to the realm of terror after the bombing attack of Casablanca in 2003. Beside this, new fields for local instrumentalisation opened up by a local reading of state references to the law in different circumstances. Finally, the fourth line of the argument of scalar interdependencies in the dealings with anti-terror legislation refers to the government's re-interpretation of local references to the law as evidence supporting the instrumentalisation of the law which state agents pursued at a transnational scale.

In order to understand the way in which anti-terror legislation was welcomed in this rural area, I will start with a short overview over the previous development. In a next step, the issue of Islamic activism and anti-terror legislation will be discussed in the context of the political processes in Morocco after the enthronement of King Mohammed VI in 1999. An analysis of state-local interplay for the period after the implementation of the new legislation will follow. Two examples of a creative access to the new legal resource in multi-scale conflict constellations beyond the 'terror and security' scope will be the core of the analysis.

In a conclusion, anti-terror legislation will be interpreted as a major incentive for the reconfiguration of mutual scalar interdependencies. It contributed to an expanded local agency and the reconstruction of local identity, while at the same time offering actors on a local, national as well as on a transnational level a new instrument, the application of which for particular purposes, however, depends on the fine-tuning between actors at all scales.

Salafi Activism in the Moroccan Souss

The regional focus of this paper is the Souss plain with its adjacent mountainous surroundings of the Atlas and Anti-Atlas in southwest Morocco. Data from different villages are included in this analysis.³ They stem from an environment where Islam in all its local variations plays an essential role for local identity and belonging, the legal arena and the organisation of daily life.

Islamic activists appeared in the rural Souss for the first time in 1999. Intervention in the Moroccan countryside started with the arrival of foreign non-Moroccan missionaries from Middle Eastern countries, who founded a *madrasa* (Islamic school) in a medium-sized town in the region.⁴ The first three missionaries to appear in one of the villages where research was done were Moroccans who had been educated in this same school. They stood out from the local population as they had beards and wore traditional clothes (*gandura*) and traditional caps. Their beards in particular were seen to be distinctive, and for this reason they have been referred to as Shablhi (*as-shab al-lihi*), beard wearers. For the rural Souassa, the Salafi were an unknown movement which seemed not to be rooted in Moroccan Sufi Islam.

Instead, the Salafiyya (from *salaf*, ancestor; companion of the Prophet Muhammad) maintains close ties with the Sa'udi ideology of Wahhabism. Nevertheless, the movement is part of the scene of Moroccan Islamism and maintains historical relations with the elites of Moroccan political and orthodox Islam, *'ulama'* and Islamic leaders inside and outside the inner circle of political power. The Salafiyya movement propagates 'Islam as the solution' (*al-Islam huwa al-hall*), the most widespread motto of Islamic activism, indicating that the adjustment of all life spheres towards the Islamic agenda offers the only escape from current misery. Its supporters promote a return to the roots of legal Islam and demand the reorganisation of social life according to Islamic core principles. They declare that they are the ones to hold ultimate authority in the judiciary and demand official acknowledgement of the Hanbali legal code by the state. Hanbali law is closely connected to Wahhabism, while Islamic law in Morocco follows the legal school of Malik. This claim implicitly challenges the Moroccan state, which also refers to official Islam as

---

3 For reasons of deontology, no concrete localisation is included and the data used remain anonymous. Fieldwork on the Salafiyya was carried out for several weeks annually between 1999 and 2005. Since 2001, the fieldwork has been part of a project within the Legal Pluralism Project Group at the Max Planck Institute for Social Anthropology in Halle on 'Sustainable Development and Exploitation of Natural Resources, Legal Pluralism and Trans-National Law in the "Araneraie" Biosphere Reserve'.
4 Proper names and toponyms are reproduced in the commonly used spelling. Arabic terms are used in simplified spelling without diacritical marks.

a source of legitimation.⁵ The Salafi criticize practices of popular Islam. Veneration of local saints (in the Salafi's interpretation 'polytheism', *shirk*), pilgrimages to the tombs of saints and moussems (*mawasim*), with its many profane concomitants, Sufi practices such as trance dancing, were particular targets of their polemics. They promote the conviction that social justice can be provided exclusively by the *qur'an* and the *shari'a*.⁶ At the same time, the Salafi condemn Western influence and warn against the destructive forces of transnational legal treaties and development cooperation.⁷ Law and order is the paramount topic of their conversation: not only hegemony within the social sphere, but absolute control over it, was the declared goal of their strategy.⁸ In order to achieve this goal they did not shy away from activating local potential for violent action or to have recourse to violence if they felt it opportune. At the same time, an essential element of the Salafi's self-image is their role as a religious movement which provides charity and social welfare.

Mobilisation of Adherents and the Setup of a Local Rural Branch

Beginning in August 1999, a new local branch of the organisation was built up in the region of research within a few months. The institutional infrastructure built up in the local communities was rather rudimental. Local groups were centred around a leading figure, called *amir,* and the internal structure was organized in accordance with a binding code of Salafi ideals (*manhaj*). In the course of time, however, the Salafi succeeded in attracting more and more local residents. A grass-roots network developed, connecting more than 20 villages and providing basic goods and services for its members. In May 2002, the Salafi had mobilized the majority in approximately half of the villages of the three rural districts in the focus area. Each local cell was also connected to a loose regional network and was under external control, as some adherents after their 're-conversion'. ('External' in this context means in contact with Moroccan and non-Moroccan urban-orthodox milieus.) During the first phase of the Salafi project, the foreign initiators of the new wave of Islamic activities seldom reached these remote areas. But later on, after the formation of local groups, itinerant preachers came and visited the new Islamist parishes regularly, in spite of their distant location. These preachers

---

5 See Eickelman/Piscatory (1996).
6 For a comparison with 'classic' Salafiyya objectives in Morocco, see the literature in Turner (2006a); Turner (forthcoming); Wiktorowicz (2006).
7 See for literature Wiktorowicz (2004: 7 f.); Turner 2006b.
8 For a more detailed analysis see Turner (2006a); Turner (forthcoming); Wiktorowicz (2006).

interfered in the internal structure of the new cells and arranged duties. Some of them gave secret instructions and criticized Moroccan politics, complaining about state persecution and secular orientation. In each village of the rural district in focus, at least one praying house (*dar al-qur'an*) was established. To discuss the manifold factors which thwarted or supported the mobilisation efforts of the Salafi would go beyond the scope of this text. In some villages, the missionaries were driven away because they so deliberately acted against local rules and behaviour patterns, in others they were not. In some cases missionaries failed to pass honesty tests villagers are used to carrying out with strangers. In other cases villagers had access to resources such as those made available by development agencies, and were therefore less susceptible to the mobilisation campaign. Furthermore, the Salafi's incessant missionary work and claim to a radical change in public and private lifestyle went on to annoy many of those who were not attracted by Salafi ideology. Suspicious to all non-adherents remained the fact that the Salafi refused to disclose the provenance of the financial means they invested in their social welfare projects. In the following, only the aspects of the Salafi mobilisation success will be addressed which are of importance for the present line of argument.

Some of the Souassa, people I have known for more than ten years, told me about their personal motivations for joining the movement. Their reasons were manifold, and not always free of contradiction. Descent ties and clan affiliation played a role. But this is not to say that Islamic activists have been particularly successful in recruiting new adherents along the lines of descent, although it is indeed quite often described in the relevant literature as one possible way of mobilizing people.[9] In the Moroccan case, another important social strategy used by local actors becomes apparent. In economic affairs, descent groups do not act as coherent units. According to local ideals of risk minimisation through diversification, many families delegated one or several of their members to join this new and powerful Islamic group for tactical reasons, in order to siphon off any newly available resources. Thus, a majority of particular descent groups in the movements' local cells could exist only to the extent that this also reflected local kin structure. In sum, conscious mobilisation patterns, tactics and strategies of recruitment combined with particular local conditions and considerations, such as those of job- and risk-sharing in descent groups. In addition, the weekly remuneration of € 10 paid to most of the adherents might help in explaining the phenomenon of success – a considerable amount of money for a pauperized rural population. Invitations to religious instruction in the evenings, coupled with copious dinners, also proved

---

9   See for literature Singerman (1995 and 2004).

very successful. This suggested the prospect of long-lasting access to sufficient food resources and raised new hopes for social security.

Remarkably indifferent during this first phase of Salafi activism in the local arena between May 1999 and May 2003 were the very different representatives of the state and the local power holders. Minor civil servants with a local background constantly tried to attract the attention of higher authorities to the complaints of many local people about the inconveniences the Salafi intervention brought about – without success. The provincial administration declared they did not intervene in religious affairs. Members of the local rural elite who held positions as elected political representatives – even if sympathizing with Salafi ideals – avoided to get in touch with the movements' prominent figures and ostensibly ignored the ongoing development. A lot of rumours circulated among the villagers about the reasons of the political leaders for their restraint. Common view was that they were waiting to see whether the Salafi would qualify as possible allies in the political arena, which was not clear at that time. For on the one hand it was clear that such a vivid Islamic activism in the rural world could not have escaped the attention of central authorities. State agents from national institutions, however, did not intervene. How was that to be accounted for? On the other hand, the Salafi heavily criticized state malpractice and corruption. Therefore it was not the right moment for local political opportunists to take up a position. The issue received a new impetus only after the implementation of anti-terror legislation, as we shall see.

When discussing the reasons why the Salafi's missionary work was so successful, one has to admit that fluctuation was quite considerable and that the 'retention period' for adherents was comparatively short. Membership did have a few drawbacks. The pious lifestyle, which was the prerequisite for the development of the new resource, has been described as 'hard work' for somebody who is actually not a fervent religious enthusiast. In this respect, the Salafiyya differs from those movements of political Islam today in which political activism outweighs the basic idea of a primordial piety to a certain extent or allows for compromises between lived religiousness and civic responsibility. Despite all displays of piety, however, the Salafi never managed to smooth out all reservations of those who criticized their hegemonic approach.

The National Political Atmosphere and Framework of Islamic Activism

The following paragraph deals with the political process which framed the development of the state's attitude towards Islamic activities during the depicted course of events in the Souss. For a long time state agents, and also external experts, did not regard contemporary Islamic international terrorism as a real threat for the country. Morocco was considered to be comparatively stable, and the position of the King as the central political authority and the commander of the faithful (*amir al-mu'minim*) was seen as an assurance against a radicalisation of Islam in Morocco.[10] The political process during which the attitude of the state administration towards Islamic activism notably changed can be divided into three distinguishable phases. Since much has been written on these developments during the past few years,[11] only the most important characteristics will be summarized here with respect to their feedback in the rural area. These phases correspond with time-marking events which required state reaction.

The first phase lasted from the death of King Hassan II and the enthronement of Mohammed VI in July 1999 to the date of the Islamist attacks against the USA on 11 September 2001. The second phase then covers the time from 11 September 2001 to 16 May 2003, the date of the bombing attacks of Casablanca. Around that time, anti-terror legislation was planned but not adopted. Finally, the last phase starting at that point in time might be called 'the reign of the anti-terror law'.

With Mohammed VI, the process of political liberalisation, which his late father had initiated, continued, even though not in the accelerated manner many had been expecting. The human rights movement, which had started to become increasingly effective in Morocco ever since the early 1990s, played an important role in this. The release of political prisoners, the return of political actors from exile, a coming to terms with state malpractice in the past were all put on the new agenda. The project of legal reform concerning gender relations was pushed forward. Expectations of powerful, external transnational actors may have contributed to these processes.

Local Islamic movements also benefited from the political spirit of renewal that characterized the beginning of King Mohammed VI's reign. It is noteworthy that at the same time the new wave of Salafi missionary activity started, or became obvious for the first time, in the rural Souss. Whether political adversaries hostile to the new King's trajectory paved the way for them

---

10 See e.g. Leveau (1976); Eickelman/Piscatori (1996); Ghazi (1997); Tozy (1999); Vermeren (2001).
11 Ben Rochd (2002); El Wardi (2003); Yassine (2003); Chaarani (2004); Kalpakian (2005); Zeghal (2005) with further literature.

is pure speculation, however based on the irrefutable presumption that without state connivance their activities would have been impossible.[12] Without further going into detail, the point is here that an increase of Islamic activism in various facets took place in Morocco at the beginning of the new millennium.

The first real shock wave in the country was triggered by the realisation that Moroccans were involved in the terrorist attacks on 11 September 2001 in the USA – not only as marginal helpers but as important leading figures. As a reaction to that the implementation of new legislation against terror was launched.[13] In fact, Morocco had already ratified the Arab Convention against terrorism in 1998, and in the following several international agreements as well.[14] However, after the attacks of 9/11 the American government appealed to different states to join the U.S.-American fight against terrorism. So the Moroccan government signalized that it would be willing to adopt the U.S.-American legislative blueprint in order to strengthen its juridical arsenal, but did not go any further. At that time, the public discourse in Morocco about the consequences the adoption of U.S. strategies might have for the political progress in the country was dominated by reservations among representatives of the institutions of civil society. A polemic arose, for instance, on a national level about the commemoration of the victims in New York and elsewhere. The Makhzen, the state apparatus, organized an official memorial service in the Cathedral of St. Pierre in the country's capital of Rabat. Representatives of political Islam attended that ceremony, as well as representatives of all religious communities and political groups of Morocco, including the PJD (Party of Justice and Development; *hizb al-'adala wa-t'tanmia*), the only political party with an Islamic background accepted by the government. The King, however, was not present. The message was clear: The Moroccan state does condemn all forms of terrorism, solidarity with the USA and religious tolerance were emphasized.[15] However, the symbolic and meaningful act of commemoration in a church instead of a mosque provoked indignation in parts of the Muslim community. A *fatwa* of 16 *'ulama'* was launched, denouncing not the intention but the site of the event. The fact that the *fatwa* became internationally known embarrassed the political scene in Morocco particularly because the official council of the *'ulama'* in Morocco had been put under state control in the 1980s and the subscribers of the document escaped its authority. Part of the content of that document was the rejection of a 'political interpretation' of the terror events in the U.S. and of the extensive definition of *irhab* (terror) used by the USA. The *fatwa* contributed to the public

---

12 Many voices were raised to that effect in the Moroccan press.
13 Bendourou (2004)
14 Benyahya 2003 (= REMALD 89, 2003); FIDH (2004).
15 Zeghal (2002: 54 and 2005: 255 f.)

discourse on anti-terror legislation, and in this way also implicitly to the diffident proceeding of the state actors. Large parts of the Moroccan public interpreted the fact that many representatives of Islamic movements condemned the terrorist attack against the USA as a sort of compensation for cautious reactions of state officials.

On 16 May 2003, five simultaneous attacks of suicide bombers on international and Jewish targets (the Jewish Community Center; the Farah Hotel; Casa Espana; Bouziatno Restaurant and the Jewish Cemetery) caused the death of 45 people, mostly Moroccans, including 12 of the terrorists. All of the latter were Moroccans. Three surviving kamikazes were arrested on the spot before they could contribute their share to the terrorist acts. The police immediately started investigations in the shantytown of Sidi Moumen in Casablanca, from where most of the perpetrators came. Also the surroundings of the transnationally active movement of Salafiyya Jihadiyya were targeted on suspicion of maintaining relations with *al-qa'ida*. Several religious experts whose sermons were evaluated as influential to the kamikaze as well as members of the group *as-sirat al-mustaqim* (the straight path, a Salafiyya branch) were arrested, too, or if already arrested for other reasons, were treated as members of a supporting milieu or even network.[16] The investigations were very soon extended to other Moroccan cities. Several networks of organized Islamist extremists were detected. The power of state reaction and the disclosures in the media based on official declarations gave the impression of a huge terrorist conspiracy against the monarchy as the authority representing both the state and Moroccan Islam. The fact that bomb factories and paramilitary training camps were discovered seemed to confirm this suspicion and left no room for alternative interpretation. In short, after the bombing attacks of 16 May 2003 in Casablanca, the spirit of renewal in Morocco made way for an uncertainty about the future, for fear and irritation. The attacks may be identified as the most memorable time marker in the collective memory of all Moroccans, apart from the achievement of independence in 1956.

The Invention of Anti-terror Law and the Continuation of Political Reform in its Shadow

Under the depicted circumstances, anti-terror legislation, which had already been formulated after 11 September 2001, came into operation very quickly by way of neglecting or, better, surmounting all political obstacles or reservations. Between January and May 2003, a highly controversial debate had

---

16 Lariège (2004)

blocked the political process of implementation.[17] After the bombing attacks in Casablanca, however, the government immediately put the project back on the legislative agenda of the parliament, with slight modifications. On 28 May, 2003, the new law became operative. It was not only implemented but consequently applied after this date. This was definitely not the right moment to oppose measures in favour of state security. A wave of solidarity against terrorism swept through the country, Moroccan artists even presented an operetta against terrorism (*la lil irhab*) in Casablanca.[18] Nevertheless it soon became clear that the civil society beyond the Islamic milieu was developing reservations both against Islamic terror and the consequences of an absolute state.[19] The reasons will become clear in a brief outline of the most important contents of the anti-terror legislation.[20]

First of all, the definition of terror (*irhab*), already criticized in the mentioned *fatwa* in 2001, is extensive enough to include all forms of disturbance of the public order, resulting in a perceptible restriction of the exercise of public liberties.[21] While most of the law's substance conforms to the U.S. American template, a central point for the present line of argument needs to be mentioned: The notion of complicity and assistance, which may be any form of social interaction with an individual identified as a terrorist at a certain moment, paved the way for collective suspicions and served the supposition of supporting milieus. So, the simple analysis of individual behaviour may result in a deprivation of fundamental rights of the suspected. This open concept of terrorist acts is flanked by a concession of remarkably extensive room for manoeuvre to state officials, like in other national versions of anti-terrorism legislation all over the world, too.[22]

As a result, the Makhzen sent controversial signals. On the one hand, there was the implementation and strict application of anti-terror legislation which led to a restriction of public liberties. On the other hand, and parallel to that, the process of political reform continued under the umbrella of that law. The reform of the family law (*mudawwana*), for instance, which had long

---

17 Bendourou (2004: 194)
18 Saâîdi captions in Le Matin; 5 May 2004: 'Composée par Said Limam et jouée le 12 mai au Rialto de Casablanca; une opérette pour dire "non au terrorisme" (http://www.lematin.ma/journal/printarticle.asp?id=33728) See also 'L'opérette "non au terrorisme" en représentation mercredi à Casablanca: Quand sons de cloche et rythmes soufis traduisent la coexistence des religions' (Le Matin, 8 Mai 2004: http://www.lematin.ma/journal /printarticle.asp?id=33853).
19 Rollinde (2004: 66)
20 Benyahya (2003) (=REMALD 89, 2003); Bendourou (2004); FIDH (2004)
21 On public liberties see REMALD 76, 2004. A whole catalogue of illegal economic and financial activities has been included in the frame of terrorist acts as well. See Bendourou (2004: 191-96 f.).
22 FIDH (2004)

been a controversial topic, passed the parliament in 2004 against resistance of important Islamic groups.[23] In the political climate at that time of the immediate adoption of anti-terror law, Islamic movements experienced quite a reduced scope for action and agitation against the reformed family law. They choked back their polemics against gender equality and similar issues laid down in the new *mudawwana* in order to prevent state repression.

A parallel development to the containment of Islamic activism is, above all, the reconciliation policy after the 'Years of Lead'. A commission was formed which had to negotiate and regulate cases of past state injustice committed during the so-called Years of Lead between 1960 and 1999.[24] King Mohammed VI had already charged the human rights association Conseil Consultatif des Droits de l'Homme (CCDH) with the organisation of a reconciliation committee on the occasion of his investiture on 21 August 1999. But the King did not actually install the commission, called *Instance pour l'équité et la reconciliation*, until 7 November 2003.[25] This was seen as a complainant gesture, advancing the integration of civil society into the war on terror. However, the simultaneity of the human rights discourse and the reconciliation policy with the proceedings against Islamic activists under the new anti-terror law became an acid test for the new liberalisation, and somewhat strange coalitions came to the fore. The left-wing oriented, critical press, which itself was put under pressure by anti-terror legislation,[26] was anxious about the human rights standards for their worst enemies, Islamic radicals who were brought to trial. Human rights activists expressed their worries about the civic rights of imprisoned and accused suspects of terrorism in the press critical of the state, and advocated basic rights for them since human rights are indivisible.

Furthermore, there was a public discussion about all kamikazes being victims of terrorist propaganda because they were uneducated people who grew up in the poorest social conditions. Measures of state intervention in the slums around the big cities were adopted, aiming at providing better living conditions for the poorest and restricting urban migration at the same time.[27] An-

---

23 Rollinde (2004: 61f.). For the development until 2002 see Buskens (2003).
24 Instance pour l'Equité et la Réconciliation (IER). Rollinde (2004: 63-65). See: http://www.ier.ma
25 The matter cannot be discussed in detail at this point, particularly not the question of impunity of state perpetrators. My focus here is on the impact the human rights agencies had on the discourse of the anti-terror legislation with their decision to watch over the legitimate rights of accused Islamists.
26 See e.g. Morocco Country Report on Human Rights Practices (2005): http://www.state.gov/g/drl/rls/hrrpt/2005/61695.htm
27 A press campaign under the motto 'lutte contre le habitat insalubre' was launched against the emergence of slums and a political milieu favouring the expansion of slums. Cf. http://www.seh.gov.ma/Habitat%20Insalubre/charte%20nationale/charte_nationale.htm

other anti-corruption campaign was initiated and welfare organisations were implemented in order to cope with the Islamic activists' major points of criticism: state corruption and the lack of public welfare. Concerning the legal sphere, in numerous articles as well as in a speech of the King in June 2003, the dominance of the Maliki *madhad* (school) was pointed out and a clear warning against all criticism of Malikiyya delivered. For local actors, most important for the strategies of containing the effects of anti-terror legislation in the rural zone was the fact that the King highlighted Moroccan culture and tradition as the best remedy against the virus of religious aberrance and terrorism.[28] All these measures were to contribute to the drying out of the same allegedly supporting milieus the anti-terror legislation was targeting.

Operative Anti-terror Law and the War on Terrorism at the National Scale and beyond

Following the terror attack, Moroccan courts passed a series of prison sentences. More than 1,500 individuals were suspected of having been involved in the attacks of May 16th or of other illegal activities with an Islamist or terrorist background. In September 2003, a total of 906 suspected Islamic extremists had been adjudged in the wake of the bombings, but the Minister of Justice, Mohammed Bouzoubaa, warned that 'the peril is still present'. Almost 50 life sentences and other heavy penalties ranging up to 30 years were handed down. As Amnesty International stated for several cases of detained Islamists, torture resurfaced under the umbrella of anti-terror legislation in Moroccan prisons. The association Human Rights Watch reported an increase of arrests for 2004.[29] To this day, local cells of Islamic activists are constantly discovered all over the country which obviously pursued a violent agenda. In the course of police operations under the anti-terror law, an involvement of military and other state officials in Islamic activism has been revealed and shocked the population.[30] The profound reshuffle in the security apparatus of the state in 2006 and the political deprivation of some of its leading figures, who had successfully accroached to themselves power as operators of anti-

---

28 An official political campaign by the government in support of local identity and culture was launched after the royal speech in July 2003: http://www.mincom.gov.ma/french/generalites/samajeste/mohammedVI/discours/2003/Discours%20du%20Trone%202003.htm
29 Human Rights Watch (2004). The report provoked vivid reactions in Morocco. See Brousky (2004) in Le Journal Hebdo N° 179 (23-29 October): 'Le rapport explosive'.
30 The group ansar al-mahdi, dismantled end of July 2006, included members of the armed forces. See e.g. Chebatoris (2007).

terror law in Morocco, were interpreted in some media as the consequence of the superiors' inability to stop the threat of terror.[31]

International cooperation in the war on terrorism also shapes the way of how different actors make use of the new legal instrument in Morocco. One year after the suicide bombings of Casablanca the devastating train bombings in Madrid in March 2004 made it clear that a Moroccan network, operating worldwide, was involved, and disagreement between Moroccan state officials and transnational investigators over its nature and origin became obvious.[32] According to newspaper interviews, Moroccan state representatives such as General Hamidou La'anigri, then Chief of Security, complained about a rather unenthusiastic support by their European colleagues after the Casablanca attacks and particularly expressed their frustration about European laws against terror being too lenient and not severe enough. The Moroccan investigators who arrested and accused [!] 2,112 suspects in the country on the basis of the new anti-terror law issued 44 international arrest warrants for suspected terrorists. They also accused European countries of being slow or unwilling to extradite captured suspects.

The need for international cooperation seems prevent the Moroccans' European partners from commenting too explicitly on the respective different standards of civil rights resulting from anti-terror legislation. Hamidou La'anigri expressed his opinion with reference to his European counterparts: 'We are victims of laws and guarantees that protect the rights of individuals at the expense of cracking down against organized crimes.'[33] In this context the Moroccan state adopted the position of its closest ally, the USA. Furthermore, La'anigri projected a version of anti-terror law which correlated to the states' own operational imperatives. By making the transnational template applicable to Morocco, he also fed this version back into the transnational pool as binding and this way upscaled Morocco's own version in an international context. In the unofficial public discourse, the dominant conviction was that the Moroccan submission to transnational anti-terror laws was particularly inspired by foreign policy strategies aimed at integrating Moroccan attempts to fight terrorist violence into a wider frame. Concerning the importance of anti-terror law for the internal repertoire of means at the disposal of state functionaries, there was a certain congruence of opinions on the national and the local scale.

---

31 Chadi and Jamai entitle an article in 2006 in Le Journal-Hebdo N° 238 (07-20 January 2006): 'Laânigri dans la ligne de mire?'; and Chadi et al. state in 2006 in Le Journal-Hebdo N° 269 (16-22 September): 'La purge?'. To comment on hints and rumours about career strategies, competitions over competences etc. within the state apparatus in connection with anti-terror legislation would lead to far in this context.
32 There is scarcely any concrete information about these developments apart from newspaper reports, interviews, etc. See Sciolino (2004).
33 Sciolino (2004)

It has been said that the Moroccan state does not actually depend on a new legislation in order to increase pressure on the terror scene; but that it rather uses the law to demonstrate its perfect conformity with transnational standards and its international acceptance. Moreover, international demands required a definite reaction, since Moroccan citizens were perceived as major actors in terrorist planning in various circumstances. Inversely, however, in the Moroccan context itself, no transnational reinsurance was felt to be necessary in order to justify state action.

Downscaling Anti-terror Legislation: Salafi and the State in the Rural Souss and the Need to Reconstruct Local Cohesion

Let us come back to the local fields of the Souss region, where the Salafiyya, the movement which is held co-responsible for the terrorist attacks of Casablanca, became active in 1999. After 9/11, the ordinary local adherents clearly expressed their condemnation of these acts, whereas the point of view of the leading persons never became publicly known. Whatever their ideas at that time might have been, there was no official interest in them. The movement reached its peak between the two time-marking terror attacks, and no connection was established between Salafi activism and international terrorism.

But before the legal impact of the anti-terror law on the rural periphery is exemplified in more detail, I will briefly outline the course of events after May 2003 with respect to state-local conjunctions. What bothered the Souassa was the question whether the rural area must be seen as a reservoir for the recruitment of new terrorists. After the bombing attack, some previously unbelievable rumours about the motives of the Salafiyya missionary activities in rural area proved to have a serious background. For instance, big amounts of old wine bottles had been bought up at very good prizes. Later, the police found several stocks of these bottles, transformed into bombs; the reason being that the glass of these old bottles is very suitable for bomb fabrication. The people who sold those bottles to Islamic activists without having any idea of the purpose were ready to take revenge for involuntarily getting involved in criminal acts. For the fact was fully recognized that this form of involvement could be interpreted as an active support of terrorism. The local activists claimed never to have had any information about these occurrences and asked for forgiveness. Suspicions started circulating. Furthermore, at least one of the Casablanca terrorists, Hasan Taoussi, 24 years old, had kin relations with Souassa, since his family, who live in the slums of Casablanca, is of Soussi origin. 20 years ago they came from the Atlas Mountains down to the plain. This news reached the rural zone in no time. It was, however, not interpreted as an undeniable connection of the Souss with the international web of terror. Instead, many Souassa argued that 'Casablanca' made him a terrorist, under the influence of transnational Salafi. Nevertheless, the mere fact of this remote connection increased the apprehension of being considered a 'milieu' by state agents and strengthened the feeling of betrayal by the Salafi.

Anti-terror Legislation, State Intervention and the Need to Reconstruct Local Coherence

The Salafi adherents in the Souss villages to whom I am referring in this paper did not openly voice a legal or religious justification of the terrorist attacks in 2003. And they never admitted it to be the declared aim of the Salafi project to integrate Morocco into a much broader context of Islamic activism. But internal tensions within the Salafi cells soon became obvious, and the deep ideological rift that opened between the recruited local members of the Salafiyya in the rural zones and the terrorist branch active in Casablanca could not be bridged afterwards. In the first months after Casablanca, even apart from, or more precisely prior to the impact of the resolute state reactions against Islamists in the region, most of the newly recruited adherents distanced themselves from the movement. Fear of state revenge may have played a role, but the feeling of having been deceived by the Salafiyya was predominant. An atmosphere of deprecation with regard to Salafi and all symbols of otherness was felt throughout the rural area. Against this background the new law against terrorism took effect.

The police closed down all Salafi mosques and praying houses and exerted strict control over their observable activities. Ubiquitous presence of security agents, police interventions and interrogations disturbed village life. One cause for consternation was, for instance, that the police started to control veiled women in order to check whether in fact it was a terrorist hidden behind the veil. State security agents were said to be active everywhere, in the mosques, on the markets, etc., and to arrest people expressing opinions which were chargeable according to the new law.

There were imprisonments, and families broke apart. Intra-familial conflicts resulted from a split of family members into Salafiyya adherents and followers of local Islam. Drunkards, hashish consumers, persons with a good local reputation and pious persons of all kinds of piety might live under the same roof. There were fathers who try to convert their sons and vice versa. As the incongruities pervaded nuclear families, there was also a – hypothetical – reference to the new legal tool in domestic affairs. A father might have said: 'I better inform the *muqaddim* (village mayor) about your clouded thoughts', or, 'you go on like this and the *shurta* (police) will come and arrest you.'

The expansion of investigations to the assumed supporting scene, as pre-traced in the anti-terror legislation, made the latter known to the overwhelming majority of the Souassa in a tangible form. Everybody who might possibly have been in touch with a terrorist was suspected of adhering to a vague supporting milieu. Therefore, as all Salafi were regarded as possible terrorists by the police, the rest of the villagers also felt encumbered by the new law. Everybody was in danger of being suspected of collaboration simply because their neighbours or, for instance, the grocer around the corner were known as Salafi adherents. Such was the apprehension of the villagers, and state representatives affirmed it very quickly through overzealous action. Youths, who full of mischief and just for fun claimed to be in touch with terrorists, were severely beaten by the police. The villagers interpreted state reaction to this kind of bad joke as over-exaggerated and inappropriate.

After the majority of the former adherents of Salafi Islamic activism in the rural Souss had defected, it was decided in the informal village councils to cede the discreet elimination of still remaining non-Moroccan prayers in the region to the investigators who were sent out by the central political authorities. Nevertheless, small groups of local Salafi adherents in the rural Souss still resisted, claiming both Souassa roots and free choice of orientation within the realm of Islam. They no longer received subsidies from outside and claimed to have no material interests. In the course of the following year they came to be perceived as part of local diversity, passing for one type of religious orientation within the local scope of the Islamic way of life. A process of careful differentiation between the 'good' Salafi and the 'others' started, and new criteria developed. Such criteria first and foremost include a local background; furthermore the suspension of all missionary activity and particularly the abandonment of any criticism of local religious and juridical practice. Salafi have to accept the local law, *'urf*. This includes, for instance, the acceptance of the role of the Aissaoua, the locally active Islamic Sufi congregation, in conflict settlement. A ban of criticism of state institutions is not included in this catalogue of criteria. However, a certain tolerance level was conceded, which is comparable to that regarding drunkards or other troublemakers with a local rooting. This process may also be read as an indication of an internal framing dispute about to what extent demonstrations of otherness or a signalling of local rooting can be accepted. Informal village councils and state representatives with a local identity exerted extreme social control over the village Islamists. At least during the first month of ongoing social restructuring, every single step of an Islamic activist would attract the attention of their neighbours. Incorrigible Salafi, who continued to annoy people in public, were threatened with denouncing them to the police. Everybody in a village was aware of the individual attitudes of each person and was averse to generalisations. The remaining Salafi activists seemed to experience a dilemma situation and expressed their feelings in various and contradicting ways. On the one hand, they recognized the protection against state intervention granted by their co-villagers and therefore accepted control. On the other hand, quarrels did, and still do, occur which must be taken seriously. The Salafi are incessantly testing the limits of the tolerance threshold, as these numerous quarrels and disputes show.

In the course of this process of re-integration, the new, or increased, state interest in local affairs resulting from an extended power of intervention called anti-terror law, proved to be extremely uncomfortable. Pressure on village life reached an extent that threatened the local reconciliation project. The villagers responded with protective measures. Since regular police controls of the village Salafi branch disturbed village life, the village council decided to suggest the Salafi should meet at night, outside of village boundaries and without attracting attention. Also, locally rooted minor civil servants contributed to the averting of danger and no longer reported local conflicts caused by the Salafiyya to higher authorities, despite still remaining tensions. Instead, the villagers now reported their problems with their incorrigible 'village Islamists', as phrased in talks with me, to the *qa'id* (chief administrative officer of a rural district). Other state agents, they felt, would only cause more problems than they were able to resolve.

Furthermore, other simultaneous political signals seemed to mitigate the restrictive effects of applied anti-terror legislation. When the King characterized local Moroccan tradition and religiosity as the best protection against terrorism and state officials had to go along with these directives, the local population hastily attempted to profit from this political hint. The Souassa referred to traditional values, for instance, in order to defend their informal self-autonomy in the maintenance of local order in the villages whenever the police or non-local state agents tried to intervene in local affairs without the villagers' consent. Integrated into local strategy, the 'culture argument' offered by the King efficiently helped to keep at bay over-officious investigators in some of these cases.

Another matter discussed intensively was the behaviour of the local political elites. After the sudden turn in policy and legislation with the introduction of the anti-terror law in 2003, the Souassa frequently asked why the powerful local policy makers in the course of more than four years never did intervene in order to defend the local way of life against religious fanatics. Their inactivity, however, did not provoke negative consequences or, in retrospect, the disapproval of the central authorities. On the contrary, their inactivity seemed to pay off. After their re-conversion, formerly fervent adherents of the movement as soon as in summer of 2003 started a political career with regional or local cut under the umbrella of the political party of PJD. These 'former' Salafi assisted in forming coalitions with local patrons, who stood for elections representing different established political parties. This triggered sophisticated conspiracy theories which reflect the opinion local Souassa have in general on corrupt political elites. Speculations concerned national politics and beyond, suggesting a financial influence of certain central authorities and foreign power holders in favour of the Wahhabi model of Islam. While on the one hand, the anti-terror law threatened village communities for the alleged forming of supporting milieus and had to be domesticated in the struggle for a reconstruction of local identity, the rural political elite and the political establishment, on the other hand, remained unaffected by these developments.

So at village level, the local people experienced the pressure of the state application of anti-terror legislation against activists and their 'milieus'; at the same time, however, they referred to that same law in order to rid themselves of non-local Salafi and used it as a hypothetical means of disciplining the remaining activists. Only in this respect is it acceptable to speak of a local instrumentalisation of the new laws at that time. This means, to successfully refer to anti-terror legislation in village affairs necessarily required keeping the gendarmes away from one's home. The project of reconstructing social cohesion had top priority, and reference to the new tool for denunciation was assessed as to whether this contributed to the achievement of this goal or not. It is true that bearded men were attacked on local markets and the police were forced to intervene to protect them against public violence. It is also true that bearded men became victims of denunciations. However, informants did not ascribe these developments to a kind of local instrumentalisation of the law against terror. In fact, these events give evidence of people taking reservations against Islamic activists seriously. The mentioned denunciations were no attempts to profit from them.

While the effects of anti-terror legislation were ambivalent from a village perspective, as a means against external Islamic activists the new legislation was welcomed. In this context it became an instrument used by rural Souassa whenever their sensitive and ambivalent relationship with migrants of Soussi origin was affected by transnational Islamic activism. Some migrants had adopted a Salafi perspective in their respective host countries. Local Souassa voiced their concerns that while Salafi missionary activities in the region have been undermined by state intervention under the umbrella of anti-terror legislation, MRE (Moroccans living in foreign countries, in France, Belgium and the Netherlands, but of Soussi origin) could contribute to a reinforcement of the Salafiyya movement in the region. This would be – at least in the Souss – a new phenomenon, since Souassa migrants who had embraced Islamic activism had not acted as supporters of the local scene during their peak time between 2000 and 2003. But this might be a local particularity.[34] In other regions, MRE Salafi played an important role in the propagation of Islamic ideas in their respective places of origin.[35] Therefore, temporarily returning migrants with a Salafi background became a particular target of local rejection in the Souss. But also in cases with different background, when underlying tensions between MRE and local Souassa openly broke out, the latter sometimes availed themselves of anti-terror legislation. These tensions reverberate that on the one hand, the local villagers feel uneasy because they depend on the investments of their MRE, but complain about the arrogant manner of some of them on the other hand. In summer 2004, for instance, MRE with beards were attacked when shopping at the market in Taroudant. The *makhzenni* (auxiliary police) were forced to intervene and brought the litigants before the *qa'id*. The latter felt uncomfortable with the situation, being confronted with a Shablhi of Moroccan origin with his French spouse claiming protection against insults of local attackers who in turn wanted to see their victims imprisoned with reference to the 'new law which allows to eliminate all of them'. This was the local reading of the law. In this case, however, an ordinary market dispute over quality and prices of goods seemed to be the true reason for the accusation. The state representative realized quite clearly that frequently, accusations of Islamic activism served the manipulation of local conflicts. Indeed, not only MRE, whether with or without a Salafi background, were accused on the basis of that law. Also local problems which must be reported to the *qa'id*, such as offending somebody's sense of honour by winking at a married woman in public, seemed to be manipulated. Sometimes, offended male relatives of such women tried to turn these events into cases of an Islamist background.

The particular given constellation described in this paragraph was also put in a wider context. One apprehension often voiced in the villages was that the rural population had to pay the bill for the pressure powerful global actors and the elite of the Makhzen exerted on state agents to produce quick results in the war on terrorism. Many Souassa, however, supported the view that the state reaction would have been similar without any legal reform. People insisted on

---

34 Cf. Singerman (2004: 157 f.). There was the persistent rumor that the Moroccan state did not allow the Salafiyya to interfere with the ties between Morocco and its migrant communities. Particularly the Salafi cash flow was to run exclusively from Saudi-Arabia to the Moroccan countryside. The investments of the MRE in rural Morocco, in turn, on which many communities depend, was not to be affected by Salafi interventions in Europe diverting the money into the transnational Salafi pool or to be detracted from the usual fields of investment. Recent reports in the media hawk the opinion that political tendencies towards an exclusion of MRE from the national elections in 2007 have to do with an assumed high proportion of voters for the Islamic PJD among them.

35 Cf. Roy (2004).

the fact that it was the locals themselves who succeeded in restricting Salafiyya influence, instead of the state, which in their eyes failed to contribute its share to this enterprise. Thus, the rural zone was not seen as being dependant on state support in managing local problems. On the contrary, the very lack of state intervention in the early stage of the Islamist appearance on the rural scene was interpreted as a deliberate strategy in order not to irritate Saudi Arabian investors, who have a bad reputation in the rural Souss. When later the police suddenly took previously dismissed complaints against Islamic activists seriously, this was said to be enforced by command of high state authorities 'in order to please the Americans'.

Anti-terror Law in Many Fields

A transnationalized U.S. American legal template not only becomes localized through the bottleneck of state implementation and interpretation and local adaptation. Its application at national and local scale by state agents is not independent of its transnational dimension. The rural Souassa, in turn, interpreted references to anti-terror legislation by Moroccan state agents for a transnational context as master models for a possible use of the legal tool for their own local circumstances. Local actors picked up hints and referred to anti-terror legislation in contexts that seem to show analogies or even connections to the transnational contexts in which state actors had mentioned anti-terror measures. The state, then, at transnational scale, interprets this local instrumentalisation of anti-terror legislation as a justified field of application, like the empirical cases evidence.

So after the experiences with anti-terror legislation at village level, the scope was broadened for further alternative fields of application. Like terrorism, these fields of conflict do not only have a transnational dimension, but also national and local ones. Two examples will briefly be outlined, showing how the anti-terror law could be useful in a wider context for both the state and ordinary local people and could serve the production of realities and certainties. One example is the linkage of the Western Sahara problem with the competition between Souassa and Sahraoui over access to scarce resources, the other the association of everyday disputes in the village with the transnational fight against internationally organized drug crime.

The first mentioned national-local field of tensions that has been affected by anti-terror legislation is caused by the exceptional position Sahraoui people originating from the Western Sahara enjoy in the whole country. This includes a relative freedom of action as well as a certain immunity, and at the same time material support and further privileges granted by state institutions. This is no official state policy, but a widespread and not officially formulated opinion in Morocco. Sahraoui rarely appear in court, even when involved in criminal cases, and if they have to, they may expect being released very soon because of this political protection. This supported a certain specialisation in activities such as smuggling or human trafficking, which can perfectly be pursued under the cover of state privileges for Sahraoui nomadic economy.[36] The reasons behind these politics are the state's attempts to integrate the population of the Western Sahara into Moroccan society and to distance them from the independence movement of the Polisario. The Sahraoui contrive to maintain their privileges and proximity to the sphere of the state, while simultaneously threatening with separation and their capacity to organize uprisings through maintaining a state of latent tensions in their homelands. So, despite all privileges, the Sahraoui are being kept under extreme state control.

Now, some Sahraoui are attracted by the Salafiyya.[37] State officials somehow seem helpless, and they did not dare arrest the leaders of the Sahraoui branch of Salafi adherents. As a consequence, a strategy was forged within the Makhzen apparatus to accuse the Polisario, the political and military archenemy in the competition over the southern provinces, of fostering Islamist tendencies in an attempt to destabilize Morocco. It is not impossible that communication between violent Islamists and the Polisario indeed took place. But apart from an Islamic background, even Sahraoui representatives of civil society associations, such as human rights activists suspected of secretly advocating endeavours of independence of the Western Sahara, were arrested under anti-terror law. They were accused of disturbing public order in Morocco and of touching on the territorial integrity of the country.[38]

---

36 See San Martin (2005). Human trafficking by the Sahraoui became a delicate issue in the context of the accelerated migration of Sub-Saharians through Morocco to Europe via the Spanish enclaves Ceuta and Mellia recently. Moroccan state officials hastened to accuse the Polisario of trafficking Sub-saharians via Algeria to Morocco and to combine this accusation with allusions to the separatists' closeness to the terror scene. This strategy fits perfectly with the U.S.-American perception of the Sahel zone as an area of concentration and withdrawal for transnational terrorism. Simultaneously, the human traffic the 'Moroccan Sahraoui' had organized, or better to say, their part of the business, has been reduced. Since then the migration flow increasingly shifted to the route from the West African coast to the Canary Islands. Latest voice in the press: Cherkaoui (2006).
37 Nevertheless, one has to point out that the specific versions of religiosity and spirituality which the Sahraoui are proud of are not actually compatible with Salafiyya ideals. Sahraoui nomads are used to drinking blood and to eating impure food such as lizards or turtles and habitually infringe upon nearly all of the rules the Islamic activists held essential. However, this does not inhibit tactical alliances.
38 Amnesty International Annual Report (2003)

The anti-terror legislation could also be instrumentalized against internal enemies. This news attracted considerable attention at the local level and was immediately downscaled. The reason is that throughout the Souss, there are lines of conflict between Sahraoui nomads and local farmers competing for access to scarce natural resources.[39] Superficially the potential for conflict can be reduced to this dichotomy. Behind it, however, there are economic interests of powerful political circles within the Makhzen. The local discourse now is on the question of whether one might accuse the Sahraoui nomads of being terrorists in order to drive them away. It is uncertain, however, how severely the state will restrict the Sahraoui scope of activity by applying anti-terror law. But how can the anti-terror legislation be activated against the Sahraoui without provoking an uprising? Locally this was considered a problem of dosage. Exaggerations and actions against Sahraoui as a collective were to be avoided. So, first anonymous denunciations of Sahraoui nomads did not refer to their illegal pasture activities. Instead, the first good opportunity was to be seized to force the police to take action against them. When the locals realized that some sub-Saharian refugees were hidden in lorries designated for camel transports, they immediately called the police, claiming that Sahraoui were helping terrorists to infiltrate the countryside. The police made an inquiry and found the refugees. On account of the anti-terror legislation the policemen refused the usual bribe and started an official investigation; the nomads were forced to withdraw from the spot and remain in custody of the state. The result in the long run was that there were no grounds for terror suspicion, and everything was swept under the rug as usual. The nomads, however, started to avoid the region where they had been denounced, and the locals celebrated their success. As a means in particular locally restricted conflicts, anti-terror legislation was found to be very helpful, and in this respect was welcomed by the Souassa on the local scene as an effective way to defeat an extremely powerful antagonist in the competition for access to scarce natural resources. Furthermore it is an option for state agents, who on the basis of local suspicions about a Sahraoui entanglement in the terror scene might instrumentalize internal power struggles between the backers of camel trading and their adversaries within the Makhzen for their own purposes.[40]

On an international level, anti-terror legislation and the Moroccan engagement in the war on terrorism provided Moroccan state officials with strong arguments against the Polisario. With allusion to local denunciations of Sahraoui, subtly encouraged by the state itself, state functionaries accused the Polisario of being part of an Islamist network reaching from Algeria to the Sahel zone and being involved in human trafficking of sub-Saharan migrants.

---

39 See Turner (2007).
40 See Turner (2007).

These arguments might be of use if the United Nations should at some point refuse to make more concessions in the conflict, if U.S. support on the international scene seems necessary, or if a counterweight against an Algerian-U.S.-American construction of alliance in fight of the 'hotbed of terrorism' in the Sahel zone is needed.[41]

The other example of how anti-terror legislation can be instrumentalized individually also reveals a subtle local adaptability and a keen sense of interpretation of political signals. After the uncovering of two huge drug dealing organisations in northern Morocco, the police and the state security realized that these groups had massively infiltrated state authorities. Now, the involvement of state agents in the hashish trade is quite common in Morocco, to say nothing of the political elite. But these syndicates were bristling with high-tech weapons and disposed of huge sums of money. State officials dispersed the information that the syndicates had connections with the international terror scene. Obviously the claim was not completely unfounded. The police in fact does not very eagerly prosecute big drug delinquency because of its close connection to political circles. On the other hand, there is an extremely high international pressure on the Moroccan state to restrain drug traffic. Both rumours and official statements in the media agreed on the point that the state referred to anti-terror legislation because of the fear that terrorists might get hold of weapons like armed speedboats.[42] Others said this was just a gesture of appeasement towards the impatient international drug investigators.

Nevertheless, the connection was established and ready to use for local application. This happened for instance in a quaint drama in a remote village. A local drug baron, who had been covered by the police, was involved in a simple car crash. He and his partner collided with the car of a small farmer. They completely lost their temper and tried to kill the poor man, who managed to escape. In a fit of rage, the two drug dealers burned down both cars and took up pursuit of the farmer. The latter, however, made it to the provincial city and informed the provincial police that a drug dealer of his village, who was the main financer of the local branch of Islamist activists, was pursuing him because of a car accident. It was obvious that the local gendarmes would never have intervened. But the state police alerted the state security, and an incredible raid took place – with explicit reference to anti-terror law. The dealer was arrested and was 'treated like a terrorist' as locals said. This is

---

41 Cf. Keenan (2005). For details on the Western Sahara conflict see e.g. Shelley (2004); San Martin (2005).
42 Bertelsmann Transformation Index Morocco (2006: 4); the latest debate was on involvement of the Islamist cell ansar al mahdi in drug business; see Jaabouk (2006).

to say that the arrested was beaten up severely by the police to force a confession from him, and then transferred to one of the high-security prisons far away from the scene of the crime.

To the international public, the police intervention could be presented as evidence that the Moroccan state took indications of a connection between drug crime and terrorism seriously, due to its widely known commitment to the war on terrorism. Furthermore, it could be emphasized how severe the state reacts to drug crimes in general. This would also invalidate reproaches of international drug investigators of the Moroccan state being too negligent of its persecution of drug crimes.

Conclusion

This paper shows how a legal template claiming transnational compliance permeated a rural environment and interlinked all scales it passed through.

With the Salafiyya intervention, the local arena had become directly connected with a transnational Islamic network and indirectly with terrorism, the latter at first without the knowledge of local actors. The successful mobilisation campaign of Islamic activists and the invention of anti-terror legislation upscaled local affairs to the global war on terror. Anti-terror legislation, implemented in order to cope with terrorism and to contain Islamic activism, developed a social life of its own and was transformed and customized when again downscaled according to divergent interests and circumstances. In the fields of local application it was destined for, it was rather perceived as an obstacle than an appropriate tool. State application of the law hindered the local process of reconstruction of local cohesion and had nothing to do with the causes of terrorism. Drawing on the parallel discourse on tradition and local values, the rural Souassa were successful, however, in preventing the new legislation from perpetuating intensified state control in the villages. At the same time the law offered the villagers a reference for disciplining local Salafi and keeping external ones away. In this respect the state increased its inability or disinterest to cope with local differentiation.

Local actors interpret state reference to the law at the national scale both as an attempt to reach results on a transnational scale which the state would otherwise hardly be successful in, and as a signal for overlapping fields of interest in which the new law can be of use both for members of the state apparatus and local groups of actors. The local feedback implicitly confirms the Moroccan version of anti-terror legislation and produces facts that may be used as arguments for state policy. In fact, local people did realize that their instrumentalisation of anti-terror legislation in many fields was not independent of implicit political fine-tuning with state agencies, and that their action would also have repercussions on government strategies. In both cases presented in the paper at hand, state agents took up local references to anti-terror legislation as evidence for existing connections between terrorism and other fields of social, political and legal problems. However, it was the state itself which had brought into play and spread these alleged connections in the first place. This evidence was useful for the argumentation of Moroccan state representatives at the transnational level of international drug crime or the Western Sahara problem.

Further to that, the following results may be summarized: National implementation of a transnational legal template empowered the local arena without weakening the state. But within both the Makhzen and the local arena, there were winners and losers of the development. As far as the Makhzen is concerned at a national scale, particularly members of the security apparatus successfully distinguished themselves through strict application of the law and this way accumulated power. At a local scale, civil servants succeeded by a selective application. Among local actors, particularly local non-Salafi widened their scope of action, while Islamic activists, but also members of the rural elite, unmasked as opportunists, had to face reduced agency. New fields of application beyond the designated frame of the global war on terror opened up by overlapping and dovetailed an interdependent course of action for both state representatives and local people. Local reference to the anti-terror law supported the state in the construction of an external terrorist threat to the country. Irrespective of the transnational consequences of this development, these scalar arrangements weaken and even absorb strategies for an intensification of state control under the analysed circumstances but in so doing at the same time acknowledge the state.

References

Amnesty International (2003): *Amnesty International Annual Report 2003*, London: Amnesty International.
Bendourou, O. (2004): *Libertés Publiques et Etat de Droit au Maroc*, Fès: Friedrich Ebert Stiftung.
Ben Rochd, R. (2002): *Le Rescapé de la Secte Infernale*, Casablanca: Déchra.
Benyahya, M. (2003): Droit du Terrorisme, *Revue Marocaine d'Administration Locale et de Développement (REMALD)*, 89.
Bertelsmann Transformation Index Morocco 2006: http://www.bertels-mann-transformation-index.de/146.0.html?L=1 (accessed 6 March 2006).
Brousky, O. (2004): 'Droit de l'Homme: le Rapport Explosive', *Le Journal-Hebdo*, 179, 23-29 October 2004.

Buskens, L. (2003): 'Recent Debates on Family Law Reform in Morocco: Islamic Law as Politics in an Emerging Public Sphere', *Islamic Law and Society*, 10(1): 70-131.

Chaarani, A. (2004): *La Mouvance Islamiste au Maroc. Du 11 Septembre 2001 aux Attentats de Casablanca du 16 Mai 2003*, Paris: Karthala.

Chadi, T./Jamai, A. (2006): 'La Purge?' *Le Journal-Hebdo*, 269, 16-22 September 2006.

—— (2006): 'Laânigri dans la Ligne de Mire?', *Le Journal-Hebdo*, 238, 20 January 2007.

Chebatoris, M. (2007): 'Islamist Infiltration of the Moroccan Armed Forces', *Terrorism Monitor*, 5(3): 9-12.

Cherkaoui, L. (2006): 'Le Polisario Complice du Trafic des Immigrés Subsahariens', *Le Matin*, 09 September 2006: http://www.lematin.Ma/Mailing/Article.asp?an=&id=natio&ida=66028 (accessed September 2006).

Dickinson, L. (2005): 'Terrorism and the Limits of Law: a View from Transitional Justice'. In: A. Sarat/L. Douglas/M.M. Umphrey (eds), *The Limits of Law*, Stanford: Stanford University Press, pp. 21-74.

Eickelman, D.F./Piscatory, J. (1996): *Muslim Politics*, Princeton: Princeton University Press.

El Wardi, M.T. (2003): Islamists and the Outside World. The Case of Abdessalam Yassin and Al Adl Wal Ihssan. *Al Akhawayn University Research Paper Series 19*, Ifrane: Al Akhawayn University.

Fédération Internationale des Ligues des Droits de l'Homme (FIDH) ed. (2004): *Les Autorités Marocaines à l'Epreuve du Terrorisme: la Tentation de l'Arbitraire; Violations Flagrante des Droits de l'Homme dans la Lutte Anti-terroriste*, Paris and Rabat: Imprimerie de la Fédération Internationale des Ligues des Droits de l'Homme.

Ghazi, A. (1998): *D'hier à Aujourd'hui. Le Champ Politique Marocain*, Casablanca: Imprimerie Najah el Jadida.

Herod, A./Wright, M. eds 2002. *Geographies of Power. Placing Scales*, Malden, MA: Blackwell.

Human Rights Watch ed. (2004): 'Morocco: Human Rights at a Crossroads', *HRW*, 16(6) [English Version].

Instance pour l'Equité et la Reconciliation (IER) ed. (2005): http:// ww.ier.ma (accessed 23 May 2005).

Jaabouk, M. (2006): 'Drogue, Sécuritaires et Intégristes', *Libération*, 14.09.06, internet edition: http://fr.allafrica.com/stories/200609140981.htm (accessed October 2006).

Kalpakian, J. (2005): 'Building the Human Bomb: the Case of 16 May 2003 Attacks in Casablanca', *Studies in Conflicts & Terrorism*, 28: 113-27.

Keenan, J. (2005): 'Waging War on Terror: the Implications of America's "New Imperialism" for Saharan Peoples', *Journal of North African Studies*, 10(3-4): 619-47.

Larìège, J. (2004): 'Les Procès de Casablanca et la Piste Al-Qaïda', *Les Cahiers de l'Orient*, 74(2): 83-91.

Leveau, R. (1976): *Le Fellah Marocain, Défenseur du Trône*, Paris: Presses de la FNSP.

Mazrui, A. (2006): *Islam. Between Globalization and Counter Terro-rism*, Oxford: James Currey.

Moroccan Government ed. (2005): *Charte Nationale de Lutte contre l'Habitat Insalubre*: http://www.seh.gov.ma/Habitat%20Insalubre/charte%20national/charte_nationale.htm

Morocco Country Report on Human Rights Practices (2005): http://www.state.gov/g/drl/rls/hrrpt/2005/61695.htm

Purcel, M./Brown, C. (2005): 'Against the Local Trap: Scale and the Study of Environment and Development', *Progress in Development Studies*, 5(4): 279-97.

Le Nouveau Code des Libertés Publiques. (2004): *Revue Marocaine d'Administration Locale et de Développement (REMALD)*, Nouveau Edition. Vol. 76.

Rollinde, M. (2004): 'L'alternance Démocratique au Maroc: une Porte Entrouverte', *Confluences Méditerranée*, 51: 57-67.

Roy, O. (2004): *Globalised Islam. The Search for a New Ummah*, London: Hurst.

Saâïdi, A. (2004): 'Composée par Said Limam et Jouée le 12 Mai au Rialto de Casablanca; une Opérette pour Dire "Non ou Terrorisme"', *Le Matin*, 5 May 2004.

San Martin, P. (2005): 'Nationalism, Identity and Citizenship in the Western Sahara', *The Journal of North African Studies*, 10(3-4): 565-92.

Sciolino, E. (2004): 'Moroccan Groups Emerge as a Source of Terrorist Activity', *New York Times* (European Edition), 24 May 2004.

Shelley, T. (2004): *Endgame in the Western Sahara. What Future for Africa's Last Colony*, London: Zed Books.

Singerman, D. (1995): *Avenues of Participation: Family, Politics, and Networks in Urban Quarters of Cairo*, Princeton: Princeton University Press.

—— (2004): 'The Networked World of Islamist Social Movements'. In: Q. Wiktorowicz (ed.), *Islamic Activism: a Social Movement Theory Approach*, Bloomington: Indiana University Press, pp. 143-63.

Tsing, A. (2005): *Friction: an Ethnography of Global Connection*, Princeton: Princeton University Press.

Tozy, M. (1999): *Monarchie et Islam Politique au Maroc*, Paris: Presses de Sciences Po.

Turner, B. (2006a): 'The Legal Arena as a Battlefield: Salafiyya Legal Intervention and Local Response in Rural Morocco'. In: H.-J. Albrecht/J. Simon/H. Rezaei/H.-C. Rohne/E. Kiza (eds), *Conflicts and Conflict Resolution in Middle Eastern Societies – between Tradition and Modernity*, Berlin: Duncker & Humblot, pp. 169-85.

—— (2006b): 'Competing Global Players in Rural Morocco: Upgrading Legal Arenas', *Journal of Legal Pluralism*, 53-54: 101-39.

—— (2007): 'Social Lines of Conflict between Pastoralism and Agriculture in the Souss'. In: J. Gertel/I. Breuer (eds), *Pastoral Morocco: Globalizing Scapes of Mobility and Insecurity*, Wiesbaden: Reichert, pp. 193-210.

—— (forthcoming): 'Salafiyya Activism in the Moroccan Souss: Legal Framing, Demand for Justice and Social Integration of an Islamic Movement'. In: M. Weilenmann/W. Zips (eds), *The Governance of Legal Pluralism. Empirical Studies from Africa and Asia*, Münster: Lit.

Vermeren, P. (2001): *Le Maroc en Transition*, Paris: La Découverte.

Wiktorowicz, Q. ed. (2004): *Islamic Activism: a Social Movement Theory Approach*, Bloomington: Indiana University Press.

—— (2006): 'Anatomy of the Salafi Movement', *Studies in Conflict and Terrorism*, 29(3): 207-39.

Yassine, N. (2003): *Toutes Voiles Dehors*, Casablanca: Le Fennec.

Zeghal, M. (2002): 'Les Enjeux Autour d'une Fatwa Marocaine: Parler du Maroc en Passant par l'Afghanistan', *Les Notes de l'IFRI (Institut Français des Relations Internationals)*, 44: 54-65.

—— (2005): *Les Islamistes Marocains*, Paris: La Découverte.

Notes on Contributors

Jan Bachmann is currently a PhD candidate at the Department of Politics at the University of Bristol, UK where he studies how the 'war on terror' is appropriated by transnational and local actors in Kenya. He is particularly interested in taking a critical view onto the convergence of Western security and development. Valuing a discourse-theoretical perspective, his driving concern is to understand the relations between Western representations of the global South in the field of security, strategies of their transformation into interventions and the possibilities of adaptation and resistance on the ground. He has been working particularly on East and West Africa.

Julia Eckert is Associate Professor at the Max Planck Institute for Social Anthropology, Halle/Saale, Germany where she heads the research group 'Law against the State' which examines the juridification of protest and the globalisation of transnational legal norms. Her research interests are in legal anthropology, conflict theory, the anthropology of the state, and social movements. She is currently writing a book on the police in Bombay focusing on everyday conflicts over norms of justice, citizenship and authority. Her work on a Hindu-nationalist movement in India resulted in her book *The Charisma of Direct Action* (Oxford University Press, 2003). Other than India, she conducted research in Uzbekistan and Afghanistan. She was a researcher at the German Institute for international pedagogical research, Frankfurt am Main, and lecturer at the Humboldt University, Berlin and the Free University of Berlin from where she holds a PhD.

Thomas M. Hawley teaches political theory in the Department of Government at Eastern Washington University in Cheney, WA. He is the author of *The Remains of War: Bodies, Politics, and the Search for American Soldiers Unaccounted For in Southeast Asia* (Duke University Press, 2005). His research interests include modern and contemporary political thought, national identity, and the politics of bodies.

Tobias Kelly is a Lecturer in Social Anthropology at the University of Edinburgh. He has carried out fieldwork amongst West Bank Palestinians, focusing on everyday conflicts over the meanings and implications of citizenship in the Israeli-Palestinian conflict, resulting in his book *Law, Violence and Sovereignty among West Bank Palestinians* (Cambridge University Press, 2006). His other recent research interests include international human rights regimes, and the relationship between law, ethics and medicine in the recognition of suffering. He received a PhD in Anthropology from the London School of Economics in 2003, and has worked at the Institute of Law of Birzeit University, the Crisis States Programme at the LSE, and the Centre for Socio-Legal Studies at Oxford University.

Frank Peter has studied Modern History and Islamic Studies in Hamburg, Germany, and then continued his training in Middle Eastern History and Arabic in Aix-en-Provence, France. His research focuses on contemporary Islam in France and the social and economic history of the late-Ottoman and colonial Levant. He co-edited with Elena Arigita '*Authorizing Islam in Europe*'(2006).

Werner Schiffauer is Professor for Social and Cultural Anthropology in Frankfurt/Oder, Germany. He has worked on the transformation of rural and urban Turkey; Turkish migration to Germany; Islam in Europe and on the comparative analysis of European multicultural societies. Recent publications: *Die Gottesmänner. Islamisten in Deutschland. Eine Studie zur Herstellung religiöser Evidenz* (Frankfurt am Main, 2000); (together with Gerd Baumann, Riva Kastoryano and Steven Vertovec) *Civil Enculturation. Nation-State, School and Ethnic Difference in four European Countries* (Berghahn Books, 2004).

Bertram Turner is senior researcher at the Max-Planck Institute for Social Anthropology in Halle/Saale, Germany. He was academic assistant at the Institute of Social Anthropology and African Studies in Munich between 1993 and 2001 where he taught anthropology with a special focus on religion and legal anthropology. He has held university teaching positions in Munich, Leipzig and Halle. He has bee doing fieldwork in South West Morocco since 1996 with a specific focus on the management of natural resources, Islamic activism and conflict settlement in a plural legal setting. His most recent monograph is on asylum and conflict: *Asyl und Konflikt* (Reimer, 2005). One of his latest journal articles was published in the Journal of Legal Pluralism 53/54 (2006): 'Competing Global Players in Rural Morocco: Upgrading Legal Arenas'.